THE QUESTION OF EQUALITY

LESBIAN AND GAY POLITICS IN AMERICA
SINCE STONEWALL

Edited by David Deitcher

With a Foreword by Armistead Maupin

Scribner

New York   London   Toronto   Sydney   Tokyo   Singapore

Scribner
1230 Avenue of the Americas
New York, NY 10020

Scribner and design are trademarks of Simon & Schuster Inc.
Designed by Bethany Johns Design, New York
Manufactured in the United States of America
10 9 8 7 6 5 4 3 2 1
Library of Congress Cataloging-in-Publication Data

The question of equality : lesbian and gay politics in America since Stonewall / edited by
David Deitcher ; with a foreword by Armistead Maupin.
      p   cm.
Includes index.
1. Gay liberation movement—United States—History. 2. Gay rights—United States—History.
3. Gay men—United States—Political activity. 4. Stonewall Riot, New York, N.Y., 1969.
I. Deitcher, David.
HQ76.8.U5Q47 1995
305.9′0664—dc20

ISBN 0-684-80030-6

Pages 4-5: Sequence of stills from Program One, *Out Rage '69*.
"Where Will You Be?" by Pat Parker, originally published in *Movement in Black* by Pat Parker
(Ithaca, New York, Firebrand Books, 1978). Reprinted by permission of Firebrand Books.
"The Moon Still Rises, the Seasons Change, and the Song Has Yet to Be Sung," by Malkia
Amala Cyril, published by permission of the author.

CONTENTS

Acknowledgements

This project has been generously supported by many people. At Testing the Limits, David Meieran, Sandra Elgear, and Robyn Hutt offered kind encouragement. The documentary's senior producer, Issac Julien, its supervising producer, Craig Paull, as well as Sarah Sheffield and Ryan Kull, saw to it that we had timely access to essential materials. Chris Hoover at Drift Distribution generously worked after hours to transfer images off of videotape for use as illustrations in the book. Thanks are due to Mimi Bowling at the New York Public Library; William Walker at the Gay and Lesbian Historical Society of Northern California; Polly Thistlethwaite at the Lesbian Herstory Archives; Walter Nagle of the Bayard Rustin Fund; Lisa Ross and Ces Nieves at the Hetrick Martin Institute; to Barbara Gittings, Kay Tobin Lahusen, Mel Cheren, Brent Nicholson Earle, and Jennifer Finlay. Special thanks to Jewelle Gomez for her hospitality during my brief visit to San Francisco; and to Mab Segrest for advice and challenging discussions. It should be noted that extraordinary demands were made of all three writers—Jewelle, Mab, and Dale Peck—each of whom came through without a hitch. I am indebted to my friend, Bethany Johns for the elegant design of this book. I received valuable guidance from literary agent Ellen Geiger, and from my own agent, the late Diane Cleaver at Sanford Greenburger Associates. At Scribner, I am grateful to Ted Lee, and, of course, to Bill Goldstein and Leigh Haber, whose commitment brought this book into being. At home, my mate and most supportive reader, Clay Guthrie, provided unstinting moral support.

Finally, this book could never have been assembled without remarkable assistance of the kind that I was fortunate enough to receive from my imperturbable co-conspirator, Ioannis Mookas. Hired as a research assistant, Ioannis went far beyond his job description to keep me focused and to make the kind of extensive contributions to the contents and design of this book that are present quite literally on every page.

— **David Deitcher**, January 1995, New York City

Preface

During a hot summer's night in 1990, three gang members from Queens went hunting for a "homo" to beat up. They killed Julio Rivera in a Jackson Heights schoolyard only two weeks after thousands of lesbians and gay men marched through the streets of Manhattan's Greenwich Village to protest the rising tide of antigay violence. These events ushered in a new phase in lesbian and gay activism. As ACT UP had brought AIDS to the consciousness of the public, Queer Nation made the public aware of gay-bashing. Testing the Limits (TTL), a video collective that had documented ACT UP and its actions since 1987, documented the community-based organizing that led to the capture and conviction of Rivera's killers. This seemed natural. Queer Nation had developed directly out of ACT UP.

In 1991, after completing a feature-length work about the accomplishments of AIDS activists (*Voices from the Front*), TTL set about producing a documentary about antigay violence. Though the murder of Julio Rivera provided the impetus for *Under Attack,* contemporary political events forced us to understand that homophobic violence was as varied in its forms as it was national in its scope. The decision to expand the focus of our project to include this wider range of political developments brought TTL to Oregon in 1992. There, for seven months, we documented a community that quite literally was under attack as a regional chapter of Pat Robertson's Christian Coalition (the Oregon Citizens Alliance) attempted to pass a virulently antigay ballot initiative known as Measure 9. Nearly one thousand cases of antigay violence reported across the state testified to the ugliness of that campaign.

Returning to New York after that experience felt like returning home from a war. Yet what we returned to was no bed of roses. Fistfights were breaking out in hearings over the ill-fated Rainbow Curriculum, New York City's multicultural program for public schools that was conceived to foster open-mindedness about difference. Meanwhile, President-elect Clinton's promise to reverse the long-standing military ban against homosexual service members triggered a heated national debate about homosexuality that divided lesbians and gay men and strained the already frayed resources of the movement.

It was in the midst of this national controversy over lesbian and gay rights that TTL applied for production funding from the Independent Television Service (ITVS) to transform *Under Attack* into a more ambitious four-part documentary series that might address all of these issues. With ITVS production funds, and additional funds from Channel Four (U.K.) and private sources, we were able to produce *The Question of Equality*.

The knowledge that this would be the first series of its kind led TTL to dedicate the better part of one year to defining the goals and the character of the series. We convened "summits," discussed our plans with scores of advisers, developed story ideas, abandoned them, developed new ones, and finally mapped out the individual programs, all the while combing the country for archival materials.

The project involved the contributions of hundreds of people—gay and straight—including volunteers and paid staff.

In the course of developing the four episodes, Blackside Productions' remarkable documentary, *Eyes on the Prize,* loomed as a tempting model. Who can blame us for aspiring to bring the struggle for lesbian and gay civil rights to national consciousness as cogently and as poignantly as Blackside's series had done with the civil rights movement? Ultimately, we rejected this idea for a variety reasons. To adopt that model would have been politically problematic, since the gay rights movement has sometimes justifiably been criticized for drawing facile comparisons between these two related but different struggles. The decision to adopt a thematic rather than chronological form, which highlights the present as well as the past, was informed by the hostile political climate in which we were working. It was also informed by aesthetic considerations. In a characteristically brilliant audiotaped message that Marlon Riggs sent to a summit he could not attend because of failing health, he urged us to beware of the pitfalls of a documentary journalism in which the meaning of historical events and of documetary representations are taken to be self-evident. This was one of the few points about which the other activists, scholars, writers, and filmmakers at the summits found themselves in agreement. Ultimately, the absence of a consensus on broader issues helped us to realize that this documentary could neither presume lesbian and gay harmony, nor shy away from the conflicts and contradictions that have marked the movement, past and present. The questions that needed to be asked about lesbian and gay equality concern internal conflicts every bit as much as they do the external challenges of people who would like us to return to the closet.

Clearly, we could not represent the movement in its entirety in four hours of television. We have treated a cross section of stories that shed light on defining issues and embrace the diversity of lesbian and gay experience and identity. The time constraints of a television documentary have also meant that much of the work that gets done must be sacrificed. One way to overcome these limitations is to create a companion book that can expand upon the series' themes and supplement the project as a whole. Scribner's commitment made this possible. David Deitcher's vision, persistence, and hard work made it happen.

TTL was extremely fortunate to receive the support of ITVS, and of its major production funding, which consists of funds provided by the Corporation for Public Broadcasting. With the CPB and public television now under attack in Congress, and with lesbian and gay representations serving as a lightning rod for the conservative campaign against public broadcasting and arts funding, the future of ambitious lesbian and gay self-representations like *The Question of Equality* is very much in doubt. We are hoping our project will stand the test of time and will inspire others to create the many works that are still needed to advance lesbian and gay civil rights, and equality for all.

—**David Meieran**, January 1995, New York City

Foreword

In November 1994, on break from a European book tour, my lover Terry and I made a pilgrimage to the Homomonument, Amsterdam's tribute to victims of homophobia, past and present. It proved to be smaller and less dramatic than we'd imagined: a peninsula of pink stone, appropriately triangular, jutting into one of the city's ancient black-watered canals. Still, we were moved by the sight, and by the scattering of memorial bouquets that other pilgrims had left behind.

As we stood there misty-eyed, envying the Dutch the casual humanity of their culture, a middle-aged man stopped and observed us, then mimed out an offer to take our picture. We couldn't know for certain, of course, but he seemed like the most ordinary sort of citizen—a banker, say, or a storekeeper, perhaps with a wife and kids at home. Thrown a little, we gave him our camera and struck a quick pose, arms wrapped around each other. He snapped the shot, then returned the camera and went on his businesslike way, waving off our thanks as he left.

We've thought about that man a lot. With one wordless act he had both recognized us as a couple and honored the long history of struggle that gay people everywhere have endured. That a stranger in a foreign country could do such a thing without batting an eye seemed all the more miraculous in light of the homophobia that has gripped our own country in recent years. Antigay measures had been replicating like a virus across the land, and Congress itself had fallen, only days before, to the likes of Jesse Helms, Newt Gingrich, and others whose nasty take on homosexuality is a matter of public record.

Earlier in the year I'd found myself squared off against these New Calvinists when the miniseries based on my first novel, *Tales of the City,* was broadcast on PBS. Though the show went on record as the most popular drama series ever aired on public television, it soon became a convenient rallying point for the goon squads of the radical right. Here, after all, was that scariest of creatures: a show that treated homosexuality as if it were the most natural thing in the world. With no apologies and no punishment for the wicked. Right there on your tax-supported station where children could see it! Homos kissing in sports cars and dancing in their underwear and cuddling in bed in the morning!

All of which played hell in several southern legislatures, where irate lawmakers vowed to punish their local PBS stations by cutting their funding. In Georgia, thanks to *Tales,* a proposed $20-million facility came perilously close to being scrapped. In Oklahoma, a rider was added to an appropriations bill forbidding the local affiliate from airing shows that cast "a favorable light" on homosexuality. The public television station in Chattanooga pulled the show an hour before its scheduled broadcast after an anonymous caller threatened to bomb the station and hunt down its employees. Even in the halls of Congress, selected lawmakers were treated to a twelve-minute bootleg videotape, featuring *Tales'* naughtiest bits, courtesy of the Reverend Donald Wildmon of Tupelo, Mississippi.

None of this surprised me. As someone who grew up in the South, I'm well aware of its capacity for parochialism. I also knew that Marlon Riggs had endured a similar attack a year earlier with *Tongues Untied*. What did catch me off guard was the cold-blooded efficiency with which PBS washed its hands of *Tales*. Rather than defend its biggest hit in years—which, typically, had arrived as a virtual freebie from Britain's Channel Four—the network fell into a guilty silence, then abandoned its plan to help finance a sequel based on my second novel. (The scripts to *More Tales of the City,* set in 1977, had already been circulating at PBS headquarters in Alexandria, so I can't help wondering if the show's impertinent treatment of Anita Bryant's Save Our Children campaign didn't hasten its demise.)

A team of PBS flacks—several of them gay, as irony would have it—was mobilized to convince the press that the network's sudden retreat from *More Tales* was simply a matter of insufficient funds, not self-censorship. A tall order indeed, considering the profile of their new boss, Ervin S. Duggan, a Presbyterian educator from North Carolina and Bush appointee to the FCC, who'd already vowed publicly to restore "balance" to the network. ("Balance," in the language of the New Calvinists, means that gay-friendly images must be countered with gay-hostile ones, since, in their eyes, our right to be heard is a shaky one at best.) So, while a number of PBS affiliates continued to profit off reruns of *Tales* by promising viewers "more fine programming like this," the death warrant for future episodes had already been issued upstairs.

A lot of average Americans, many of them straight, wrote me in praise of *Tales,* grateful for a show that embraced the whole human family while espousing such currently outmoded values as tolerance and compassion. It was refreshing, they said, to see a miniseries without a moment of violence or explicit sex that explored, among other things, a tender romance between two sixty-year-olds. The new PBS president and his gay helpmates might have said something like that when *Tales* came under attack, but they chose instead to run for cover, fearful for their jobs, letting a two-bit hatemonger from Mississippi have the last word.

This is old news, of course. I rehash it only to illustrate how many widely disparate agents conspire to keep honest depictions of gay lives from entering the American mainstream. Our most formidable foes in the culture wars are not the Donald Wildmons of the world but a host of others who, because of self-interest or cowardice or greed, let the Donald Wildmons rule the day.

Such foes almost surely await *The Question of Equality,* the ambitious documentary series to which this book relates as a companion volume. The producers of *The Question of Equality,* like those of *Tales of the City,* had to assemble their funding with assistance from a foreign source (once again, the exemplary Channel Four), working in conjunction with the Independent Television Service. If the series is ever to find its way onto American public television, it will most likely do so through the good graces of enlightened individual affiliates, since in the current climate, a "national feed" from PBS Central in Alexandria seems a remote possibility.

Our visibility remains, as ever, the disposable card in the poker game of American life. We learned that the hard way when Bill Clinton caved in to his own generals with the Don't Ask, Don't Tell fiasco. We learned it again this year when, fearing the wrath of the farm bloc, "sympathetic" senators like California's Dianne Feinstein voted for an agricultural bill with a Helms-sponsored antigay clause attached. Our expendability is driven home every time we see films like *Philadelphia* or *And the Band Played On* that deny us even the briefest glimpse of the love they purport to defend. We are bludgeoned by compromise and equivocation on a daily basis, while social scientists jimmy with our numbers (a laughable 2 percent at the latest count) as if to diminish our claim to a place in the human race. "Annihilation by blandness" was the term Christopher Isherwood coined for this wholesale dismissal of our existence, and it couldn't be more apt today.

But there is still reason to hope. Our movement, after all, is rooted not in politics or in art but in the basic human drive to love and be loved without intimidation. Most people will fight for that when push comes to shove. Indeed, nothing makes an activist like a bully with the upper hand. My own commitment to gay rights—like Terry's—was launched by the aggressive homophobia of the Anita Bryant campaign, and there are young queers today responding in similar ways to the social terrorism of the radical right. It saddens me, of course, to see that some things haven't changed much in twenty years, but at least the chances of our being heard are far greater than ever before.

A growing number of lesbians and gay men living happily out of the closet has finally given us a voice in the culture with which to air our grievances and shape our dreams. And that's cause for rejoicing. Our visibility has provided the perfect bogeyman for the radical right, but it has also helped us win the hearts and minds of reasonable people everywhere. Judging by both our friends and our enemies—and by this book and its accompanying series—I'd say we're still on the right track.

— **Armistead Maupin**, December 1994, San Francisco

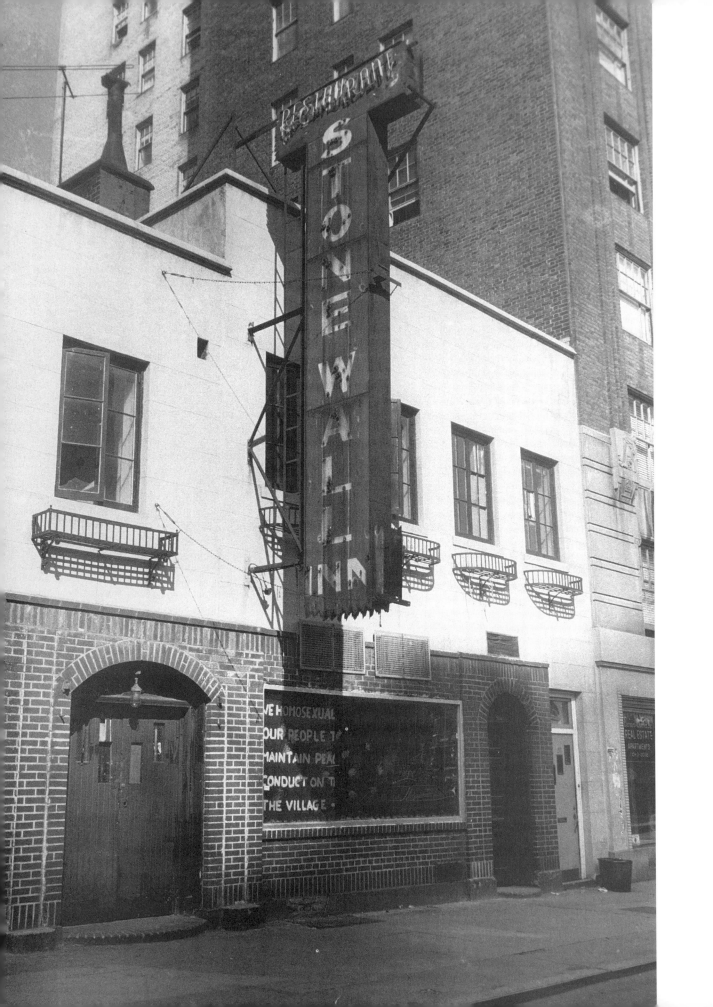

Introduction

by David Deitcher

In the introduction to *Gay American History,* published in 1976, Jonathan Katz reflected on the tumultuous times during which he had prepared his pioneering book. In the seven years since the 1969 Stonewall uprising, Katz observed, the individual and collective self-perception of lesbians and gay men had undergone a profound transformation:

Starting with a sense of ourselves as characters in a closet drama, the passive victims of a family tragedy, we experienced ourselves as initiators and assertive actors in a movement for social change. We experienced the present as history, ourselves as historymakers. In our lives and in our hearts, we experienced the change from one historical form of homosexuality to another. We experienced homosexuality as historical.

Gay American History was one of a number of early books that helped to foster this shift in lesbian and gay self-regard from passive objects to active subjects of history. Katz's book gathered together masses of historical documents, every one of which testified to the variety and tenacity of lesbian and gay experience in America from the seventeenth century onward. In this way it fulfilled an essential human need: the need of a people for a past. In Katz's words, gay men and lesbians had been "the silent minority, the silenced minority—invisible men, invisible women."

Coming to understand the many ways in which "homosexuality was historical," we have also had to learn that history itself has been heterosexist, and not simply the impartial result of archival burrowing and evaluation on the part of disinterested university professors and scholarly amateurs. It was during the 1960s and 1970s, in the earliest skirmishes of what has since been dubbed the "culture wars," that African-Americans, women, and then queer men and women set about the difficult process of exposing this myth. Modern history had attended principally to the exploits of straight white men (like the historians themselves). Gay and lesbian history had to be rescued from the oblivion to which it had been consigned, along with the men and women who had suffered it.

Nearly two decades after the publication of *Gay American History,* the production of *The Question of Equality*—both the documentary television series and the book—offers further proof (if any were needed) that lesbians and gay men have indeed become subjects of history. Yet precisely what kind of history is recorded here warrants a brief explanation.

But other parts of the story will soon be history, exactly the kind of details of a life that we always want to know. What does it feel like? I've read the newspapers for that weekend, both the dailies and Sundays, and nothing of what I remember is mentioned. Nothing of my experience of that weekend merited a public record. There is no evidence of that weekend.
—Neil Bartlett, *Who Was That Man?*

Facing page: The Stonewall Inn, the bar on Sheridan Square in New York City that has attained mythical status since the uprising there on June 28, 1969. Photo by Diana Davies.

I was among three dozen activists, academics, and artists who were invited by the New York–based video collective Testing the Limits (TTL) to attend a "summit" late in July of 1993 to consider what kind of documentary should be produced with the funds that TTL had been granted for that purpose by the Independent Television Service. Since this was to be the first documentary series ever to deal with the lesbian and gay rights movement, and since the conservative political and cultural climate in the U.S. suggested that this might well remain the only television series to deal with this subject for some time to come, these decisions were neither simple nor easy to make. Ultimately, the producers' approach to the series was determined by a combination of practical, aesthetic, and, above all, political circumstances. The context in which we were meeting to discuss the project was dominated by the continuing AIDS crisis, by an epidemic of homophobic violence, and by antigay rights campaigns that Christian right and secular conservative groups were conducting nationwide. Add to this the legendary divisiveness that is known to erupt among lesbians and gay men along the barbed boundaries of gender, race, class, ethnicity, and political persuasion, and the task of devising a single documentary to represent such a movement becomes an especially daunting one. Nevertheless, it was this context as a whole that informed the producers' decision to create *The Question of Equality* as a work that examines contemporary challenges to the lesbian and gay rights movement in relation to a treatment of the movement's history. It was hoped that such a reflective, even self-critical, account of the movement's most pressing issues could serve educationally and politically to advance the cause of equal rights (in *every* sense) for lesbians and gay men.

After being commissioned by TTL in the spring of 1994 to edit a companion volume for the series, I set out with the producers' encouragement to assemble a book that would function more as a supplement than as a typical documentary companion. The four authors who have written the essays that anchor each of the book's four sections were encouraged to adhere to the overall subject matter of the related program; but they were also encouraged to go well beyond its parameters. This volume includes works of art and poetry, comic strips, and documentary "sidebars" that do not appear in the series. Similarly, only a fraction of the photographs that illustrate the book appear as stills in the documentary. On the other hand, the book incorporates individual images and sequences of images that come directly from the series. Transcribed and edited interviews that were originally shot by the producer/directors of individual shows were made available to the book's writers, for whom this material could serve as primary resources. Yet the extensive oral-history material that appears in each section of the book under the heading "In Their Own Words" may figure in the shows in only a fragmentary way, or not at all. Salvaging the valuable material that would otherwise have been sacrificed as a result of the documentary's four-hour time limit is therefore only the most literal way in which this book supplements the series.

If history before Stonewall was heterosexist, then the gay history that followed it was not infrequently sexist and racist. It is with this in mind that in Chapter One ("Out of the Past") Jewelle Gomez examines the formation, the subsequent fragmentation, and the re-formation of the lesbian and gay civil rights movement. She outlines the principal concerns and accomplishments of the pre-Stonewall homophile movement and highlights the defining conflicts throughout the turbulent years between Stonewall and the dawn of the Reagan era in order to clarify the character of this movement that represents the interests of people who have so much, and yet so little, in common. In Chapter Two ("Visibility and Backlash") Mab Segrest investigates the concept of "visibility," which was constructed in the post-Stonewall era as both the principal strategy and goal of the struggle for lesbian and gay rights. Segrest ponders the consequences of increased visibility at a time when the AIDS crisis results in an epidemic of gay-bashing; and when antigay crusaders shrewdly sidestep the great queer constituencies in the nation's urban centers to undermine support for lesbian and gay rights in small-town settings nationwide. In Chapter Three ("Law and Desire") I assess the relationship of queer men and women to institutions that have defined the American mainstream as heterosexist: the law, religion, family, and the military. I consider the shift in recent years in the allocation of the movement's energies and resources away from AIDS activism to a concentration on issues that concern the law, marriage, family, and "gays in the military." In relation to such institutions, which situate us either inside or outside the mainstream, I question the lesbian and gay reflex to categorize one another as "radical" or "assimilationist." In Chapter Four ("Making History") Dale Peck evaluates the situation of queer youth today. He reviews evidence of the emotional burden that bedevils queer youth in the age of AIDS, notes the presence of a handful of lesbian and gay-operated institutions that offer support to the queer offspring of parents who shut them out, and investigates the homophobic causes of the movement's broad failure to deal effectively with the turbulent passage from queer youth to adulthood.

Finally, a note regarding the tone of this book: the book's authors address their topics from a personal perspective; often, they weave personal accounts into the historical reportage and analysis that forms the basis of each chapter. As long as the most intimate details of lesbian and gay experience remain the object of institutionalized scrutiny and proscription, queers will not have the option of distinguishing private from public life. In this specific sense, lesbians and gay men can take advantage of a bad situation to try to restore to history the receptive kind of memory invoked by Neil Bartlett. It has long been a queer cultural project to valorize certain aspects of art and life that the majority culture discards as worthless. (Think of camp.) But as gay men and lesbians remain swept up in the whirlwind of plague and political backlash, the inclination to impress upon the histories we write the particularities of everyday experience becomes urgent as well as poignant. Under these conditions, threads of individual revelation can be woven to form the humane connective tissue of queer history that helps to sustain us as we continue the struggle for justice and equality.

CHAPTER

1

OUT OF THE PAST

Out of the Past

by Jewelle Gomez

The Private Place Made Public

The most common phrase repeated by lesbians and gay men over forty years of age as they tell their coming-out stories is "I always thought I was the only one until . . ." Around the country each of us believed that we alone had been blessed (or cursed) with our desire to love someone of the same sex. John Donne's axiom "No man is an island" was a taunting lie as we floundered around our hometowns or in strange cities searching for a place to put our feelings. We were part of a vast, scattered archipelago, whose neighboring islands were not even within shouting distance. To imagine those islands reconvening, coming together and forming a solid body, is to envision the natural geographical process shifting into reverse. A volcano gaping open, not to spew out molten lava but to take back into itself the tons of matter that dot the sea around it.

Yet this is exactly what the lesbian/gay movement is doing—reaching across that glittering sea that separates each of us and drawing us back toward each other, creating a whole with recognizable shape and focus. Each of us has been terribly alone because few heterosexual families actually prepare anyone for the possibility of gayness. We spend our early years trying to manufacture a context, a mode of expression for deeply rooted emotions that everyone around us pretends don't exist. In that way we were islands isolated by the sea of compulsory heterosexuality.

This couple posed in front of a plaque mounted by the City of New York in 1979, the tenth anniversary of the Stonewall rebellion. The plaque remained in place only briefly, before being destroyed by vandals. Photo by JEB (Joan E. Biren).

After years of treading water, struggling to make a space for the expression of love, lesbian/gay activism offered us the chance to look to one another for solid ground on which to stand against the attitudes that kept us separated from each other and hidden from the rest of society. Our movement is different from others; we have little shared, public history or culture. In fact we, as a group, are made up of all of the various other groups that have been in direct competition with each other in this society. And a most important difference—our oppression is rooted in this culture's fears about sexuality. It is this unruly diversity that is so difficult and so extraordinary. Our movement is about reaching past the barriers society has erected and reconnecting that which has never really been connected before. And all we have in common is our passion.

It was in words that I first found passion, the fiery rhetoric of the civil rights movement, which I initially heard on the television news and in the eloquent language of the printed page, available at every turn. I devoured, indiscriminately, Boston's *Record American* and *Globe, The Saturday Evening Post, Sepia, Ebony,* and *Jet* along with whatever paperbacks my relatives

Overleaf: A crowd of thousands overflowing the Sheep Meadow in Central Park following the first gay liberation day march in 1970. Photo by Diana Davies.

discarded. Among a stack I found at my father's house when I visited him one weekend was a copy of *The Well of Loneliness*. Its elegiac cover featured a figure of indeterminate gender entreating what I've come to think of as a "high femme." My reaction was visceral—this was a book about me, what I knew myself to be. And as I devoured the closely spaced type that was written by Radclyffe Hall as an apologia, to elicit sympathy for the homosexual cause, I, at fourteen years of age, recognized myself. And despite the objective differences between my reality and that of the protagonist, Stephen, that book helped me know whom to look for.

Later lesbian activists interpreted Stephen as a reinforcement of the stereotypical image of the pitiful, neurotic lesbian. But alone, listening for the whisper of any voice, I heard within the story a philosophical parallel to the civil rights movement I'd watched on television and then participated in when it touched Boston's black community in the 1960s. In my naïveté I didn't then understand why black leaders didn't take up the call, which would have included women like Stephen and me. In fact they seemed determined to squelch any attempts to recognize black gay life. Even premier black playwright, poet, and activist Amiri Baraka (then LeRoi Jones) used his limited access to the pages of the *New York Times* to call the gay movement "plastic." In the slight coverage such pronouncements were given dwelled the complete dismissal of a segment of the black population I knew existed. I felt in those words a betrayal of the basic principles of the civil rights movement and (unknowingly) saw the seeds of masculinist traditionalism that were later to define the limits of civil rights activism. The ease with which homosexuals were rendered untouchable was replicated in the unconscious way black women were relegated to support positions in the civil rights movement and pushed outside the circle of public leadership.

In my reading of *The Well of Loneliness* my imagination did not just take in the individual pathos of the story but extrapolated an understanding of both the history and possibility of my lesbian life. In fact the actual story became almost irrelevant to me when considered alongside the transformation it wrought within me, a believer in words. It helped give a name (even if it was a poor one) to who I was and offered the hope of a lesbian life. It became a significant indicator for me— something that points toward growth, progress, that illuminates some value being overlooked or new path that may be taken. Throughout life I keep looking for the significant indicator and make the assumption that it won't necessarily be found in the most expected places.

If I'd chosen based on the cover alone, there'd have been little reason for me even to open that old edition of the Radclyffe Hall novel. Too often we're convinced that the significant indicators are only available to us from a narrow range of sources, only from people who look like us, or speak our language, from the established order or proven methods. We close down our imagination expecting that an answer will be on the path we're taking just because we've taken that path.

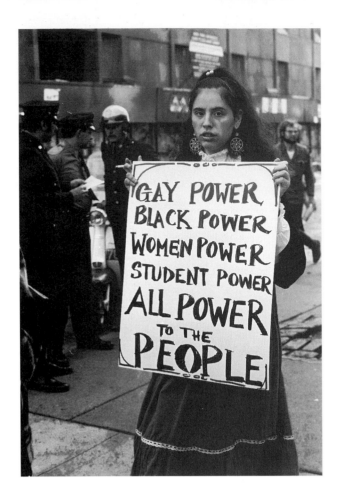

Activists in the early 1970s, such as this student demonstrator at New York University, were quick to invoke the commonality of shared struggles, but the complex and all-too-real differences of race, gender, sexuality, and class could not be overcome quite as easily. Photo by Diana Davies.

In trying to devise a political philosophy that encompasses the multitude of identities that I am—African-American, Native American, lesbian, welfare raised, college educated, urban, Bostonian, female, etc., etc.—I have a number of sources to which I can turn. I have to believe that we can dwell in more than one place at one time since more than one place dwells within me.

Often the really interesting insight comes from the unexpected place, from the things not said, the event not reported, or the perspective not widely considered. In keeping open to these, we avail ourselves of the really wide variety of options for problem solving, and living, that are available to us. The lesbian/gay movement offers us those insights. We have aligned ourselves with an array of people that represents the full spectrum of life in the United States. Our gayness gives us a connection we would otherwise never have in heterosexual society. And in that connection we can share experiences and knowledge that others ordinarily do not. I believe there is a new world in that place where the expected and the unexpected meet. As poverty and violence erupt around us, we have the only movement that presumes the inclusion of all types of people working together despite historic animosities. What lessons can we learn from the success and the failure of such presumption? Over the past twenty years I've worked in collaboration with Irish feminists, Southern gentlemen (both black and white), an Israeli editor, Sri Lankan poets, Caribbean dancers, Chicano performance artists, African-American professors and cabdrivers, and more. What drew us together was our gayness. Figuring out how to keep us in coalition is part of what a movement is about. And in learning that lesson I believe we got a picture of a bigger, wider-reaching politics, which has the possibility of changing society.

I always made the connection between the liberation ideals of black people and gay people in my mind, even if black leaders did not. Each movement had something that was important for me. But having made this connection, whom was I looking for? A blond butch called Stephen who lived on an estate? Not in the economically depressed black community where I lived. Stephen's world was remote not just because of its Edwardian and European setting. It was a white world, a wealthy world, so different from my own that it and the hope for a lesbian life remained only a fantasy to me for many years.

The media saw the story of gay liberation as filler, if it saw us at all. Coverage of the civil rights movement, rightfully, swelled newspaper pages and television screens, but news of gay activism was scarce and skewed. I remember the Stonewall riot as a tiny squib in the local paper, with few political overtones. And the same was true later, in 1970, when New York police raided a gay after-hours bar, arresting 166 men; among them was Diego Vinales, an Argentinean. In his fear he tried to escape the precinct house and was almost killed as he jumped from a second-story window, impaling himself on a fence below. The subsequent medical efforts to save his life and the street full of protesters were widely covered, but nowhere was it mentioned that the victim, the raided bar, and the protesters were gay. By refusing to identify the protest as the response of a group with a common interest, the media focused the public's attention away from the movement and onto what appeared to be isolated incidents. The public reading an account saw only a story about a mob of irate bar patrons, not the activism of concerned citizens. It is as if the arrest of blacks for drinking at white water fountains had been reported as simple trespassing.

In ignoring the political context, the press helped to short-circuit the momentum the gay movement had been gaining for more than a decade and left the general public completely uninformed about an aspect of the political climate that had far-reaching consequences. No wonder black leaders looked upon gay activists as simply Johnny-come-latelies trying to cash in on black activism.

But the gay movement had, from its inception, looked to the civil rights movement (consciously or unconsciously) for its inspiration and its tactics. In the 1950s, organizations such as the Daughters of Bilitis, ONE, the Mattachine Society, and SIR emulated the goals of the National Association for the Advancement of Colored People (NAACP) and the Southern Christian Leadership Conference—securing civil rights within the existing system. Lesbians and gays did not have the shared history of the Middle Passage, slavery, or jim crow laws. But the strategies and spirit of the civil rights movement provided the perfect model for gay activists. They organized educational projects to help lesbians and gay men learn their history and self-respect and encouraged us to be visible. Just as picketing was used by the early labor movement, civil rights activists and then lesbian/gay activists hand-lettered their protests in block print on cardboard and put on their walking shoes. A major difference was that blacks were always visible, even when not acknowledged. But gays were like ghosts who suddenly materialized, marching on the steps of government buildings. Gay demonstrators were fewer in number, and although FBI and CIA records show the movement was subjected to surveillance and infiltration, the press looked upon it as an oddity rather than a threat.

In the nineties, when lesbians and gays have our own merchandising catalogs, commercial sea cruises, and entire sections in Barnes and Noble, it's difficult to imagine the medieval atmosphere in which most lesbians and gays lived and the important role played by those groups. Even those of us who didn't go to the

The Ladder $1.25

HOMOSEXUAL AMERICANS DEMAND THEIR CIVIL RIGHTS

EQUALITY FOR HOMOSEXUAL CITIZENS

NORTH AMERICAN CONFERENCE OF HOMOPHILE ORGANIZATIONS

JUSTICE

OCTOBER / NOVEMBER 1969

This picket line in front of Independence Hall in Philadelphia was one of many organized by homophile groups through-out the 1960s. At top left is Barbara Gittings, a prominent early figure within the Daughters of Bilitis and an editor of their journal, *The Ladder*. Photos by Nancy Tucker. Collection of the Lesbian Herstory Archives.

meetings can see that little we have accomplished since then would have come about without those few who dared to take those steps out of the closets.

In 1968 I worked for the public television station in Boston on *Say Brother*, one of the first black, weekly television programs. We featured music, news, and interviews with activists like Stokely Carmichael and Amiri Baraka. At the same time I also secretly scanned the back pages of the local alternative weekly, check-ing every edition just to glimpse the announcement of the meeting for the Daughters of Bilitis. I was not brave enough to go. The group seemed as remote and unconnected to me as did Stephen and her anxious affluence. But their small ad and the knowledge of their presence was a beacon I turned to every week.

In retrospect, it may not be easy to recognize the courage it required for those women to come together to attend meetings that were disguised to sound as if they were being sponsored by poetry societies, or for Lisa Ben to publish the first lesbian magazine, *Vice Versa*, in 1947. But for me, who could not bring myself to take that first step toward myself, her efforts seem monumental. She disseminated words to the hungry, to be gobbled up, digested, and used for building strength. The value might have been hard to recognize in the hand-typed and -distributed periodical that only lasted for nine issues. But for the first time contemporary lesbians saw the possibility of representing ourselves in print. We were no longer simply figures of pulp fiction or doctors' theories. With the passion and conviction that fuels many liberation movements—the knowledge that this has never been done before—Lisa Ben provided a significant indicator. Publications such as *Vice Versa, One*, and *The Ladder* provided a bridge between the islands. Their existence implied that we were not alone, there were enough of us to warrant a publication. They further provided a forum in which we could explore our commonalty. The articles, stories, and editorials were the soft ground where we would first tread to see if we recognized each other. So tenuous was the safety of such public appearances, many who attended meetings or wrote for these publications did so pseudonymously—Lisa Ben was an anagram for *lesbian*; Barbara Grier, founder of Naiad Books, edited *The Ladder* as Gene Damon. Henry Gerber, a founder of the early homophile organization the Chicago Society, wrote anonymously to *One* magazine. Lorraine Hansberry, the first black woman to write a play produced on Broadway, wrote anonymously to *The Ladder* in 1957 to express her joy that the publication existed. And just as she did not accept the isolation of black people from mainstream society, she believed lesbians had a role in world politics: "I think it is about time that equipped women began to take on some of the questions which male-dominated culture has produced." Fostering these connections was still such an anathema to the established order of society, anonymity was often the only security.

Seven years after *Vice Versa* was published, in October 1954, the Los Angeles Post Office banned *One* magazine from its mail service. Our words were considered too dangerous, not food but poison. Or as the Los Angeles postmaster had declared: "obscene." In silencing our "obscenity," the post office was isolating us from each other and again making lesbians and gays invisible to the rest of the country. The U.S. Supreme Court ruled on the case brought by *One*, finally making it possible for lesbian and gay publications to be mailed through the postal system.

It is here, in the question of visibility, that many in the black civil rights movement felt distant from the struggle for lesbian and gay rights. Blacks were not only visible but targeted. The black community perceived lesbians and gays as too easily assimilated into mainstream culture to be considered oppressed. Still the connections between the two movements were undeniable. Many out lesbians and gays were, like Joan Nestle, Candice Boyce, and Bob Kohler, also veterans of the civil rights movement. And just as the goals of civil rights organizations were grounded in the already articulated rights of the U.S. Constitution and Bill of Rights, so, too, were the goals of the early homophile organizations. Emulating the tactics of civil rights activists, lesbians and gays were counseled to dress and act like mainstream, middle-class citizens, to reassure the establishment that we were responsible members of society. We were just like everyone else.

On television we'd all seen pictures of prim, crisply dressed black children under police protection, as they tried to integrate schools and lunch counters. In contrast the segregationists were wild-eyed and rabid, screaming epithets, throwing garbage. The image of the black students presumably gave some who were undecided an opportunity to think about integration. What could be so wrong with such a clean little child, or an elegantly suited and coiffed young person? The student was made a symbol of our ability to fit in, to be a credit to our race. But could such an approach open the eyes of a mob? The complexities of race and class are not so easily swept away. How realistic was that expression?

The opportunity for the success of such a tactic was even more questionable for early lesbian and gay demonstrators. Admonished to dress conservatively and not hold hands, lesbians and gays walked picket lines in front of the White House, Independence Hall, and the United Nations under the aegis of our homophile organizations during the same time as the Woolworth sit-ins and voting-rights demonstrations. But they had little chance of making it to the evening news. Even as they daringly presented themselves for the public, their actions were kept closeted by sporadic and thin coverage.

The significance of these demonstrations may have been more personal than public. Stepping from the closet out into the open air gave each person walking the picket line a chance to see herself within the context of her country, not just her lover or other bar patrons. Each picketer was also able to see others like himself; not imagined shadows in a fantasy book or back room, but adult men walking on a public street. The picture may be an ordinary one, yet without that vision little organizing would ever have been possible. Being open in the world was a truly

The forceful and highly successful opposition to the U.S. war in Vietnam created an atmosphere of radical political possibilities from which the many divergent movements at the time—including black power, the women's movement, and gay liberation—derived inspiration and strength. Photo by Diana Davies.

revolutionary act because the isolation enforced by our invisibility in the larger society was also a type of stasis. It led lesbians and gays to see ourselves as perpetual victims, hoping only to escape the notice (and punishment) of authority. For the individual lesbians and gays who dared to march annually in front of Philadelphia's Independence Hall, and for those who heard about it, taking public space was a life-affirming step toward casting off the mantle of victimization. To stand in the open, in front of a monument to democracy representing uncountable other lesbians and gays, was a simple act that ripped the veil from our own eyes, made us look in our mirrors and see ourselves and each other out in the open air for the first time. This seeing is the fuel of change.

Even without attention from the press, such conciliatory tactics as a march made sense in the atmosphere in which many of the groups had been born. The mania of Joseph McCarthy and anticommunism was a defining factor of the 1950s. Suddenly private political beliefs, whose expression was guaranteed by the U.S. Constitution, were being held up to public scrutiny, along with aspersions on private sexuality. It was natural for homophile groups to stress the qualities about lesbians and gays that were the same as the rest of society. The national organizations were not just attempting to make the "other" appear to be just like everyone else, they were strategizing for survival in a society that threatened to eat us alive.

Homophile groups were, at the same time, equally, significantly, providing an alternative to the bars, bathrooms, and parks that were the only public social settings lesbians and gays had in which to make contact.

But, most importantly, by insisting on commonality among gays, homophile groups were providing a political context for what had, until that time, been considered by many (even some homosexuals) aberrant sexual behavior with only personal, not political, ramifications. The political aspect of the development remained muted, as many groups focused on social activities. In fact most lesbians and gays would never have described themselves as a political body. At best they would have seen themselves as individuals who just happened to have sex with people of the same gender; at worst they would have accepted society's assessment of themselves as sick and depraved. In an attempt to draw lesbians and gays out of the bars and other places that encouraged society's definition, homophile organizations provided not just a social alternative but a political context for our lives, for the first time in this country.

The emergence of this most "other" of the others may have been unexpected, but it was an intrinsic part of the evolution of urban culture and national politics in this country. Our emergence from the closet was part of the groundswell of activism that included the national antiwar movement and the free-love constituency. And the more publicized radical methods of antiwar protesters and the outrageous behavior of flower children created the atmospheric preconditions for Stonewall.

The dichotomy between the established methods of civil rights activism as embodied in the activism of early homophile organizations, and the idea of confrontation represented by the counterculture, antiwar activists and others, is a theme that is repeated through most of the history of U.S. political movements. I remember being conflicted when the Black Panthers and Malcolm X rose in popular influence. Their pronouncements directly contradicted and sometimes condemned the work of people like Martin Luther King and Fannie Lou Hamer, activists who'd first led the black population to the idea of a common identity. On one hand we were being told blacks were a natural part of the fabric of U.S. life and must assert our rights to "have a place at the table." The American pie was being redivided to provide African-Americans with a bigger share. On the other hand, black nationalists like Huey Newton, Kathleen Cleaver, and Malcolm X stressed looking to ourselves rather than to the larger society for our identity and our survival. They were also not shy about reminding us of the brutal history of slavery and segregation. They hoped to use the newly articulated black anger to instill black pride and from that establish the institutions that would be a refuge from continued racism. They were no longer interested in the pie at all.

In a traditional fashion, these differing approaches are always set up in opposition to one another. Each faction had to discredit the other in order to maintain its legitimacy. Little thought or public discussion was given to how the differing tactics and philosophies might each serve African-Americans. The magnitude of the problem did require more than one approach. Instead much energy was spent on emphasizing the dichotomy between working for reform and working for revolution. And, later, in the lesbian and gay rights movement that dichotomy and competition were repeated just as forcefully.

Boys with No Eyebrows

I remember Judy Garland dying, but the riot at Stonewall was not as big in my consciousness. Boston, where I lived, was rife with civil rights activism. Especially following the death of Dr. King in April of 1968, the African-American community was focused in on itself and little attempt was made to forge connections with other political struggles, except for some links to contemporary African politics. The imprisoned Nelson Mandela became a rallying point for black students on U.S. campuses. The takeover of Alcatraz Island by a coalition of Native American activists in the fall of 1969 was also a significant incident for many liberation groups. But somehow in the worldview of people who were not directly connected, the meaning of Stonewall and the event itself were lost. It had to be more than simply the media's obfuscation of the riot and its significance. I think those factors lie within us and within our individual fears.

Activist Sylvia (Ray) Rivera says that as a young boy, he experimented with his transvestitism. His mother drew the line at his altering his facial hair, exclaiming, "Now, boys can't really run around without eyebrows." And in some ways Rivera's mother's voice echoes deep inside all of us. That cautious side of us plays an active role in how we perceive the movement and how we frame our relation to it. That admonitional voice has many elements. Part of it is our wanting to ensure survival in a world we know to be hard and merciless toward the "other." Another aspect of us doesn't want to risk losing whatever ground we have already personally gained.

Legendary drag queen Marsha P. Johnson, who participated in the 1969 Stonewall uprising, remained a lifelong activist until her death in 1992. Photo by Bettye Lane.

We also fear seeing our own vulnerabilities reflected in others. A woman whose son shaves off his eyebrows is herself exposed. A part of us doesn't want to be embarrassed.

The story of Stonewall is much like the incident that sparked one of the pivotal events of the civil rights movement, the Montgomery bus boycotts. Not the famous scene where a dignified Rosa Parks refused to leave the whites-only section of a city bus. The photograph of her in the Montgomery jail remains an inspirational, iconographic image for most African-Americans. But earlier that same year—1955— a fifteen-year-old, Claudette Colvin, was dragged from a Montgomery bus by police and arrested after she and an elderly woman refused to give up their seats. The NAACP came to Claudette Colvin's defense and was gearing up to take the matter to court and to use that incident as a rallying point until it was dis-covered that their symbol was pregnant. Claudette Colvin was no longer suitable; her sexual behavior might reflect badly on all of us. Abandoned by the civil rights movement in pursuit of a purer, more appropriate heroine, Colvin remains barely a footnote, although it was probably her youth, her anger, and her marginalization that gave her the courage to rebel.

These censorious aspects of ourselves helped to shove Claudette Colvin to the side. In 1969 they let some of us ignore the Stonewall riots, or some of us even to condemn them. Because of all those boys with no eyebrows. The specifics of exactly who was there have varied in the telling, but it is clear that this was not an Ivy League crew. They were not neatly starched students but rather hustlers and street people living a rough life—not one that we wanted to see on television. Many were not white, spoke with accents, took drugs, or drank too much. As tawdry as the middle class or professional members of the community may have thought it to be, the Stonewall was their territory, a place of excitement and familiarity.

For many the bars substituted for family and provided a place where individuals could voice support for each other, play at the glamour that everyone moves to New York City for, and bring their private lives out into the public. As Joan Nestle says importantly, unlike the political organizations, the bars had sexual energy. The element most lesbians and gay men identified as the root of their difference from society was understated in most homophile groups. In the bar, sexual energy was allowed free rein. It was a place of regeneration. Women standing on bathroom lines, or men slyly dancing, forced bonds that reinforced their right not just to a gay life but to a sex life.

The riot outside such a bar brought the public face-to-face with the reality of private sexual desire. With its aggression and flamboyance, this group was the embodiment of that sexuality we feared had made us completely unacceptable.

Like Claudette Colvin, Sylvia Rivera and all the others there that night were lightning rods for our fear of our difference in what Amber Hollibaugh has described as an "erotophobic" U.S. culture. In each case, in 1955 and 1969, puritanical proscriptions against sexual expression made movement heroes unpalatable. Gay revolt against police harassment on that summer night was an embarrassment to some of us. But its very tawdriness, its ragged, urgent quality, was just the energy we needed to move into a new period of activism.

More significant than the first night of rioting at the Stonewall was, I think, the second. It is one thing to have an explosive, spontaneous reaction growing out of a generalized sense of long-term abuse, quite another to decide to return to the streets, to be joined by many others who were never there, and to engage in open conflict with police. The rioters' return is what turned Stonewall into not just a riot but a political protest. Craig Rodwell has said the second night was a "public assertion of real anger by gay people that was just electric." That signaled our ability to embrace a complex identity and, with the bonds forged among us, to sustain our anger long enough to organize.

I wish I had read about the queens and street people more explicitly in 1969. I would easily have seen them as related to me. They were much like some of the men who were patrons of the bar in which my father worked when I was a teenager. Located in Boston's racially mixed South End, the Regent was host to musicians, hospital workers, prostitutes, maids, taxicab drivers, black working people in general. Several of his customers were openly gay and held a protected status in that community. I can imagine Miss Kay, whose shoes and sweaters I had often inherited, kicking up his heels and demanding his rights in Sheridan Square. But it was exactly that which would have made them recognizable to me that would also have made them untenable to many others—just as Claudette Colvin was to the largely middle-class leaders of the NAACP.

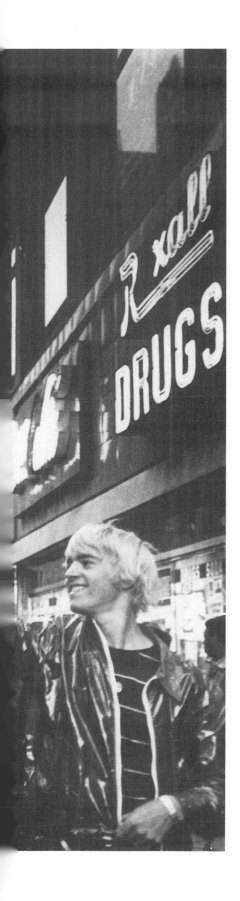

In September 1970, the Black Panther Party sponsored the Revolutionary People's Constitutional Convention in Philadelphia, which brought together supporters from across the country, including members of the Gay Liberation Front (GLF). After some negotiation between the two organizations about the role GLF could play in the revolution, on August 21, 1970, Huey Newton, Supreme Commander of the Black Panther Party, published a letter in the party's newspaper that caused quite a stir in black nationalist circles. In it he stated that "maybe a homosexual could be the most revolutionary." He articulated his recognition of the level of oppression women and gay people face in this society and of the need for African-Americans to resist their insecurities and respect the participation of lesbians and gays in the struggle for liberation. The Black Panther Party had worked to redeem many members of the black community and to forge a bond between liberation struggles worldwide. It was not totally out of character that lesbians and gays be included, though resistance to their presence was vociferous enough to cause most GLF women and some GLF men to walk out.

Earlier opportunities to deal with homosexuality within the context of the black struggle for liberation had not been so direct. Bayard Rustin was one of the organizers of the March on Washington where Dr. Martin Luther King Jr. gave his historic "I Have a Dream" speech. When Sen. Strom Thurmond denounced Rustin as a homosexual, draft dodger, and communist on the Senate floor in 1963, there was debate among civil rights leaders about whether Rustin should be allowed to continue his public work with the committee organizing the march. The support of Dr. King as well as A. Philip Randolph kept Rustin on

Some of the street kids who fought back during the Stonewall uprising, in part because they had little to lose, marching here under the banner of the Gay Liberation Front, the first major lesbian or gay organization to emerge following Stonewall. Photo by Diana Davies.

**Statement of Demands
to the Revolutionary Peoples
Constitutional Convention**
from the Male Representatives
of National Gay Liberation

We Demand:
1. The right to be gay anytime, anyplace.
2. The right to free physiological change and modification of sex upon demand.
3. The right of free dress and adornment.
4. That all modes of human sexual self-expression deserve protection of the law, and social sanction.
5. Every child's right to develop in a non-sexist, non-possessive atmosphere, which is the responsibility of all people to create.
6. That a free educational system present the entire range of human sexuality, without advocating any one form or style; that sex roles and sex-determined skills be not fostered by the schools.
7. That language be modified so that no gender take priority.
8. The judicial system be run by the people through people's courts; that all people be tried by members of their peer group.

9. That gays be represented in all governmental and community institutions.

10. That organized religions be condemned for aiding in the genocide of gay people, and enjoined from teaching hatred and superstition.

11. That psychiatry and psychology be enjoined from advocating a preference for any form of sexuality, and the enforcement of that preference by shock treatment, brainwashing, imprisonment, etc.

12. The abolition of the nuclear family because it perpetuates the false categories of homosexuality and heterosexuality.

13. The immediate release of and reparations for gay and other political prisoners from prisons and mental institutions; the support by gay political prisoners of all other political prisoners.

14. That gays determine the destiny of their own communities.

15. That all people share equally the labor and products of society, regardless of sex or sexual orientation.

16. That technology be used to liberate all peoples of the world from drudgery.

17. The full participation of gays in the Peoples Revolutionary Army.

18. Finally, the end of domination of one person by another.

board, but discreetly so. The issue of Bayard Rustin's homosexuality was frequently used as a weapon against King by other black leaders. Despite efforts by the closeted FBI director, J. Edgar Hoover, to exploit this inflammatory issue, it remained largely unspoken when the big march was discussed in the black community. But neither King nor any of the national organizations ever issued a statement of solidarity on the magnitude of Newton's. And on *Say Brother*, which provided a platform for most of the issues bubbling up in the black political organizations of the late 1960s, the question of homosexuality was never raised.

To my mind the Panther Party's community-education and free-breakfast programs provided practical, class-relevant action that suited its revolutionary rhetoric. Its emphasis was on self-determination, pride, history. Its somewhat radical suggestion that African-Americans dress not in suits or demure dresses but either in all-black, paramilitary, or African garb indicated at least an intuitive understanding of "costume" and how it shapes our thoughts and actions. It did not seem an unfounded leap to embrace lesbians and gays who were straining against some of the same boundaries as they worked for liberation. But the focus of the civil rights and black power movements was severely constricted, and our identities as "black" remained tenuous. People were still arguing about how skin color affected your ability to be a revolutionary. Presenting an argument to support the inclusion of lesbians and gays (if the discussion ever came up) would have been as unthinkable to me as letting my co-workers know I had a lesbian lover.

Another prominent element that made an alliance between black nationalists and the lesbian/gay movement impossible at that time was racism. Although people of color participated in the early lesbian/gay rights movement, having all the people of color crowd to the front to represent the group may not have met with any more success. Groups such as the GLF were predominantly white.

Less than a year after the Stonewall rebellion, sexism led to a split within lesbian/gay organizing. Civil rights organizations and nationalist groups had not been interested in shifting the emphasis of the discussion to include an examination of the role of sexism in society. Black activism placed racism at the center of society's ills, the presumption being that once black citizens were given our rights, everything else would fall into place. After some flirtations with the more complex interconnections suggested by socialism in the 1930s, black

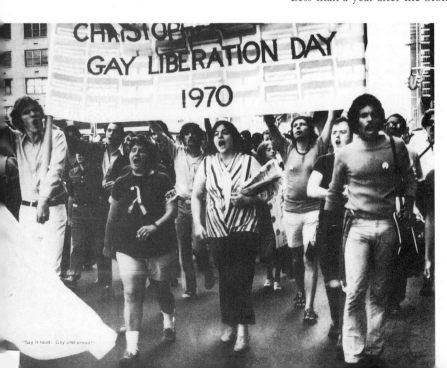

"Say it loud: Gay and proud!"

The first of what would become an annual march through the streets of New York to commemorate the Stonewall uprising. From "Gay Freedom 1970," a photographic essay published in *QQ Magazine*.

leaders eschewed analyses that made racism one of several oppressions to pursue a single-focus agenda.

The issue of sexism, probably more than class, struck a raw nerve. It left civil rights and black power activists in a position of having to consider their own beliefs and behaviors, not just those of white oppressors. In fact sexism's identification of a black male power structure was, in itself, probably too much to handle. When Stokely Carmichael laughingly announced that the position for women in the movement was prone, many perceived his remark as a joke. But many others did not. And the lesbians of GLF didn't take as a joke the routine sexism of gay liberationists or black nationalists.

Despite Huey P. Newton's enlightened engagement in print with the questions of sexism and homophobia, women from GLF felt sexism was never honestly addressed at the Constitutional Convention or raised among members of the Gay Liberation Front. GLF support of the Black Panther Party proved a significant factor in persuading the lesbians of GLF to form their own organization. And because the concept of a revolutionary alliance with the Panthers struck many GLF members as irrelevant to their goals, it also precipitated their departure and the formation of the Gay Activists Alliance.

But the attempt to make this revolutionary alliance had been important. Across the country, in smaller cities, with varying degrees of success, lesbian and gay groups were attempting to forge just such alliances with black organizations. Philadelphia's Homophile Action League, which was always more ethnically diverse, had made outreach an intrinsic part of its plans, even though it also cautioned against wholesale support of groups that did not show reciprocal support for the lesbian/gay movement.

By participating in the Constitutional Convention, GLF was attempting to establish lesbian/gay politics as a part of a national coalition. It was, in some ways, another step outside of the prescribed territory we had been permitted by society: outside the closet, outside the bar, outside the closed community. It was an impressive act of faith for a young movement and an indication of early political sophistication that has been difficult to regain. Newton's historic document remains valuable, especially today as the tide of nationalism surges again for black youth. It has resonance, too, for lesbian and gay youth who are looking for support around the issues of education and housing. The statement stands as a documentary indicator of the broad political base that is possible, and of the ways of thinking about liberation that can take root if there is someone willing to put them into words. The next step, standing behind them, is where we most often falter. The importance of Newton's statement lay not in the groundswell of support that it failed to promote, but in its simple recognition that alliances must be formed if social justice is to be attained, and that there is much to be learned from even the most transitory coalitions.

"A Letter from Huey to the Revolutionary Brothers and Sisters About the Women's Liberation and Gay Liberation Movements," *The Black Panther*, August 21, 1970.

Whatever your personal opinions and your insecurities about homosexuality and the various liberation movements among homosexuals and women . . . we should try to unite with them in a revolutionary fashion. . . . We say that we recognize the women's right to be free. We haven't said much about the homosexual at all, and we must relate to the homosexual movement because it's a real thing. And I know through reading and through my life experience, my observations, that homosexuals are not given freedom and liberty by anyone in the society. Maybe they might be the most oppressed people in the society. . . . A person should have freedom to use his body in whatever way he wants to. That's not endorsing things in homosexuality that we wouldn't view as revolutionary. But there's nothing to say that a homosexual cannot be a revolutionary. And maybe I'm now injecting some of my prejudice by saying that "even a homosexual can be a revolutionary." Quite the contrary, maybe a homosexual could be the most revolutionary. . . . When we have revolutionary conferences, rallies and demonstrations there should be full participation of the gay liberation movement and the women's liberation movement. . . . The women's liberation front and the gay liberation front are our friends, they are potential allies and we need as many allies as possible. . . . We should be careful about using those terms that might turn our friends off. The terms "faggot" and "punk" should be deleted from our vocabulary, and especially we should not attach names normally designed for homosexuals to men who are enemies of the people, such as Nixon or Mitchell. Homosexuals are not enemies of the people. . . .

This pastoral outing in Central Park was one of several public activities organized by women of the Gay Liberation Front, who strove to create women-only spaces. Photo by Ellen Shumsky.

You Are What You Cruise

Any good therapist will tell you that the breakup of a relationship is never the fault of just one party. She would also tell you that sometimes a breakup is a good thing. The Gay Liberation Front, born in the raucous aftermath of Stonewall, shared the revolutionary atmosphere with other progressive movements. The lesbians of the GLF were working within the context not just of gay liberation but of feminism. The initial argument may not even have been about sexist "behavior" per se. Women's insistence on their right to create a women-only space within the GLF was met with puzzlement by most of the GLF's male members, who, like the Panthers, were not ready to address their own privileged position as men. Some, like Jim Fouratt, who was grounded in an older leftist movement, understood the importance of consciousness-raising and the other matters that women raised. He didn't want "to sit at a table with just a few people that look[ed] like me."

Some GLF members grudgingly conceded that women had the right to their own space, but ultimately no one ever really understood what the other was feeling. The fundamental fact of sexism was not taken seriously by most of the men, and the women had no patience with men's fears about breaking up the group. After repeated efforts to gain not just the acquiescence but the active support of the men in GLF, lesbians established the GLF Women's Caucus and then their own organization: Lesbian Feminist Liberation (LFL). The women of GLF focused on developing feminist consciousness within the lesbian community as well as on providing specifically women-oriented services such as battered-women and rape-crisis intervention, health clinics, legal aid for lesbian mothers, and literary and political publications. They were also struggling to bring home the issue of homophobia to feminist groups such as the National Organization for Women.

That conflict is more prominent in my memory; maybe the press was happy to exploit a possible split among "women's libbers," or maybe it just found the split ridiculous. Maybe I was paying more attention to feminist events and issues. I had spent months, along with thousands of others, worrying about Angela Davis's welfare. She was in my consciousness not just as a black revolutionary but as a woman revolutionary. Her case provided an unconscious bridge to feminism for me.

Despite the progressive outlook of feminism, lesbians were publicly dyke-baited by many feminists, including Susan Brownmiller and Betty Friedan, who, in the mainstream media, had referred to lesbians at first as a "lavender herring" that diverted attention away from the women's movement and then as the "lavender menace" that overtly threatened the movement. The women who formed the GLF caucus decided to confront feminist homophobia. At the second annual Congress to Unite Women (sponsored by NOW, 1970), the GLF women's contingent plunged the auditorium into darkness, seized control of the microphone, and brought the lights back up to reveal dozens of women sporting T-shirts emblazoned with "lavender menace." They held the floor, laid out their case against homophobia in the women's movement, and served notice on heterosexual feminists that lesbians would no longer do the work and be quiet about their issues. They wouldn't do it for men and they wouldn't do it for straight women.

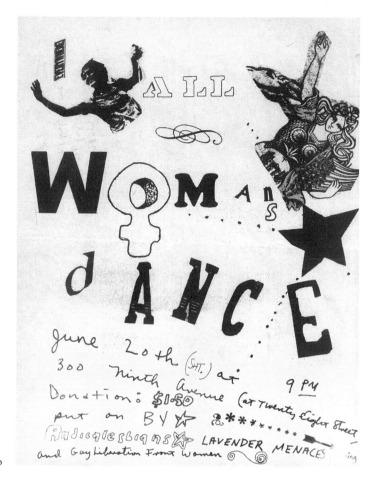

Flyer in the collection of the Lesbian Herstory Archives.

Increasing estrangement from the male-dominated workings
of the Gay Liberation Front resulted in the formation of
Radicalesbians, a group whose influence still endures through
"The Woman-Identified Woman," a collectively authored
manifesto that became a cornerstone of lesbian feminist
thought. Photo by Ellen Shumsky.

The Woman-Idenitified Woman

What is a lesbian? A lesbian is the rage of all women condensed to the point of explosion. She is the woman who, often beginning at an extremely early age, acts in accordance with her inner compulsion to be a more complete and freer human being than her society—perhaps then, but certainly later—cares to allow her. These needs and actions, over a period of years, bring her into painful conflict with people, situations, the accepted ways of thinking, feeling and behaving, until she is in a state of continual war with everything around her, and usually with herself. She may not be fully conscious of the political implications of what for her began as personal necessity, but on some level she has not been able to accept the limitations and oppression laid on her by the most basic role of her society—the female role. The turmoil she experiences tends to induce guilt proportional to the degree to which she feels she is not meeting social expectations, and/or eventually drives her to question and analyze what the rest of her society more or less accepts. She is forced to evolve her own life pattern, often living much of her life alone, learning usually much earlier than her "straight" (heterosexual) sisters about the essential aloneness of life (which the myth of marriage obscures) and about the reality of illusions. To the extent that she cannot expel the heavy socialization that goes with being female, she can never truly find peace with herself. For she is caught somewhere between accepting society's view of her—in which case she cannot accept herself—and coming to understand what this sexist society has done to her and why it is functional and necessary for it to do so. Those of us who work that through find ourselves on the other side of a torturous journey through a night that may have been decades long. The perspective gained from that journey, the liberation of self, the inner peace, the real love of self and of all women, is something to be shared with all women—because we are all women.

It should be understood that lesbianism, like male homosexuality, is a category of behavior possible only in a sexist society characterized by rigid sex roles and dominated by male supremacy. Those sex roles dehumanize women by defining us as a supportive/serving caste in relation to the master caste of men, and emotionally cripple men by demanding that they be alienated from their own bodies and emotions in order to perform their economic/political/military functions effectively. Homosexuality is a by-product of a particular way of setting up roles (or approved patterns of behavior) on the basis of sex; as such it is an inauthentic (not consonant with "reality") category. In a society in which men do not oppress women, and sexual expression is allowed to follow feelings, the categories of homosexuality and heterosexuality would disappear.

But lesbianism is also different from male homosexuality, and serves a different function in the society. "Dyke" is a different kind of put-down from "faggot," although both imply you are not playing your socially assigned sex role . . . are not therefore a "real woman" or a "real man." The grudging admiration felt for the tomboy, and the queasiness felt around a sissy boy, point to the same thing: the contempt in which women—or those who play a female role—are held. And the investment in keeping women in that contemptuous role is very great. Lesbian is the word, the label, the condition that holds women in line. When a woman hears this word tossed her way, she knows she is stepping out of line. She knows that she has crossed the terrible boundary of her sex role. She recoils, she protests, she reshapes her actions to gain approval. Lesbian is a label invented by the Man to throw at any woman who dares to be his equal, who dares to challenge his prerogatives (including that of all women as part of the exchange medium among men), who dares to assert the primacy of her own needs. To have the label applied to people active in women's liberation is just the most recent instance of a long history; older women will recall that not so long ago, any woman who was successful, independent, not orienting her whole life about a man, would hear this word. For in this sexist society, for a woman to be independent means that she *can't be* a woman—she must be a dyke. That in itself should tell us where women are at. It says as clearly as can be said: woman and person are contradictory terms. For a lesbian is not considered a "real woman." And yet, in popular thinking, there is really only one essential difference between a lesbian and other women: that of sexual orientation—which is to say, when you strip off all the packaging, you must finally realize that the essence of being a "woman" is to get fucked by men.

The message was, in many ways, in direct opposition to earlier political approaches: lesbians were refusing to be "nice girls." Some feminists decried their methods, which were demanding, loud, and effective. Lesbians could not be ignored. Unlike the female-to-male ratio in the gay movement, lesbian participation in the women's movement was high. The resultant negotiations made feminism an enduring part of lesbian organizing and vice versa. While some women continued to work with gay men, much lesbian energy went into projects considered part of lesbian nation building. The emergence of a group of women—the Lavender Menace/Radicalesbians—who were willing to take on the reputation of troublemakers gave women the space to begin to develop their own methods and most importantly their philosophy of liberation. Educational programs were devised to give women skills in trades. Health facilities sensitive to lesbians such as the St. Mark's Clinic in New York City and the Lyon-Martin Clinic in San Francisco sprang up. The annual national conference on women and the law provided a regular forum for the examination of issues facing lesbians such as partnership and inheritance rights, child custody, and discrimination in housing and the military.

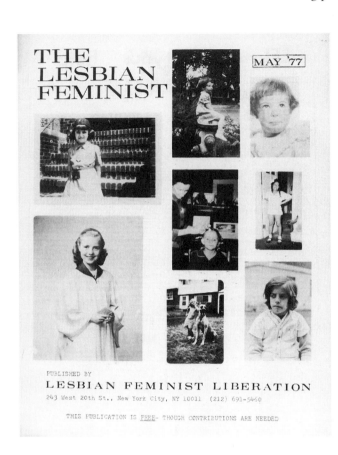

The Lesbian Feminist, published by Lesbian Feminist Liberation. Collection of the Lesbian Herstory Archives.

To me, one of the most exiting developments was the emergence of so many magazines and presses. In the 1970s the number of lesbian publications grew to tremendous proportions and included periodicals from almost all sections of the country: *Ain't I a Woman* (Iowa City), *The Furies* (Washington, D.C.), *Lesbian Tide* (Los Angeles), *Lesbian Connection* (Lansing, Mich.), *Conditions* (Brooklyn, N.Y.), and *Sinister Wisdom*, which moved with the rotation of its editors. These publications helped women who felt completely silenced by heterosexual society find their voices, and disseminated news and cultural information.

Consciousness-raising, which helped individuals come to terms with difficult identity and personal issues, became a valuable though lately parodied road that lesbians took to enlighten themselves and to survive as writers, editors, and publishers. But consciousness-raising was a sore point for men in the GLF, and another of the reasons some of them decided to split and form the single-issue Gay Activists Alliance (GAA). The issue of what political and administrative approach to take in GLF meetings had also struck a nerve. Some members felt the GLF meetings were too anarchistic, that the mission—reaching out to all oppressed people—was too broad, or that the underlying leftist/socialist philosophy was more radical than their positions. The establishment of the Gay Activists Alliance provided a venue for activism more directly tied to reformist democratic politics, and the meetings were somewhat easier on the nerves. The two organizations often worked in tandem, but the belief that one tactic was better than the other was never far beneath the surface.

The split reflected a mode of thinking that also pervaded the civil rights movement. The premise is that a movement really needs only one method—moderate or radical, reform or revolution. That type of either/or approach was exactly what lesbian feminists were trying to get away from. Male resistance to consciousness-raising was a refusal to examine the issue of sexism and to explore how far-reaching the goals of the movement could be.

Feminism remained a difficult issue for gay organizations because it asked that members struggle internally with their own privilege as well as externally with other causes of oppression. The initial surge of enthusiasm of the lesbian/gay movement could not obscure the fact that each of us had been raised in a racist and sexist society and that the commonality of homosexual desire and the institutional injunctions against it would not be enough to keep us together. Here at this moment of the splintering, the real questions were first raised but never fully articulated: How could we develop a politics that would unite us in support of a fully developed position on our issues in more than a piecemeal fashion? What belief system could do more than unite us against adversaries whenever they arise to give us the means of attaining something completely new?

The broad-based organizations like the North American Conference of Homophile Organizations (NACHO), and the East Coast Homophile Organization (ECHO), were beginning to fall prey to factionalism as a younger generation of activists emerged. New organizations such as the National Gay Task Force (founded in 1973, later the National Gay and Lesbian Task Force) worked tirelessly on a variety of issues, but like GAA stayed mainly within the arena of gay politics. This contraction of political ambitions overlooks that more precarious place where gay concerns intersect or clash with those of other oppressed people in this society. But that is often where new approaches to problem solving are found. The movement that had its roots in the spirit of revolutionary change began to lose that sweeping historical perspective and to narrow its vision. In this, it reflected the common narrowing of political visions as the United States turned to the relative insularity of "self-realization" during the period after 1972 when our participation in the Vietnam War ended.

Marty Robinson, who left the homophile Mattachine Society of New York to participate in the revolutionary Gay Liberation Front, went on to found the Gay Activists Alliance, an overtly reformist alternative to the GLF. The Gay Activists Alliance adapted GLF's confrontational strategies to a more structured organizing approach focused solely on gay rights and visibility. Photo by Bettye Lane.

Where Will You Be?

I heard Huey Newton speak in Cambridge in the late sixties, and when asked about some changes in the Black Panther Party, he responded with a humorous double entendre: "Flux, everything flux." He pointed out what I think is the heart of any revolutionary movement. Just as we activists ask the establishment to change, so, too, must we be changing, reevaluating, and updating the information about who we are and what we want, about how we change the world. The questions that we put to the oppressor we must also periodically put to ourselves if we hope to effect real social progress. This was the essence of consciousness-raising for political groups and the plea that lesbian feminists were making to their gay brothers.

The shift in attention to lesbian feminist organizing by the women of GLF and GAA was more than the fallout from confrontations with sexism, it was an essential part of their evolution. They needed to take on an identity that was fuller than gay, that reflected the other areas in which lesbians were oppressed. A number of others within the lesbian/gay movement who encountered oppression in their lives for reasons other than just being lesbian or gay experienced a parallel shift. STAR, Street Transvestite Action Revolutionaries, was the work of Sylvia (Ray) Rivera and Marsha P. Johnson, two street queens who knew the oppressions of race and economics as well as sexuality. Their first order of business was to try to create a home for their homeless. The Third World Caucus of GAA soon emerged to create a feeling of racial solidarity for the vastly outnumbered people of color. A black lesbian caucus also met sporadically. Several incarnations followed until the establishment of Salsa Soul Sisters in 1974. Salsa Soul Sisters embarked on an impressive program of education, activism, and cultural and social events that, for the first time, centered on lesbians of color. Salsa Soul Sisters' success lay in its ability to meet black and Latina lesbians on their own ground. Although its first meetings were held in church-donated space in the West Village, it drew women from Manhattan, the Bronx, Brooklyn, Staten Island, Queens, and New Jersey because it created one of the things impossible for lesbians of color to find— a comfortable social space. Dances, picnics, bus trips, literary readings, as well as

FAGGOT:
bundle of sticks
used for kindling

JANUARY 27 & APRIL 6:
Metropolitan Community Church
Los Angeles, CA

GAY PRIDE DAY:
The Exit Bar
San Francisco, CA

workshops and professional speakers, had women of color at the center rather than as simply an afterthought. For women whose frame of reference was the civil rights movement, Salsa Soul provided the cultural grounding, such as music, food, socializing, that was familiar to black activists. It was just the right mix of the personal and the political.

Salsa Soul Sisters continues now, more than twenty years later, under the name of African Ancestral Lesbians United for Societal Change. Around the country the need to work within a recognizable cultural frame of reference emerged in many communities. Eventually Unidas was formed in Los Angeles, Las Buenas Amigas in New York, Sapphire's Sapphos in Washington, D.C. Later, Asian Lesbians of the West Coast and the East Coast sprang to life.

The Gay Activists Alliance made its home in the Firehouse (above), a building that was equal parts political headquarters and social hangout. In 1974 the Firehouse was destroyed by arson, one casualty of a series of fires that ravaged lesbian and gay centers around the U.S. Fran Lebowitz reported in *Interview:* "At 3:04 A.M. on October 8, 1974, the fire alarms sounded alerting the boys in rubber to the fact that the Gay Activist Alliance Firehouse at 99 Wooster Street was burning down. . . . No one was hurt so thank God we won't be hearing any tasteless remarks about flaming faggots." Photo by Bettye Lane. Sequence of stills (below) from Program One, *Out Rage '69.*

JULY 27:
Metropolitan Community Church
San Francisco, CA

In October 1974,
the GAA Firehouse in
New York City was
destroyed by arson.

gay activist

The Combahee River Collective was a Boston-based black feminist collective that was founded in 1974. As a series of unsolved murders of black women in Boston occurred in 1978–79, Combahee members mobilized women of color to protest police indifference. At center is Barbara Smith. Photo by Tia Cross.

The Combahee River Collective in Boston was an example of the central difference between the organizing focus of people of color and other lesbians or gays. Endemic to the mission of Combahee was "solidarity around the fact of race." The group was a way to build the sense of self black lesbians need in a racist society and to facilitate unity with other black people. White gay and lesbian liberation groups recognized little need to reconnect with the communities from which they'd come. But doing so was essential for the emotional health of people of color.

Within the larger lesbian movement an idea began to take root that paralleled the needs expressed by the actions of people of color—lesbian separatism. The premise was that lesbians should withdraw from male contact and domination by coming together in communities that are devoted exclusively to lesbians. Separatism was not a completely new idea for white lesbian and gay men. In 1970 there was at least one ambitious plan—the Alpine Project—for a mass migration to establish a lesbian/gay takeover of a sleepy town in central California.

Lesbian separatism was somewhat different. Women first established women-only festivals, and many later combined their resources to purchase land. This evolution was significant for lesbians who became separatists and for those who did not, as well as for the men they left behind. Gay men were left to ponder their role as oppressors as well as being oppressed themselves—an opportunity for critical reflection that not many took advantage of. Lesbians found themselves working and living for extended periods in proximity to other lesbians who had determined that the only true way for a lesbian to be liberated was to isolate herself from society more deliberately than lesbian life already had. Separatism seemed even more radical than feminism to many lesbians. It pointed up the need for a philosophy that was based not just on the presence of an oppressor but on the formation of a common focus, shaped by lesbian vision, on the goal of a nation free from oppression.

When I attended the Michigan Womyn's Music Festival, I went with excitement and openness, not knowing what to expect. A picture of Woodstock floated somewhere in my head, but even that was incomplete since my images of Woodstock had all come from *Life* magazine. The level of energy rose about one hundred points as soon as I boarded the Salsa Soul Sister bus in Greenwich Village and we started what seemed like an endless journey. When I finally got off the bus on the land in Michigan and started putting up my tent, the energy went off the scale. And before the four days were over, I felt as if I could levitate.

Yes, the sanitation was not the best; yes, not all the pathways were accessible; yes, I ate more peanut butter and tofu than I'd seen in my entire life. Yes, it rained, but I'd been carefully instructed on how to put up my tent to avoid disaster. The only thing akin to the psychic joy I felt at the festival was my visit to Ghana and Dahomey when I was twenty-three years old. A completely new world opened up. I could see the past and the future all at once. My life was in a totally new context, one of power, not victimization.

In the middle of Michigan, eight thousand women, trying to get to know each other, trying to get a date, just trying to get along, was an amazingly arduous yet similarly liberating experience. That women were willing and able to take on the emotional, financial, legal, and political responsibility of such a massive project,

not just once but every year, left me feeling that I could accomplish anything. It was here that some of the first workshops on and organizing for the establishment of women's land happened.

Years later when I stage-managed at the New England Women's Music Festival, it was a smaller but no less intense experience. From the inside it is not the nirvana it seems to a young dyke who is just listening to the music or going to the workshops and cruising women. But the radical (in this society) idea of women controlling our own space—deciding where everything goes, how things should proceed, what is valuable—made it worth the hassles of trying to figure out where to put the smokers and drinkers and how to protect practitioners of sadomasochism from the wrath of the anti-S/M contingents. Making the decision to have a separate space under women's control—whether it's the festival grounds or an ongoing community like The Pagoda in Florida or Camp Sister Spirit in Ovett, Mississippi, or the many other rural enclaves of lesbian separatists around the country—is a brave act.

Throughout the 1970s lesbian feminists forged a unique culture and community. One of its greatest achievements was women's music, a genre rooted in folk arts, which brought messages of self love and affirmation to thousands of lesbians drawn to concerts and festivals across the United States. Attending the Michigan Womyn's Music Festival has become an annual ritual. Photo by JEB (Joan E. Biren).

Women's music superstar Alix Dobkin recorded the breakthrough album *Lavender Jane Loves Women,* which helped to establish lesbian-owned recording labels as commercially viable enterprises. Photo by Lynda Koolish.

The utopian vision of a lesbian nation, made of completely self-sufficient women's communities, led to the founding of experimental lesbian-separatist communes in the 1970s. While many communes dissipated, some have not only endured but continue to spring up, such as the embattled Camp Sister Spirit in Ovett, Mississippi. Photo by Lynda Koolish.

One of the most difficult aspects of the idea of women's land is that it is a distinctly rural vision. Everything must be built from the ground up, an alien concept for most urban lesbians. The physical stamina and money such construction and maintenance require is not readily available to many. Another aspect to be faced is establishing an egalitarian system that can accommodate the wide variety of personal experiences—vegetarians, meat eaters, varying spiritual beliefs, raised poor, raised middle class or wealthy, women's music, soul music, loud, soft, chemical user, drug free, boy children, needs of the elderly, access for those with disabilities. All of these "isms" taught to us by our parents go with lesbians onto the land. And with the amount of physical work that usually needs to be done, there's little time for the meticulous processing of prejudices. One of the issues women have not been taught to deal with realistically in this country is money. Yet the purchase and use of land begins and ends with a mortgage. Romanticizing the return to nature, the presumption that lesbianism would smooth all the rough places, has left many women burned-out, broke, and bitter.

Yet for many women the possibility of making and keeping agreements with each other is enough to inspire them to leave mainstream society. It is in confronting all those changes that separatists find their lives. In the ordinariness of its goals, it's an experiment offering unparalleled empowerment.

That is some of what separatism is able to do for women and was expressly what was needed by women emerging into power in the 1970s and still today. When it works well—that is, the skills and patience are in balance with the vision, women learn to trust and rely on each other—the accomplishments of separatism can remove our doubts about ourselves. For those who've worked within a separatist context, lived in separatist communities, or given the concept the serious consideration it deserves, there is a maturation that comes with trying to fit an idyllic vision with the hard realities. Learning how to hold on to feminist principles in a misogynist world is not as easy as putting on a button or showing up at a demonstration. Keeping in mind the precepts of self-sufficiency and cultural independence that are at the root of separatism, even a lesbian who doesn't choose separatism has in hand valuable guidelines for a successful life. Lesbian separatism is much like the vision black nationalists had for black people—establishing a community that was not dependent on those who'd perpetuated oppression. Not an unreasonable idea. But it, like black separatism, seemed to strike terror in the hearts of men and some feminists.

For me, separatism was a compelling idea but socially problematic. My survival has always been intertwined with all the members of my ethnic group—contemporary and historical. Even when black men have been

rude, abusive, or willfully ignorant, our historic bond and our resistance to white supremacy stood firm. To break away from those who've been part of our survival is a leap many women of color could never make. Moving into a separatist community has often meant leaving behind not just men of color but other women of color as well. We often become the one dark face, bearing the brunt of everyone's racism, whether conscious or not. I've felt that the white separatist's dismissal of those ethnic bonds and false "color blindness" epitomize racism. As time has passed, I continue to insist that white separatists acknowledge and respect my history. But I've also come to recognize the need for me to loosen some of the bonds

Lesbian poet Pat Parker, seen here reading at the first Country Woman festival in Albion, California, in 1972. Photo by Lynda Koolish.

Barbara Smith *(l)* has continuously integrated her feminist activism with her commitment to writing. Seen here with her sister Beverly, she cofounded the Kitchen Table: Women of Color Press to make the writings of Third-World lesbians widely available. Photo by JEB (Joan E. Biren)

that keep me taking care of men, even men of color who haven't done the consciousness-raising work I still believe is necessary. I also have my own set of anxieties about nationalism, that its exclusionary political philosophies suit only a single ethnicity, gender, nationality. I do need spaces that can nourish the many constituent parts of who I am, such as being among black women hanging out together or attending a lesbian concert—these are the times and spaces that give me the energy to go on. But not one of them can offer me a place in which I can dwell exclusively.

Many see this proliferation of identity groups, of lesbian separatists, black causes, as splintering the movement, siphoning off the energy, destroying the unity. And in some ways that has been true. It left groups like GLF, GAA, and LFL looking more white than ever, free to absolve themselves of the need to examine racism or sexism. It also gave the movement the appearance of being white, since these were the groups to which the media responded.

The divergent paths taken by lesbians and gay men in this period produced an equally divergent set of accomplishments. Women used cultural activities and broad-based social concerns to develop their political ideologies and activism. The legacy of Lisa Ben and *The Ladder* was inherited by publishers like Naiad, Diana Press, and Daughter, Inc. Where there was once a desert, now an oasis flourished. Romance, murder, manifestos, utopian visions, and poetry sprang up at the growing number of women's bookstores. A later development, made possible by the groundwork these presses laid, was the founding of Kitchen Table, the first press devoted to women of color in this country. Founded by a multicultural group of women including Audre Lorde and Barbara Smith, the press responded to the writings of women of color with several groundbreaking anthologies. *Home Girls*, a black feminist anthology, and *This Bridge Called My Back*, writings by radical women of color, have become classics in the feminist, lesbian, and, increasingly, gay male communities. Cherrie Moraga said in her introduction to *Bridge*: "We begin to see ourselves all as refugees of a world on fire." For the first time lesbians of color—these "refugees"—were producing work that was then internationally distributed, incorporated into women's studies courses, and used as reference works and anchoring points for the general feminist community.

The development of women's cultural activity was an indication of the significant level of repression women felt in this society. Women's music and comedy festivals, magazines, and publishers became the focal point of lesbian energy, along with antinuclear power activism, breast-cancer awareness, and other women-identified issues. The sharp edge of lesbian comics like Maxine Feldman, Robin Tyler, and Pat Bond was honed in these lesbian-centered spaces, and in turn their humor helped lesbians keep doing the work. The social and the political realm were an interactive space, generating energy and shaping philosophy.

Gay men, on the other hand, were in a position to see their participation in the movement through more commercial eyes. They were more firmly ensconced within the existing sexist power structure. Even when closeted, they felt their influence. Developing male space has never been difficult in this society. Making it palatable to gay men who no longer see themselves as pariahs is another story. Corrupt (official and unofficial) heterosexual control of gay space had seemed like a given for more than a generation. But achievement of limited success in securing openness for a gay male subculture also brought business opportunity. The gay world began to include a Horn-and-Hardart array of social meeting places—bathhouses, bars, restaurants, discos, and resorts catering to an assortment of clientele—clones, S/M queens, but less and less "fats and femmes." The image of the Village or Castro Street clone—tight jeans, flannel shirt, closely trimmed hair and beard—became nationally recognizable. This middle-class interpretation of a working-class look suggested that gay men were not nellie queens anymore but tough, well muscled, and not to be messed with. It was the look that almost any gay (white) man could adopt and still keep his job; a look that the press—gay or straight—found more acceptable, more marketable, than the previous gay iconography.

A significant development for gay men was the creation of disco—the music and the clubs. The concept gave the music business a major shot in the arm and pushed the image of gay men farther into the general population. The music was designed for specific tastes and circumstances. Its high-pitched vocals and extraordinary lengths contributed to an almost trancelike state aided by innovative lighting,

Sylvester was the only openly gay performer to achieve crossover success as a reigning diva of disco. Photo by Rink Foto.

mirrored balls, and large quantities of marijuana, quaaludes, cocaine, and poppers. It was music for the young and adventurous that spoke to a wide spectrum of men, from opera queens to body builders. The disco was the complete antithesis physically and psychically to most gay bars. It was not a dark, clandestine, shameful room, but expansive—a ballroom and a place of celebration. Discos courted the patronage of almost everyone. Celebrities went to Studio One in Los Angeles and to the Paradise Garage in New York City. The media picked up the images of whirling, athletic, handsome gay men, making them look almost like the boy next door—but better. The actual physical place was not usually distinctive on the outside. The Garage, as it was usually called, was an old taxicab facility in downtown Manhattan's far west side: inconvenient to get to and nondescript from the outside to uninitiated passersby. But inside was something else. It's oil-stained floors and walls were camouflaged with ramps and carpeted platforms creating endless vaulted spaces awash in moving light. The effect was that you were Cinderella finally at the ball with Prince Charming there at your fingertips, somewhere among the crowd. Finally, the Garage had a reputation not just for transcendent music but for transcending the boundaries of race and class that other clubs reinforced. In the minds of many, it was the disco equivalent of utopia.

With the musical crossover gay icons, the Village People, it became clear just how closely gay dreams paralleled those of the rest of the country. Dressed as a motorcycle cop, a construction worker, an Indian chief, a motorcycle gang member, a cowboy, etc., the Village People embodied the lustful fantasies of gay men, some of which had been explicitly eroticized by Tom of Finland. At the same time they parodied the stereotypical Hollywood images of macho that had been sold to generations. The overlap made them palatable to almost everyone in the mainstream. And before there was k. d. lang out on the airwaves, there was Sylvester, blending black gospel with disco diva drama, selling records by the millions. Sylvester, tall, brown, and plump, represented the fantasy world of elegance and romance that was appealing to even the most tweedy gay man. Yet his earthy blackness was not overpowered by the glitter of rhinestones. His presence in the gay community of San Francisco was solid, and the seriousness of his approach to his art was obvious. His balance of fantasy and reality was his hallmark. "You make me feel mighty real"—my favorite refrain—gave voice to both the starry-eyed quality many of us still had as we approached the possibility of an openly lesbian/gay life and suggested that the fantasy of "regular life" was not beyond our grasp. Perhaps even in *our* lives there could be the comforting rhythms of the everyday.

Some lesbians found the music, lights, and space of male discos liberating. It was like having Michigan all year round, not just a week in August—and no rain. The emergence of a gay male space opened a window for lesbians and the straight world and provided a new common ground for lesbians and gay men of all ethnicities.

The immediate impression might be that women and men are just different and want different things with their money and leisure time. That is true, in part, but this development was also further indication of the very real economic differences between men and women. Women, statistically, just did not have the financial resources or supportive contacts that would have allowed the proliferation of women's bars. In some cases, like Maude's, a woman-owned bar that opened in San Francisco in 1966 and operated for over twenty years, the creation of a lesbian social space was successful. But it was more likely that a women's bar be managed, not owned, by a woman. And many lesbian feminists insisted that the bars were too much like a colonized territory. Lesbians who wanted to dance in a predominantly women's disco space had to wait till the eighties and then make due with traveling dances sponsored by groups like Cinnamon Productions and Shescape.

For some gay men, too, the trendy disco was outside their economic reach. The gay street people and hustlers who frequented the docks and Times Square may have had a place of their own at the Stonewall Inn, but lavish members-only establishments like the Saint or Flamingo were not putting out the welcome mat. They were more likely to find themselves in a place like Blues, a more old-fashioned establishment on Forty-third Street, which over a decade after Stonewall erupted suffered more than one brutal police raid. In September 1982, the mostly black and Hispanic clientele—many drag queens among them—fought back, but the location did not make Blues an easy flash point. It had none of the accoutrements of a trendy disco and fit in easily with the seedy bars on the neighboring blocks. Its only distinction aside from its location across the street from the *New York Times* building was that its customers were nonwhite gay men. Protests against the harassment and police brutality at Blues were organized ten days later, and fifteen hundred protesters showed up, but Blues easily got caught up in the perpetual cleanups of Times Square by the law. While the disco era offered a new way of being lesbian and gay together and made "gay" life at least more newsworthy, bars like Blues still thrived, thereby pointing up the vast economic disparities between women and men, as well as the uneven economic and political development among men.

A peak moment at the Paradise Garage in New York, one of the defining gay discos of the 1970s. Photo courtesy Mel Cheren.

A typical weekend gathering in San Francisco's Castro district during the late 1970s, where gay male street styles were on parade. Photo by Rink Foto.

One of the things that lesbians and gays were beginning to understand, just from looking around our communities and from increasing mainstream attention to the "gay lifestyle," was that one of our greatest strengths is the immense diversity of the lesbian/gay community. It's like the television ad for the Bell yellow pages: "If it's out there, it's in here." But the full attention never really wavered from gay men. Other lesbian and gay communities—those that were not centered on either coast or did not take well to instant makeovers—were left in the shadow.

The reality is that the diversity of the community offers little common ground and that sustained organizing for all of us is a nightmare. Ethnicity, class, and gender were always unresolved questions within the movement. But as the mainstream media focused its attention on lesbian and gay images, these questions were pushed even farther into the background. National network films about lesbians

(*A Question of Love*, 1978) or gay men (*That Certain Summer*, 1972) attempted to make homosexuals acceptable to the mainstream audience, which meant erasing any of us who lived on the margins. The portrait of lesbians and gay men as middle-class professionals and artists with discretionary income was as inaccurate as the picture of all blacks as drug-dealing welfare recipients. It was a mythic representation that did as little to help others to see us as it did to help us to see ourselves.

An archetypal leather couple at the Folsom Street Fair in San Francisco. Photo by Rink Foto.

Fruit Juice

There's a classic scene in the 1930s James Cagney film *The Public Enemy* in which he's having an argument over the breakfast table with his "gun moll." Abruptly he reaches out and pushes half a grapefruit into her face. It's shocking how naturally the act catches his punishing rage. I have to admit that from 1977 on, whenever I thought of that film, I saw not the pert blonde but Anita Bryant, spokesperson for the Florida Citrus Commission, coughing and sputtering as her mascara runs in

Members of Salsa Soul Sisters, a pioneering organization of African-American and Latina lesbians founded in 1974, demonstrating in opposition to Anita Bryant's homophobic crusade. Photo by Bettye Lane.

acidic streams down her face. She was actually hit in the face with a cream pie in Iowa, by a gay activist, an event covered extensively in the media. But the situation left journalists a little confused as to what tone to take. Their homophobia and sexism kicked in all at once. They couldn't take her too seriously. She was just a former Miss America, and she looked silly with the cream on her face. But the

journalism establishment had to take Bryant seriously or it would look as if they were siding with homosexuals. We, too, had to take her seriously. As Candice Boyce of Salsa Soul Sisters said, "The homophobia of Anita Bryant was the homophobia of the country."

If in the words of the Radicallesbian manifesto "Woman-Identified Woman," lesbianism is the rage of all women condensed to the point of explosion, Anita Bryant seemed to be the parallel condensation of straight, middle-class frustration and emptiness. Bryant effectively undermined support for the Dade County (Miami) gay-rights ordinance, launching the first salvo from what a friend of mine has termed the unapologetic right. Like conservative politician Spiro Agnew, who recommended the "benign neglect" of people living in poverty, and like religious (Christian) leaders from the pope to Jimmy Swaggart who cloaked their bigotry in words of concern, Bryant called her campaign Save Our Children. Bryant, and then John Briggs in

In 1977, entertainer and born-again Christian Anita Bryant spearheaded a crusade to repeal a Dade County, Florida, ordinance that guaranteed equal housing and employment rights for lesbians and gay men. Her campaign, and a similar initiative led by then-senator John Briggs in California the following year, foreshadowed the efforts by the religious right to eliminate the rights and protections afforded lesbians and gay men in the 1990s. AP/Wide World Photos.

California, played on resentments and fears that all U.S. citizens are raised with to demonize lesbians and gay men. In the process they laid the groundwork for the subsequent national antigay campaigns of fundamentalist Christian right-wing groups. The Anita Bryant crusade also restored a sense of common political destiny to lesbians and gay men and helped establish within the movement awareness of urgency and of the need to organize. The national boycott of Florida orange juice had the focus and energy of the grape boycotts in support of Cesar Chavez's farm-worker union. Lesbians and gay men took to the streets, this time with picket signs, and this time we made the 11 P.M. news.

In 1978, a nationwide support network helped local activists defeat the Briggs initiative, which would have locked lesbian and gay teachers out of California's classrooms. The national response to the attack from conservatives was a valuable energizer for the movement. Unfortunately, we did not review our history nor did we take a lesson from the right and begin to articulate a broad-based strategy to initiate national campaigns. On the local level we did well, seeing the election of many first-time lesbian or gay officials, such as Elaine Noble to the Massachusetts State Legislature (1974) and Harvey Milk to the San Francisco Board of Supervisors (1977). But unless we were reacting to an external crisis, we remained fractured as a movement. This was a structural "given" in a movement that consists of a network of pocket publics scattered throughout all sociological and geographical strata of society.

But neither did we respond at all to the indicators in society that pointed to a conservative backlash. After all, the man who became president of the United States in 1969, the same year as Stonewall, was a politician whose paranoia was legend: Richard Nixon. The mood of the country was no longer expansive but defensive and surly. Men were being defeated in a war that they were proclaiming they would win.

The National Gay Task Force did begin to set a national agenda, creating several local civil rights offices that could help to present a lesbian and gay response to both governmental and individual manifestations of homophobia. But the national focus seemed to lose sight of the grassroots elements that made Stonewall and the response to the Briggs campaign as effective as they were. When the Gay Liberation Front was organized in New York City, other branches quickly sprang up around the country, often with the assistance of GLF members who traveled to communities and campuses to share philosophy and strategies. The design of the organization gave it a grassroots base. Members could respond quickly, independently, yet remain part of a larger body and mount national actions. Examined closely, this method is also similar to the grassroots strategy of the religious right. The growing influence of Christian fundamentalists and the increased alienation that people felt from government suggested that the movement had to look to its past in order to prepare for the future. The "old-time religion" approach had to be joined to the pie in the face.

At a press conference in Des Moines, Iowa, a gay activist from Minneapolis delivered a pie in the face of Anita Bryant. AP/Wide World Photos.

Private Club

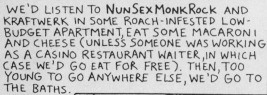

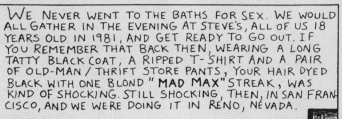

WE NEVER WENT TO THE BATHS FOR SEX. WE WOULD ALL GATHER IN THE EVENING AT STEVE'S, ALL OF US 18 YEARS OLD IN 1981, AND GET READY TO GO OUT. IF YOU REMEMBER THAT BACK THEN, WEARING A LONG TATTY BLACK COAT, A RIPPED T-SHIRT AND A PAIR OF OLD-MAN/THRIFT STORE PANTS, YOUR HAIR DYED BLACK WITH ONE BLOND "MAD MAX" STREAK, WAS KIND OF SHOCKING. STILL SHOCKING, THEN, IN SAN FRANCISCO, AND WE WERE DOING IT IN RENO, NEVADA.

WE'D LISTEN TO NUN SEX MONK ROCK AND KRAFTWERK IN SOME ROACH-INFESTED LOW-BUDGET APARTMENT, EAT SOME MACARONI AND CHEESE (UNLESS SOMEONE WAS WORKING AS A CASINO RESTAURANT WAITER, IN WHICH CASE WE'D GO EAT FOR FREE). THEN, TOO YOUNG TO GO ANYWHERE ELSE, WE'D GO TO THE BATHS.

WE HATED RENO WITH THE RIGHTEOUS PASSION OF THE YOUNG, BRILLIANT AND TRAPPED. NO ONE AT THE BATHS WOULD SLEEP WITH US—THEY WERE CLONES, THEY WERE MEN. WE WERE FAGGOTS, AND PROUD OF IT, LONG BEFORE ANYBODY EVER INVENTED QUEERS. NO, WE WENT TO THE BATHS FOR THE MUSIC.

AT THE SAN FRANCISCO BATHS LOTS OF HOT MEN WERE FUCKING THEIR BRAINS OUT, BUT MORE IMPORTANTLY, THERE WAS A D.J. THERE MAKING TAPES OF THE BEST MUSIC IN THE WORLD, WHICH HE SENT TO THE CLUB BATHS IN RENO. WHERE ELSE COULD WE HEAR THE MUSIC WE NEEDED? A.M. RADIO RULED THE WORLD, WITH POCKETS OF HEAVY METAL ON F.M. AS THE ONLY ALTERNATIVE. SO WE'D GO TO THE BATHS AND DANCE THROUGH THE HALLS, RUNNING INTO EACH OTHER'S ROOMS TO ASK, "WHO DOES THAT SONG?" AND SMOKE CIGARETTES AND SHRIEK LIKE THE 18-YEAR-OLD MISSIES WE WERE.

"Private Club" by Robert Kirby, story by Orland Outland.
From *Strange-Looking Exile*, no. 5.

IT'S WHERE I FIRST HEARD JOY DIVISION AND THE FIRST NEW ORDER SONGS, LIKE "CEREMONY" AND "EVERYTHING'S GONE GREEN." KLAUS NOMI AND GARY NUMAN AND OMD, SO LONG BEFORE ALL OF THEM WERE ANYBODY ANYONE HAD HEARD OF BUT US.

SOME SONGS, WE NEVER FOUND THE ARTIST. I WOULD PAY A FORTUNE FOR THE ONE THAT GOES "CAN I HAVE A TASTE OF YOUR ICE CREAM / CAN I LICK THE CRUMBS FROM YOUR TABLE / CAN I INTERFERE IN YOUR CRISIS?" THAT SONG WAS OUR MANTRA; OUR RELIGIOUS DUTY WAS TO SING IT ON BUSY DOWN-TOWN STREETS, TERRIFYING TOURISTS WHO EXPECTED NONE OF THIS IN THE BIGGEST LITTLE CITY.

SMALL WONDER I DIDN'T GET INFECTED UNTIL 1989 — I WAS TOO BUSY DANCING AND SCREAMING TO HAVE TIME FOR SEX. WHEN THEY CLOSED THE BATHS IN S.F. THERE WERE NO MORE TAPES. FOR A WHILE THEY PLAYED THE OLD ONES, BUT ONE DAY I WENT IN AND THEY WERE PLAYING THE A.M. STATION - EVER TRY TO WANDER A DARK HALLWAY IN YOUR TOWEL, TRY-ING TO LOOK EXOTIC AND FORBIDDING, TO THE STRAINS OF "MY BABY TAKES THE MORNING TRAIN"?

BESIDES, WE WEREN'T 18 ANYMORE, ABLE TO GET IN-TO BARS AND NO LONGER QUITE SO SCARED OF MEN. WORST OF ALL, IT WASN'T SCARY TO BE PUNK ANYMORE - EVERY SUBURBAN MALL RAT WHOSE LIFE CHANGED WITH HIS FIRST DEPECHE MODE RECORD THOUGHT HE INVEN-TED THE PUNK LIFE. I GUESS WE WERE LUCKY TO HAVE HAD OUR SECRET WORLD, PUNK FAGS IN THE MIDDLE OF NOWHERE; AT LEAST WE LOST OUR WORLD TO TIME AND OTHER FACTORS AND NOT TO THE MACHINERY THAT EATS ALL TRENDS AND MAKES THEM SOFT ENOUGH FOR MASS CONSUMPTION.

I SHOULD HAVE LOVED CLUB URANUS WHEN IT OPENED, DISCOVERED THE WORLD OF PUNK FAG-GOTRY REBORN THERE, BUT IT WAS TOO LATE. I'D DONE IT, IT WAS OVER, AND BESIDES, IT WAS AN S.F. THING, WHICH MEANT IT WAS ABOUT BEING PRETTY MORE THAN ABOUT BEING PUNK. THEY COULD HAVE PLAYED THOSE OLD TAPES AT URANUS ONE NIGHT AND THEY'D'VE SOUNDED JUST AS FABULOUS, BUT IT COULD NEVER BE THE SAME.

In the spring of 1982 over eight hundred women attended a conference, "Toward a Politics of Sexuality," at Barnard College in New York City, which was part of an annual series—The Scholar and the Feminist. A group of women swooped down on the conference, leafleting, disrupting sessions, and blocking entrances in order to silence discussion of issues they'd deemed inappropriate—butch/fem relationships, sadomasochism, pornography. The panelists weren't engaging in any act, simply talking about them. The following weeks saw the harassment of a number of lesbian feminist writers and activists including Joan Nestle, Dorothy Allison, Gayle Rubin, and Amber Hollibaugh. The question of sex rose up before us, that specter that the lesbian and gay movement kept trying to push to the background. Just as queer demonstrators of the fifties were advised not to show any affection publicly, we were now told that some forms of affection were inappropriate, incorrect. Conservative heterosexual male repression has always elicited a militant response from those being attacked; the conservative feminists' imitation of heterosexual male repression ignited the "sex wars." A flurry of articles, books, and panels debating the dangers or benefits of various aspects of lesbian sexual life and identity was precipitated. The good news was that lesbians had something to debate.

In 1985 a presidential commission was appointed, headed by Attorney General Edwin Meese, to travel the country and gather data about the harmful nature of pornography. The New York City session I attended was a carefully orchestrated antiporn forum that cost the country an enormous amount of money but elicited little new information that would be of use in protecting women from violence. Although the methods and targets of the antiporn attacks were generally ill-conceived, the activism did open up the important discussion of the commodification of female sexuality and the commercial violence connected to it.

In direct response to the attempt to shut down discussion of certain aspects of female sexuality, *On Our Backs*, the nation's first lesbian sex magazine, was founded (1983) in San Francisco. It was followed shortly by the publication of other erotic anthologies and short-story collections, as well as erotic literary readings. The sex wars may have seemed beside the point for lesbians not that interested in erotic writing or the esoterica of S/M, or those who were simply living their lives outside of the urban spotlight, not naming their identities or behavior. But in a culture in which the objectification of women and our sexuality is a dominant theme, the addition of sex as an aspect of lesbian life was important to helping lesbians understand our fullest selves. The phenomenon also helped to infuse the lesbian movement with an energy not really experienced since the old Lavender Menace days. In the antiporn movement lesbian activists again encountered heterosexual feminists who were unable to see lesbians fully and, worse, some lesbians who were willing to sacrifice lesbians they didn't approve of.

Although it was repeatedly shown that antiporn campaigns almost always injured lesbian and gay bookstores or embargoed lesbian or gay periodicals, rather than *Playboy* or *Penthouse*, a generalized erotophobia kept the controversy going for years. The campaign made it possible for conservatives and members of the religious right to ally themselves with antiporn feminists in developing legislation (for example, in Minneapolis) whose purpose was to protect women, and that legislation was often implicitly and explicitly antigay.

As lesbians were fighting to protect our rights to express and experience sexuality, the appearance of HIV sparked a still more dangerous set of conflicts for gay men. Panic over the spread of the disease led city officials and some gay leaders to demand the closing of gay bathhouses and bars with back rooms used for anonymous sex. But like the wholesale condemnation of pornography, this demand promised a false solution. It suited the need that some had to condemn promiscuous sex, thereby answering to our most censorious and guilty consciences, but it arguably promised to do little to halt the spread of HIV. Rather than throw the captive audience out into unregulated settings, I had thought the baths and bars a natural place to educate gay men about safer sex.

The public attacks against the baths raised the ire of lesbian feminists who were already fighting to protect lesbian sexuality from antiporn activists. More than lesbian separatism, the sex wars left each faction—prosex or antiporn—shocked and surprised at the other's position. The unexpected alliance of lesbian feminists and gay men who demonstrated to keep the baths open continued the revelation of how complex the movement and its politics were. This moment of mutual political recognition between lesbians and gay men signaled a new era of activism. The historical tendency to downplay sexual expression in the movement was now challenged by the need to valorize our sexual identity against unprecedented hostile circumstances.

In 1985 my boss and friend, Gregory Kolovakos, urged me to come to a meeting of a group of people who were strategizing to fight the *New York Post*'s campaign to close the baths and its inflammatory misrepresentation of the AIDS epidemic in which large headlines like "AIDS DEN" screamed at us from newspaper stands. Gregory's world had been focused on translating Latin American literature and reading poetry aloud. It was hard for me to imagine him tromping around with a picket sign outside a sex club. I didn't know how I was going to fit one more meeting into my life, but then I bumped into a pal, film theorist and activist Vito Russo, and he, too, urged me to come. Then I heard that Jim Owles, who'd helped found the Gay Activists Alliance, was part of it all, so I showed up. When I became the treasurer of the Gay and Lesbian Alliance Against Defamation (GLAAD), I knew that the next two years of my life were spoken for.

At a large demonstration outside the *New York Post* building, the rallying cry came from GLAAD member Darryl Yates Rist. He screamed, and everyone took

It was around ankles and wrists that bath-house patrons wore the keys to the lockers and private rooms they rented. Nine years after the New York City Department of Health shut down these establishments, until February 1995 the keys still hung in a gay bathhouse vestibule. Photo by Ira Tattelman.

up the chant: "Stop the lies!" For many of us this was a demand made not just of the newspaper but of ourselves. We could no longer *not* see the threat of AIDS, nor could we allow our sexual lives to be repressed, recloseted, because of the society's and *our own fears* about sexuality. As a community, we had to acknowl-edge desire and embrace it as a right. Even as ministers like Jerry Falwell were preaching that AIDS was a punishment for gay sex, and antiporn activists were dictating the correct ways to have sex, we had to accept the challenge of being sexual and responsible simultaneously.

GLAAD's frontal attack on a major news publication attracted national attention and led to the establishment of a network of GLAADs, which moni-tored the media coverage of lesbians and gays. For the first time we were not beg-ging people to pay attention, we were giving grades for the quality of attention. American society is shaped by mass communications that transmit information of dubious veracity and value. GLAAD's goal of intervening and influencing that flow of information was a crucial direction for the movement to take, one that had been tried in more modest—though no less creative—ways in the GAA. There had been relatively little that lesbians and gays could do to respond to the misrep-resentations and distortions of who we were before we were forced by AIDS to stand in the spotlight. As we began to speak for ourselves, about ourselves, what we had to say remained a question.

Gregory was the executive director of GLAAD for two years before his health started to deteriorate because of AIDS. Before then he had successfully balanced an array of urgent activities: guiding GLAAD to its incorporation, meeting with media representatives, fulfilling his duties as director of the literature program at the State Arts Council of New York, and championing the work of Spanish-speaking writers to the English-speaking literary establishment. In that time GLAAD grew from a local committee sifting through news clippings to an organization with national chapters and development directors. After having spent most of his adult life fighting in one way or another for literature and for love, Gregory died on tax day, 1990.

The idea of GLAAD seems to have been a success. But once we've altered our lives to combat media misrepresentation or conduct an orange-juice boycott, to write letters to congressmen and senators, to arrive at buses at dawn to make the demonstration by noon, how do we then transform these actions into an ongoing influence on our daily lives? How do we live the activism, not simply show up for it?

Blood Is Thicker Than Water

In 1982 I was staining bookshelves in my new apartment in the Bronx when a friend called to tell me about the first person I knew personally to die from this illness with no real name, only initials. Robert, a beautiful and brilliant black actor, had been part of my world since I'd moved to New York City in 1971. I could barely imagine him not being there, not being anywhere. I was angry with myself for falling into the trap of believing the news media's false construction of the gay community as white men only. With Robert's death I understood for the first time that they weren't the only ones dying.

Expanded awareness of the epidemic deepened the mobilization of lesbians and gays again, but this time with more ramifications than the pie in the face. Five years after my friend Robert's death, the emergence of the AIDS Coalition to Unleash Power—ACT UP—returned its members to the old GAA model of organizing. Its sustained attack on bureaucratic walls of indifference was needed to awaken lesbians and gay men as well as politicians to the tragedy and magnitude of the crisis.

For more than twenty years the women's movement had attempted to influence the medical establishment by demon-

In 1987, AIDS activists initiated a campaign of marking the streets of New York with indelible body outlines to remind passersby of the crisis to which many remained oblivious or indifferent. Photo by Bettye Lane.

ACT UP extended the patient self-empowerment model of the feminist health movement, revived the media-savvy "zaps" of the Gay Activists Alliance, and rehabilitated nonviolent civil disobedience as a central political strategy. Photo by JEB (Joan E. Biren).

strating and lobbying for safer standards in birth-control products, for healthier and more humane procedures in detecting and treating breast cancer, and for improved prenatal care for women without access to ongoing medical treatment. In her 1980 book *The Cancer Journals*, Audre Lorde spoke for many survivors: "I do not wish my anger and pain and fear about cancer to fossilize into yet another silence." But sexism made the efforts of the numerous women's organizations invisible. With the appearance of ACT UP and its vociferous, media-savvy, and confrontational methods, attention was focused nationally on the crisis in American health care.

The questions were large but specific: Where is the money? Where exactly should money go for research? How do patients get access to new drugs and enter drug trials in spite of the Federal Drug Administration's red tape? How can pharmaceutical companies be made answerable for high prices? How do women and people of color get access to drug trials that systematically exclude us? How can the 40 million people who live and die without health-care coverage get access to it? But the extensive nature of the activism and the media's coverage soon made the questions even larger. Organizations lobbying for better approaches to detection and cures for breast cancer had many questions of the same nature, and ACT UP's example—including the example of its audacious lesbian members—reignited their efforts. Unlike previous participation in gay organizing, lesbians have been an important part of ACT UP and have helped reveal that faults in the medical and insurance establishments had permitted AIDS to become the crisis it is to this day and also had perpetuated a crisis in women's health issues. By the 1992 presidential campaign, five years of demonstrations and premature deaths and the establishment of municipal liaisons to the lesbian/gay community as well as AIDS agencies within many city governments made it possible for health care to play a key role in the political agenda for the first time since Roosevelt's New Deal. It was an issue tailor-made for a Democrat and at the time a perfect target for the Republicans who like to appear to be against more government or federal subsidies.

The Bill Clinton campaign team and his early administration pursued research that many hoped would lead to a complete overhaul of the medical and the insurance establishment in this country. Republicans and lobbyists for the AMA and the insurance companies spent a lot of money to oppose such a transformation. It will be years before the issue even receives the attention it deserves, but the groundwork laid by early advocates of birth control, cancer care, and AIDS awareness is directly responsible for bringing the idea of broad-based health care before the nation.

Although few talk easily about this, it will also be a long while before we fully appreciate the extent of the losses the lesbian/gay community has suffered. First, expressly through the HIV-related deaths, we have lost the larger part of a community of men, from all age groups. Gone are men who made possible Castro and Christopher Streets, haute couture, camp, some of the finest literature, theater, and visual art of our generation. Those with the economic advantage to help give gays a visibility in the economic world, as well as those who simply overcame their fear and showed up for the marches, have died. And each year we still lose hundreds of lesbians to various forms of cancer, which still remains insufficiently targeted by the medical establishment. The baby boomers and beyond who helped to create the culture of feminism and showed us how to organize a march, or provide support systems for abused sisters, are having mastectomies, lumpectomies, hysterectomies, some not surviving beyond the projected five years.

This is the first period in our movement to witness such a broad spectrum of out lesbians and gay men. From adolescents to members of Senior Action in a Gay Environment (SAGE), lesbians and gays are taking part in the movement. This is an exiting development, but it also creates special demands. We can no longer view ourselves from a single perspective (as if we ever really could) with a single purpose: gay rights now! I read an article in a lesbian magazine in which the writer referred to me sarcastically as a "pillar of the community." I, who think of myself as made eternally young by struggling against oppression, was stunned to realize that a generation of lesbians saw me as the old guard, antiquated, somehow standing in their way. She needed to rebel against me as she rebelled against her parents. Figuring out how I continue to assess and affect the movement from this new perspective will be a challenge.

Among the many issues such an evolution makes us all face are health care for the sick and dying young, housing and social lives for those of us who are aging and have not yet returned to the heterosexual fold of our family, the education of our young children, the explosion of lesbians and gays having children, and the economic survival of all of us. The financial power of the "unapologetic right" and the growing influence of conservative lesbians and gays who now stake a claim to the movement indicate some new philosophies and strategies are long overdue. These losses and demographic shifts have not really been addressed within most lesbian/gay organizations.

The universe in which lesbian and gay activists do our work is light-years away from that which saw gay men trying to convince psychiatrists they were normal (some remain unconvinced) and lesbians remained invisible. HIV and AIDS has forced us to a new level of activism and self-awareness. It has also moved straight society to another level of consciousness. Out of the horror of AIDS, lesbians and gays have renewed a sense of affinity and coalition. There has been much bitterness, of course, as each confronted the other with his or her own idea of what kind of work was to be done and how.

Overleaf: In October 1992, thousands gathered in Washington to view and participate in ceremonies at the Names Project AIDS Memorial Quilt. Photo by Marilyn Humphries.

The day after the Names Project AIDS Memorial Quilt was unveiled in Washington, ACT UP members converged on the White House, bringing the ashes of their deceased loved ones to spill on the White House lawn in the first of several "political funerals" for people with AIDS. Photo by Marilyn Humphries.

One place where the organizing around AIDS seemed less tainted was the initiation of what is probably the largest art project in the world—the Names Project Memorial Quilt. I spoke in New York City's Central Park at the dedication of the New York section of the quilt. Before going backstage I walked through the park, examining the panels. I'd seen other sections, but this one felt different simply because it was from my town. I moved cautiously, afraid that I would walk up on a panel bearing the name of someone I knew, someone I thought was still alive.

I didn't, but I was fascinated by an object that felt so familiar yet unknown. Later I realized that what held me was not just the individual panels themselves, but what the Quilt might represent. There in the middle of Central Park, as a monument to the many who'd died, the vast majority of them men, but not all, was a representation of one of the most womanly arts—a quilt. Most monuments are quintessentially male—carved in stone, meant to defy time and to last forever. But the quilt is woven of cloth, shot through with ephemera, words, letters, snapshots, it is enduring yet transitory; artful and utilitarian. So many of the panels were like the love letters that many included, testifying to those who cannot speak for themselves.

A quilt is a nurturing thing, taking hours of arduous work, and is ordinarily made for a family member we cherish. It's meant to keep us warm and safe, to lift our spirits with its beauty and to be handed down through the generations. In this quilt I saw the theory and practice of family laid out for all to see, and in it a unity of body, spirit, and politics within the lesbian/gay community.

Some people have dismissed the Quilt as sentimental busywork, "AIDS kitsch," empty New Age spiritualism, or at any rate a retreat from activism. Of course, for some the Quilt will be any one or all of these things. But it is also a ritual of creation and display, and ritual is one of the cornerstones of any culture. It is a way for individuals to build bridges to each other. The devising of each panel as well as the organization it required to bring it before the public are unifying rituals that help to sustain communal spirit. It may be a mistake to extrapolate anything symbolic from this living monument. But it would be a worse mistake to ignore its implications regarding coalition and action.

It is easy not to hear the meaning of the words in the emotional tributes offered. It is not just the mourning for our lost friends and lovers, or for the carefree past, that is given voice. What I see when I look at the Quilt is what we still hold in reserve within the lesbian/gay community—our skills, strength, subtlety, and audacity. We are no more and certainly no less than each of the panels the Quilt weaves before us. If we can look at it and see the work behind it, we arrive at a more complete sense of who we are as a community. If we look at each action we take as a community (even the ones we don't like), from storming the steps of City Hall to helping to feed shut-ins, we will not be fooled into believing the media's narrow representation of who we are. All the indicators of who we are and where we're going are not right there on the surface, in the beadwork or headlines. We are a much more complicated people than that. The uneasy or unknown parts will yield much more about our wholeness, about our future. We are those scattered islands, each so different but still connected. If we take the time and do the work to look closely, we see not simply emotional response but the layers that make us who we are. A quilt is complex work. It can speak to us in the way Radclyffe Hall's character Stephen spoke to me—as a voice of "demand like the gathering together of great waters."

Members of ACT UP unfurl the Silence = Death banner in the New York Lesbian and Gay Pride March in 1988. Photo by Michael James O'Brien.

Sylvia (Ray) Rivera was one of the patrons of the Stonewall Inn who made history on the night of June 28, 1969, by fighting back when Deputy Inspector Seymour Pine and seven other officers from the Public Morals Section of the New York City Police raided the West Village bar. A fierce presence in the Gay Liberation Front and the Gay Activists Alliance, in 1970 Rivera cofounded STAR (Street Transvestite Action Revolutionaries), which offered shelter and support to street kids.

Before gay liberation, if you didn't want someone to bash you, you would look away. You actually looked at the ground. It's like the black person who looks away from the white man. . . . I grew up on the Lower East Side in the Spanish community. That's my heritage. Starting to come out of the closet in my culture, gay people were always belittled and put down. I used to hang out with, and even went out with, a couple of the boys, but in public they would not acknowledge me and I could not acknowledge the fact that we had been together. . . . Learning how to hustle was easy after leaving the neighborhood and going to Forty-second Street, but then I was really dealing with a different kind of straight society. I was used to what my people were saying about me, but dealing with the outside world was completely different. I got into lots of trouble just for looking at straight boys, you know, like saying to myself, "Well, this is a beautiful man." Not trying to pick them up or anything, but all of a sudden I'd find a pistol in my face because of the way I walked or the way I acted. . . .

Drag queens and effeminate men never were in a closet. What kills me as a drag queen is that I can go into a gay bar and listen to these so-called macho gay men, "Oh, Mary this, and Miss Thing that." But as soon as I walk into a bar, they know where I'm coming from, and right away I'm shunted aside.

Stonewall was basically a hustlers' bar, not the drag queen bar and not a black bar. It was a hustlers' bar for whites. Only a select few drag queens went there. Mostly you'd get third-world people and drag queens at the Washington Square Bar on Third Street and Broadway. That was one of your big third-world drag-queen bars. . . . The Stonewall was a very nice campy little bar owned by the Mafia—

the type of gay bar that was typical of that era. You just went there to party and get high and pop pills and do drugs and drink watered-down drinks. I went to the Stonewall maybe tops ten, fifteen times before it was raided. . . . I was there because we used to make the trip in from Jersey and stop off, have a drink, and then shoot over to the Washington Square Bar. But I'm glad I was there that night. It must have been fate.

I was partying. I was spaced out on black beauties and Scotch. We were dancing, my lover and I, and the next thing we know the lights came on, and lights coming on in a gay bar back then meant, "Hey, we're being raided." And, as usual, cops were checking IDs and I started freaking because I didn't think I had my ID, but my lover had his. I had just gotten my draft card, which said I was 4-F, and I was really proud of that. . . . Besides being into drugs, everybody was into politics and into changing the system. My feeling is I was fed up doing and fighting for everybody else. That night I could feel the tension inside and I'm sure everybody else that was there was feeling it, too. It was time for us to get our nook in the people's revolution, to show the world that we are human beings. We were sick and tired of being put down, and things just started happening. . . . It was bad enough that you had to go to these sleazy-ass clubs, but when you had to knock on the door, pay three dollars to get in, get one watered-down drink for the three dollars, and, if you wanted a second watered-down drink, you got it for four bucks. Everybody was just angry. I can only speak for myself, but I felt that I couldn't leave the area until everything was over. I had to see what was going to happen.

Queens started being filed out, being put into police cars, and the loose change started flying—you know, everybody

started throwing it as payoff to the cops. And then the words, the cursing: "Hey, fuck you, pigs. We're not moving. We're tired of this bullshit." You know, all this was happening, and I guess you could taste a bit of freedom before it even happened. Because I know I was feeling good, just for the change being thrown at the cops, for gay brothers and sisters and drag queens and street kids and hustlers just throwing this money at these people like, "You've been treating us like shit all these years? Uh-uh. Now it's our turn!" . . . It was one of the greatest moments in my life.

When the first brick and bottles started flying, I'm like, "Oh my God, the revolution is here. Thank God. I'm here and I'm part of it." So I enjoyed being there that night. Every outrageous thing that I did I did out of anger because society had fucked me over for so long. . . . And it was amazing that within ten minutes there were like thousands of gays in the street ready to rebel and fight the police. People were taking a lot of knocks. There was a lot of bloodshed that night.

A lot of people got hurt, but people kept coming back. . . . Someone handed me a Molotov cocktail and I had never seen one except on the news about riots. And I'm like, "What am I supposed to do with this?" And this guy said, "Well, I'm gonna light it and you're gonna throw it." And I'm like, "Fine. You light it, I throw it, 'cause if it blows up, I don't want it to blow up on me." It's hard to explain, except that it had to happen one day. . . .

The police knew they were in trouble. They barricaded their asses in there when we started our shit outside, and when they couldn't get backup for forty-five minutes, they were ready to come out shooting. Guns had been drawn. I don't know where the parking meter came from, but we did ram the door open. Molotov cocktails were flying into the bar. Telephone lines somehow mysteriously got cut. You know, through the years no one has figured that out. It's very interesting because Inspector Pine called and asked for backup, and in the middle of his phone call, according to

Activists Sylvia Rivera *(l)* and Marsha P. Johnson *(holding umbrella)* participate in one of the many protests and zaps that the members of GAA organized to advance Intro 475, which would have added *sexual orientation* to every clause of New York City's Human Rights law. The New York City Council only extended antidiscrimination protections to lesbians and gay men in 1986. Photo by Diana Davies.

what's been said, the line was cut. And it took forty-five minutes for the Tactical Police Force to get there, and within that forty-five minutes there were so many brothers and sisters out there ready to riot. Traffic had already been stopped, and Molotov cocktails were flying, windows were shattering.

For the first four years of the gay liberation movement, Lee Brewster put up the money for the bond for the parade. Bebe [Scarpi], another drag queen, worked behind the scenes and planned the first four marches. There were a lot of drag queens behind the scenes that could not be seen in front lines. . . . But the drag queens were doing a lot in the background. . . . Well, my dear girlfriend Jean O'Leary, a founder of Radicalesbians, decided that drag queens were insulting to women. In 1973 the 82 Club show queens were in the march. Side by side with the Queens Liberation Front banner and the STAR (Street Transvestite Action Revolutionaries) banner. I had been told I was going to speak at the rally. And that's when things just got out of hand. I'm very militant when it comes to certain things, and I didn't appreciate what was going down with Jean O'Leary stating that we were insulting women. There was too much stuff going down that day. Bette Midler was there and Vito Russo—may his soul rest in peace. . . . It was supposed to have been a great march. To this day, I still have people come up to me from the old days and say, "Well,

you trashed us on the fourth anniversary." I say, "No, I just stood up for me." . . . Mama Jean and I are still dear friends. She told Vito Russo to kick my ass onstage . . . but I still got up and I spoke my piece. I don't let too many people keep me down. Especially my own. . . .

I'm a very boisterous person, obviously with a temper. Instead of just going up to people and asking them to sign a petition, I would stand in the middle of a block and say, "Excuse me, could you please sign my petition to stop discrimination against homosexuals in housing and in jobs?" And people then would sign any petition. There was a peace rally one night and it was broken up at Forty-second Street and Bryant Park, and the people were pushed down towards Seventh and Eighth Avenues. The Tactical Police Force was out that night, as usual. And I'm standing there doing my thing and the next thing I know: "You're under arrest." I said, "For what?" I said, "I'm not hustling." "Well, you're under arrest." I said, "But for what?" "Well, you can't petition." I said, "But wait a minute. It's in the Constitution that I have the right." I got angry because I know that I'm being arrested for being gay, not because I'm out there soliciting signatures. . . . The first time that I had to appear in court after I was arrested for soliciting the signatures, I had no idea that there were going to be people there to back me up. I walked into this courtroom and all these brothers and sisters that I had never seen

and who were all from GLF stood up and applauded. I said to my friend Josie, who was with me, "Who are all these people and why are they standing up here applauding me?" She says, "Oh, girl, you don't have a lawyer and they're probably gonna throw you in jail and you don't even know it." I said, "Well, if I go to jail, that's fine, too. Who cares?" That's what first turned me on to GLF.

Marsha [P. Johnson] and I always had this dream. When we had STAR House, we tried to make it come true. When Marsha and I got the building on Second Street, the only person that came to help us put that building together was Bob Kohler of GLF. Bebe Scarpi came to do what she could. She would bring us groceries. She would take clothes from her mother's house and things for us to keep for the kids for sleep. . . . I've always known that through the years I have lost my brothers and sisters between drugs and living out on the street. Then I lost Marsha two

years ago . . . she had no reason to be out on the streets. She was an icon of the movement. Everybody thinks Sylvia Rivera, but Marsha was higher than me and had no place to live. Randy Wicker took her in. She helped so many people out. Marsha was a front-liner like myself. She was never afraid to take a knock or lay down in front of a police car. Marsha would go out and hustle. She'd be out hustling at night and come in with all the coffee and Danish for the people at STAR House. "All right, girls, I made all this money 'cause, see, this is for our movement." She tried to give all that help when we had STAR House despite all the bad things, including things with me. . . . But I still play little mother hen up there in Westchester in my apartment. When you come up to my apartment, what do you see? A bunch of drag queens on my floor. They come to me, "Mother Sylvia, do you have something to eat? Can I crash in your house?"

BOB KOHLER

Bob Kohler ran a talent agency on West Fifty-seventh Street during the early sixties that was notable for the number of black artists it represented. He became a confidant and supporter of the young hustlers and street queens who congregated at the park on Sheridan Square, which is where he was on the night that the Stonewall erupted. Kohler was a prominent early participant in the Gay Liberation Front before he became manager of the Club Baths on First Avenue. Today he owns a clothing store near the site of the old Stonewall Inn.

In the spring, a bunch of very young gay youths descended upon the park in Sheridan Square. They sort of set up homes there. Until May, the park was pretty much taken over by these kids and older Italian women from the Village who used to give them money and sit and talk with them. I had a particular route I'd take with my dog past the park, and sometimes they'd stop me and talk and I got friendly with them. It got to the point where I'd go in the park and listen to their troubles. . . . These street kids were terrible. They fought constantly, with each other and with anybody who just looked at them. They stole and broke windows, but I could get along with them. In retrospect, a lot of it had to do with the fact that I had no interest in them sexually, because sex was all that their lives were predicated on. That was how they lived. They would sell themselves down at the piers. They were not drag queens per se—not as we know drag queens today. . . . They'd tie a rag around their head or steal a blouse and have on silly bell-bottom pants and fright wigs that they'd steal from merchants on Fourteenth Street. It was not a pretty sight. But they felt that they could make more money that way when they'd go down to the piers at night. A lot of them never went in drag, just in cutoffs as effeminate boys. . . .

On June 28, I was walking my dog as usual, and when I turned from Waverly Place, I saw a small commotion and a paddy wagon and I thought, "Oh, that's a raid." I didn't quicken my steps. I just walked up to the park, and the kids were all on one side of it and some were putting on their makeup and not paying attention, but others were. It was commonplace to see raids. I stood there with them and then the police started bringing patrons out of the bar, and the kids knew some of them and would wave and yell to

them, things like, "Don't worry, you'll have a roof over your head," because these kids slept in doorways, on rooftops, in the park, wherever they could. Everything was very festive. Everybody was calling out to each other, "Bye! I'll see you in a day or two." And without any reason that you could see, a riot started. Now, it took very little for these kids, who were very angry. They were not all minorities—that's a myth—they were white as well as Hispanic and black. Some of them even came from good homes they'd been thrown out of or been badly abused in. Anything could set them off.

Everything happened all at once, which it does in a riot or disaster. Your first thought is self-preservation. I had my dog with me, so I was worried about him and about one of the street kids. I was trying to keep them both out of harm's way. It just started with bottles, windows breaking, trash cans, fires, then the fire engines—everybody was pulling false alarms. It just erupted. . . . The police were totally at the mercy of the crowd. There were eight police and the crowd was what appeared to be thousands—of course it wasn't, but you know those little streets. All you could see was people and it was panic time. When the cops retreated into the bar, they dragged in what they thought was one of the rioters, and it was Dave Van Ronk, the folksinger, who at the time just happened to be passing by, and they beat the hell out of him. The police have admitted that they had their guns drawn, ready to fire on the crowd. A fire did start inside. Somebody threw a Molotov cocktail or something. So the cops called for reinforcements. They were ready to shoot their way out when we heard the sirens coming from the Tactical Police Force (TPF). Which just accelerated the riot even more, because they came for blood. Up until that point people had been throwing things at the Stonewall because the cops were in there. But when the TPF came, who were the brownshirts of their day with their helmets and clubs and I think two buses, that's when things got really bad, bloody, and mean. That's when people got hurt. They came swinging their clubs, just running into the crowd and whoever was there didn't matter. That was their tactic. They broke up riots. At Kent State they called in the National Guard. In New York it was the TPF. . . .

The parking meter, again, is myth because I happened to be standing right by it and it was just loose in the ground. But they did pull it up and use it as a battering ram, trying to break down the door of the Stonewall. No one had any idea what we would have done if we had broken it down. With those eight cops, it could've been a disaster. They could have been killed because there was a frenzy and the kids were no longer in control. . . . When the TPF came, a bunch of the kids lined up in the street opposite them and formed a Rockettes line. They had a little song: "We are the Stonewall Girls. We wear our hair in curls. We don't wear underwear. We show our pubic hair." And they would kick like the Rockettes and the police would go crazy and run after them. Five or six kids would run down the street and cops would go after them, but then five or six more kids would run behind them and taunt them, too, so it became almost like a ballet. . . . One queen did grab a billy club from one of the cops. He was a very young Hispanic cop and he tripped, or she knocked him down, and she said, "How'd you like this billy club up your Puerto Rican ass?" The humiliation was greater than any cop could ever have imagined. There had been many riots during the radical sixties with all kinds of people, but no group had ever had the cops on the run. It was the first time that cops ran and barricaded

themselves—and they ran and barricaded themselves from fairies.

Eventually people just got tired and bloody and had to go to St. Vincent's [Hospital], and I remember sitting on the curb. They put up police barricades around the park. There was a place on Washington Street called the Silver Dollar, which was a hang-out, and we all went down there and talked about it like it was no big deal. There would be no more. And during that day, people started showing up with leaflets. The first leaflet I saw said, "Are homosexuals revolting? You bet your ass they are!" They were calling for meetings and calling "Gay power!" and "Off the pigs!" which was a Black Panther slogan at the time. The second night you did have—and I use the word kindly—provocateurs. . . . Things were actually worse. More people got hurt. It was a rebellion. For the kids, it was just another night of fun. . . . They would read all these leaflets and go, "Oh, great, great, great, off the pig, off the pig!" They did have a lot of problems with the cops because they were beaten up a lot and were treated like dirt by them. So any excuse to fight them was great. But the second night was more planned. You had Trotskyites, you had crazies and yippies. You had almost every gay person that had ever had a radical thought turn out. That's why I think it was worse—because it was more planned. The first night was spontaneous. . . . But these people knew what to do when you get cops cornered: beat the hell out of them. By the third day, you had people leafleting all over the place.

A group started meeting at Alternate U., which was a radical movement center, a free space in a loft on Fourteenth Street and Sixth Avenue. It was just a small nucleus of people who were determined to carry this thing along, to seize the moment and keep the rage and not let this be just another case of gay people being beaten up and then crawling back to thank the Mafia for letting them return to the bars. . . .

When people talk about Judy Garland's death having anything much to do with the riot, that makes me crazy. The street kids faced death every day. They had nothing to lose. And they couldn't have cared less about Judy. We're talking about kids who were fourteen, fifteen, sixteen. Judy Garland was the middle-aged darling of middle-class gays. I get upset about this because it trivializes the whole thing.

Marty Robinson, Michael Brown, and a few other people formed this action committee that Mattachine New York had allowed. Then it got a little too hairy for Mattachine, so those people left and formed this new group, which met at Alternate U. Martha Shelly came up with the name Gay Liberation Front. They wanted to make it as radical-sounding as possible. It was going to be a bunch of faggots and dykes and we weren't coming on as some homophile society. We were coming on as the Gay Liberation Front, which was a scary name during the Vietnam War. . . . There were no leaders. There was a new chairperson every week. If you wanted to be chair, you threw your name into a hat and the hat went around and they jiggled it up and somebody picked a name and said you're the chairperson. The majority ruled, or the loudest mouth . . . it was total anarchy. No rules of any kind. If you came to a meeting, you were GLF. We did insane things. We actually went to Philadelphia

in 1970 and confronted the Black Panthers at their People's Revolutionary Constitutional Convention where there were Panthers from all over the country. We just barged in and accused them of being sexist and racist and everything else, and we did get a statement from Huey Newton at the time saying, yes, you have a point, and we'll see what we can do, and we do acknowledge you as a revolutionary organization and want to work with you. Basically, we went where angels feared to tread. . . . We organized marches and participated in other people's marches. We had fistfights with the Communist Party at a demonstration once because they said we were embarrassing them by being there.

The Gay Activists Alliance (GAA) came out of a vote for supporting the Black Panthers. There was a group of people in GLF who said we should be a one-issue organization. . . . We had voted overwhelmingly to support the Black Panthers, and that's when people who later became GAA walked out to form their group. They worked within the system where we worked outside of it completely. We did not acknowledge that the system existed. I know that sounds stupid, and it was, but that was the way we worked. We were looking for alternatives to everything. . . .

We had no money. We didn't have dues. We didn't have any way of getting money. So we would give a dance at Alternate U. We got the space and charged two dollars admission and fifty cents for beer. If you didn't have the two dollars or the fifty cents, it didn't matter. We would have somebody out in the hallway. I remember once it was Sylvia [Rivera], who sat with a huge butcher knife in her panty hose because we were ready for problems, which we sometimes did get. . . . We advertised the dances as an alternative to gay bars, so the Mafia was very unhappy. It was a struggle just to get the dances going. We tried to take an ad in the *Village Voice*, but they would not let us use the word *gay*. They said the only word they would use was *homophile* and we refused to use it. We picketed the *Village Voice* from six in the morning until six at night and finally they gave up. I remember Lois Hart went up to negotiate and waved a white handkerchief out the window . . . it created a great deal of excitement and we did get our ad placed every week. I think the dance was every Friday night. We would sometimes make as much as a thousand dollars, which was a lot of money in 1970. Usually the money during the dance was kept in Sylvia's panty hose or in my back pocket. We used the money as bail. We'd get a call that two Black Panthers had been arrested. One of us would take money, go down, and bail them out. Or women were striking at the telephone company and one was arrested and beaten up. Or someone wanted to start a youth organization. We'd throw a dance and give them the proceeds. What little money we saved we'd keep under my bathtub because we were afraid of banks.

JOAN NESTLE

I came out in the bars as an eighteen-year-old working-class femme, and the bars were under such total surveillance by the forces of the state; and by that I mean the police, the vice squads, the Mafia. It was a very tense, heightened, and dramatic place, and as a young woman searching for touch in a certain sense, it was there that I learned how to love women, and there that we all learned what we had to do in order to find each other. It was older women telling me really what was expected of me as a woman in this community, so it was a very profound experience. When you see the police come in and see women beaten or thrown up against the wall and stripped, there's both a sense of horror and of camaraderie, a grittiness. And I spent from fifty-eight to seventy in those places. When I walked in, the women I was there with would be butch/femme women, prostitutes, bar girls, women who were basically working class: taxi drivers, hairdressers, telephone operators (the telephone company was a big employer of women in those days). When I walked into Daughters of Bilitis (DOB) with the balloons and this sort of gentle music playing and everybody looking the same, I felt no sexual tension. The women spoke a different language, and I was very class conscious. It seemed to me that they really would be ashamed of a woman like myself. They certainly would have been ashamed of the women I was with in the bars. I mean, no prostitute would have walked into DOB and felt comfortable. . . . Being a bar woman, I was exactly what DOB had come into being to provide an alternative to. DOB says in its charter, in its code, that we want "to educate the sexual variant," to provide an alternative to the bars. That's one of the sadnesses of how the movement developed. . . . There were whole

Writer, teacher, and lesbian activist Joan Nestle traveled to Selma, Alabama, in 1965 in the company of many other Jews who similarly contributed to the civil rights struggle. She cofounded the Lesbian Herstory Archives with Deborah Edel in 1973 in their apartment on New York's Upper West Side. Today the Herstory Archives occupies its own building in Brooklyn's Park Slope, where it preserves the world's most comprehensive "nonjudgmental home for all markings of lesbian life."

The Lesbian Herstory Archives was created in 1973 to collect and preserve evidence and documentation of lesbian experience. Seen here are founders Joan Nestle, Deborah Edel, and Valerie Intyre. Photo by Bettye Lane.

generations of women, very strong, mostly working-class women, who could have added, and who never entered the movement via groups like DOB or the feminist organizations because of this sense of class judgment. . . .

There was a ritual for us—a ritual of control but also a ritual of education—called the bathroom line. There was a butch woman, and I remember her as being the same butch woman every time I was there—short, stocky, dark-haired—who would stand right outside the bathroom door, and there'd be this long line. The Sea Colony was made up of two rooms, which was something else: the front room, which was legal, because everybody was sitting down and that's where the bar was, and then the back room, which was illegal, because that's where we danced. But this line for the bathroom reached all the way from the front room and snaked all the way to the back, and when you got to the front of this line, that woman was standing with a roll of toilet paper and—I'll remember this image until my dying day— around her fist she would wrap an allotted amount of toilet paper and hand it to you. Now that moment of transfer of the toilet paper, which basically said, "We control your most private moments," became harder and harder for me to take. Because in the sixties I was active in the civil rights movement, in the antinuclear war movement, I knew the power of the people saying no. But I had not yet said no to that allotted amount of toilet paper.

I'm still in awe of the young woman—seventeen and eighteen—in what would have been 1958, living on the Lower East Side in this really grungy apartment with a bathroom in the hall, who made her way to this bar called the Sea Colony, on Abingdon Square, usually at twelve, one, or two in the morning.

Now remember the fifties, remember the messages to women just about going to a bar. It meant taking on fifties America. It meant being a woman who was different from the protected, domesticated woman. It felt subversive going out in the streets at two o'clock in the morning, knowing that I was going to a place that was illegal, a place that I had to prepare my body for because of the three-pieces-of-clothing rule. For such a simple thing as to find someone to make love to me, I was willing to risk everything. I'm still in awe of the courage of every woman I met there, who, with no family power behind them, no money power behind them, and no social status behind them, would find their ways to those bars. There were many powerful worlds existing within a framework of oppression before Stonewall.

I certainly don't see gay and lesbian history starting with Stonewall, and from my own life and work with the Lesbian Herstory Archives, I don't see resistance starting with Stonewall. What I do see is a historical coming together of forces, and the sixties changed how human beings endured things in this society and what they refused to endure. . . . Certainly something special happened on that night in 1969, and we've made it more special in our need to have what I call a point of origin. People seem to need points of origin, but it's more complex than saying that it all started with Stonewall. . . . Gay people have a long history of resistance in small towns and large cities in many different ways going back to the early dances of the fifties, going back to the forties to *Vice Versa*, the lesbian journal that was put out by Lisa Ben, going back to the turn of the century. I'm a witness to the courage of another generation. I can't allow the idea that it all started with Stonewall to go unchallenged, not because I'm a historian and care about dates, but because I care about the women who were with me in those bars who then were in their fifties and sixties, meaning that they form a public community that goes back to the thirties. That's the loss we endure if we say that it all started with Stonewall.

The bar of origin for me, where I learned my ways, was the Sea Colony, and that was a so-called rough bar. Now one step up—these are fine gradations—but one step up was Kookie's, and how I remember Kookie's on Fourteenth Street! One night I was sitting there with a group of friends, and a sound caught my attention. It was the sound of demonstrators. I had been on demonstrations already for ten years. But I never thought I would hear demonstrators outside of a lesbian bar, and the next thing I saw was a group of women, younger than myself, not dressed butch or femme, sort of in flannels and jeans, and they came in with flyers that they wanted to hand out. There was this moment of confrontation: Kookie was actually shoving them out the door. You heard the tinkle of glasses as everything just went on, but for me something changed. I got a copy of the flyer and I had mixed feelings about it. My first feeling was, who are these women and why are they invading my territory? Then I looked at the flyer—it was announcing a GAA meeting, though the women themselves might have been from GLF. I think it was within a month that I started to go to GAA at the Firehouse, because at that point I couldn't deny my own historical sense. I couldn't accept being inside while there was a social movement going on outside—not when I had been a part of those other social movements. So for Kookie's, that night was my Stonewall. It led me to another way. . . .

GAA took up its wonderful craziness in a firehouse that the city was no longer using on Wooster Street. At the time, nobody would ever go to SoHo except to go to the Firehouse. It had wonderful double doors so the fire engines could get in, but now they were filled with queers, and it had an embankment outside so you could sit, and cobblestone streets in front of that. There'd be mass meetings—it was like ACT UP before ACT UP—where everybody would be screaming, "We should do *this!*" You could already see the tensions. There was the left group, which I identified with; there were the assimilationists; but basically it was like a New England town meeting. They tried *Robert's Rules of Order*, but then the tensions would come up. There were committees, which I never worked on. But eventually I remember women saying, "There are too many men here. It's not lesbian-specific enough. We need to do something for ourselves." And the most wonderful thing that came out of that was Lesbian Sundays. On the second or third floor there was this huge room, and it had a kitchen and I spent a lot of time in that kitchen making coffee for hundreds of women. There were round tables we'd put tablecloths on and fix up with candles. That was really amazing for me: to see lesbian women, not in a bar, not living with the fear of the police, talking to one another in this way. I also noticed that there was a whole generation of women who were not there: all my bar women. There were mostly young white women and I noticed the differences, but I was intoxicated with what was possible. For instance, they would have weekly discussions, and there was one discussion on lesbians and their mothers—the first one ever—and my mother came to that discussion.

When you walked into a GAA meeting, the first reaction you would have would be white male queer hippies, though there were some wonderful drag queens as well. At any given meeting there could be anywhere from fifteen to twenty-five women, but when we formed our Sunday groups, there were hundreds of women, so that really spoke to the need for separatism. I didn't really feel the lack of women because—remember—I had come from women-only bars like the Sea Colony, and lesbian bars were like lesbian separatism before there was such a thing. Many of the women coming in had never been to a bar, and when they walked into GAA, what they saw were all these men. . . . The women were meeting to form this new organization that would turn into Lesbian Feminist Liberation (LFL). We would meet in little concentric circles. Those in office would be right in the center, then the members would be in another circle, and then there was an outer circle for women who somehow just found themselves there. One night I was in the second circle—the coffeemakers' circle—and two older bar women came in. They were gray-haired and wore DAs, which is a cut that was very popular in the bars, and they were very butchy-looking and sat on the outer ring. I just happened to leave the room to go to the bathroom, and there were younger women standing in front of me from the inner circle and one turned to the other and said, "Did you see those two gray-haired women? Why do they have to look like men? I hope they never come back." I overheard this and I knew at that moment that one world was dying and another was being born. I didn't say, "Why are you saying that? They should be here, too, you know." I accepted that in order to be in one world you had to let go of another. It's taken a lot of work—particularly my work with the Lesbian Herstory Archives—to make up for that moment for myself. . . .

The Firehouse was like a living organism—like the nerve center. For instance, if on the radio I heard that Morty Manford had been kicked down the escalator steps by the head of the firemen's union, I didn't have to wait for a call. I knew that we'd all be at the Firehouse that night and that there would be what we called a zap—a spontaneous demonstration. It would flow out of the Firehouse and usually go to the Village, and nobody had planned it and it was an incredibly cathartic experience. There were a lot of actions that I didn't take part in, wonderful kind of humorous things like when LFL created the purple dinosaur for the Museum of Natural History. . . . If you go to the museum, you know it's dominated through and through by the male pronoun. So these women built this huge, purple papier-mâché dinosaur—a woman dinosaur—and they pulled her through Central Park to the museum. I got there afterwards, in time for the dancing. . . . It was the liberation of a territory that's spatial but also political and emotional. The territory that was liberated that day was the front of the museum, where all of those lesbians were dancing. It was like a ballroom dance in the middle of the afternoon. It's hard, I think, for some gay people to understand now what it meant at that time because you're used to thousands of people marching on a sunny Sunday afternoon. But to me, any open-air demonstration of same-sex community was amazing. For so many years I had lived in the darkness of bars.

When I started the Lesbian Herstory Archives in 1973, I now understand that what I was really doing was looking for my home, and my home really couldn't be LFL. I had felt the pinch of judgment. They wouldn't take all of me and I needed a place that would take all of me—all of my decades of history. So I made such a place. . . . Sensing that there were whole communities of women missing, several women and I started to discuss something that came to be called the Lesbian Herstory Archives: a nonjudgmental home for all markings of lesbian life. In my head it meant I could reconnect with the women of the forties and the fifties and make generational dialogue. . . . The whole time this was going on, the bar women didn't die or go away; they were still going to bars, still creating their culture and community. There were whole communities of African-American women who didn't come to the predominantly white LFL. Salsa Soul Sisters, for instance, gets started in 1974. Asian Lesbians of the East Coast got started a little later. And there were older groups of women—for instance Mabel Hampton, a friend of mine who died a few years ago in her eighties. Her whole lesbian life was lived either in Harlem or the Bronx, and in every decade of it there was community. . . . I've learned that there are many parallel communities, but it's only those who have access to the media or to the written word who are considered "the community."

CANDICE BOYCE

I became involved in the black civil rights movement but never denied being a lesbian, not even as part of the Black Panther Party. . . . There was something within me that couldn't deny it, that said, "Whether it's right or wrong, I can't deny who I am." But there was also part of me that believed it was wrong. I always was a tomboy and had to prove myself because of that. But when I came out as a dyke and as a butch, everything was intensified. I didn't have the safety of the neighborhood even though we were all still black people. People in the neighborhood were turning on me because I was turning into something they didn't understand. I was fighting every day with some of the people I grew up with because now I wasn't the girl that someone was going to marry. I was a dyke.

People say, "You were at Stonewall!" Well, in all honesty I was not. I was in the Village at a women's bar on West Fourth Street called Bonnie & Clyde. That park there on Christopher Street was a stop-off spot for me. The queens always had the best reefer. It was their park. That night in Bonnie & Clyde, I had a few drinks and somebody came in and said, "There's a fight on Christopher Street." Those were the first words I heard. When I hear people talk about Stonewall and the movement that grew out of it, I sometimes flash back to those words. "There's a fight" because that's what it was—like, "Oh my God, the drag queens are at it again." . . . After a while we got ourselves together to go see the fight. But when we got there, we knew that this was more than a fight. We didn't know it would lead to a movement, but we knew it was more than a fight. For me there were mixed feelings, like, "We're not going to be able to walk in the streets because the police are going to make us pay for this." But it was also like, "Good! I hope we hurt a few of them." . . . The next day everybody was back, and the amazing part of Stonewall is how many people started coming down

Harlem-born and Bronx-raised activist Candice Boyce joined Salsa Soul Sisters in 1974, the year of its formation. Today, she heads the board of directors for the organization, which is now called African Ancestral Lesbians United for Societal Change. Since 1993, Boyce has also coordinated scheduling for the scores of other groups that also use the facilities at New York's Lesbian and Gay Community Services Center.

there as word spread. People came from every borough, people who never came to the Village were there. And if you were there, you were part of it, and that's why you hear so many people saying they were at Stonewall.

For the first time I was talking to strangers. I'd been around a lot of white women, but it was my first time to talk with a white gay man about a shared experience. That was unheard of, not just because of the segregation but because my experience was "You white men have the power. Don't say nothing to me." It didn't change any of our prejudices, but we did stop and talk about what was going on and about what we had to do. It was a survival thing that we had to be quick to learn. And we needed to bail people out. . . . Before then our relationships with whites had been sexual but never political in this sense. Many people had interracial sex, but when the sex was over, we still went back to the South Bronx, to Brooklyn, to Bed-Stuy, to Harlem, and that was the end of it. They were still our masters. But now there was this new issue . . . being free had to do with something other than race and gender. It also had to do with sexuality.

Black women didn't have the time for the Gay Activists Alliance. We didn't have the time to sit on the fence while our people were dying. There's no other way of putting it, because if I could get ten women to come out with me, half of them would be drunk or high or would be putting needles in their arms. GAA was not what I needed at the time because they didn't understand the depths of what we were experiencing. They were trying to survive in another area. Many of us did stay connected to GAA, but at arm's length. I know that it took every ounce of my energy and finances to support and educate black lesbians. . . . We were always walking out of GAA meetings. "Don't come to me now," I'd think, "after you haven't even asked me to be a part of planning some action." I'd look around and find almost no people of color. Women were being silenced by men who would just jump up and talk, talk, talk. There was a love/hate relationship. You were always fighting with them about their ways, and there were many men there who knew it and asked, "Well, what can we do?" I didn't feel like I had time to teach them what to do. I remember saying this with other women at meetings and conferences: "You need to go off and learn what to do because we're not here to teach you. We're here to see what we can do so that we can bring new information back to our communities." And as I say it, I can see in retrospect that the men in GAA pushed us out. We had other things to do—women who needed help—but it wasn't comfortable there. They did good work, but they just didn't know how to be inclusive. To be a white male in America and to realize your gayness and find out that you're oppressed is a very different thing than being oppressed all your life as a woman of color.

There were women who said, "Let's get together." Rev. Delores Jackson was saying we need an organization for black women, and she planted the seed. Some women started getting together and saying, "Well, why don't we just meet and talk? Nothing deep. Nothing big, just something comfortable." I could still go out and run the streets, and then I could also get this other side of myself off, too. We started sitting in a church basement and talking about anything that came up: your mother, your lover, anything. And then the room started filling up because these women needed this space so badly. And we moved from the church basement to West Fourth Street. The three women who actually pulled it all together were Sonia Bailey, Harriet Austin, and Luvinia Pinson. I came because a friend of mine said, "I found a place for you where you can go run your mouth off and stop bothering us." I had come out of a militant movement and I saw women doing nothing and I was always preaching. I went down there and right away I knew this was what I was looking for and it just snowballed. There was no other place for women of color to go and sit down and talk about what it meant to be a black lesbian in America. . . .

They called themselves Salsa Soul Sisters, which is important because they wanted to connect the Latina and the black women. . . . When I first came in, everybody was just talking at the same time, and there was this energy. I felt everyone was looking at me, though now I'm sure no one was. I was shy and quiet and sat in a chair in the back and waited for someone to say something to me. I just sat there and wrote my feelings down. I've kept journals for years. And these women were talking about their mothers and coming out, and I'm writing

my feelings down. And finally Harriet Austin said, "What are you writing? Who are you? Are you the FBI or something? We're going to get you to talk." Now I was not used to people grabbing me and hugging me. That's an amazing thing that I had not noticed until then. I was always aloof, very self-contained. And this woman, who was nothing to me sexually, grabbed me and hugged me. I must have pushed her away: "What is your problem? So *this* is what this organization is about." I was suspicious at the beginning, but every time I came she would grab me and hug me until I realized that she didn't want my body. She just wanted me to relax, and eventually I did. Then I started talking, and the first time they heard me speak they said, "She has to be on the board." Emotions just came out of me like out of a faucet. So I got on the board and I've never left it. . . . I was an alcoholic—that's what I had needed to survive. And these women embraced me and told me I was smart and that I wasting my life. . . . I had already been talking about what we had to do for our sisters, not realizing that I was one of them. My sisters taught me that you are warm to a person, that you don't assume that everyone knows what it is to be cared about and to be loved; that this is what they need but to give them space if they desire it. This was a revelation. It was amazing for me to learn that there was something else going on inside of me besides just being a lesbian in the streets who knew how to survive. I came out in Salsa Soul as a poet. That was another coming-out process. We had a group called Jemima and we did all the coffeehouses and women's groups on the East Coast, reading poetry. Though I had thought that I was out before, that was my big coming out.

Where Will You Be?

by Pat Parker

Boots are being polished
Trumpeters clean their horns
Chains and locks forged
The crusade has begun.

Once again flags of Christ
are unfurled in the dawn
and cries of soul saviors
sing apocalyptic on air waves.

Citizens, good citizens all
parade into voting booths
and in self-righteous sanctity
X away our right to life.

I do not believe as some
that the vote is an end,
I fear even more
It is just a beginning.

So I must make assessment
Look to you and ask:
Where will you be
when they come?

They will not come
a mob rolling
through the streets,
but quickly and quietly
move into our homes
and remove the evil,
the queerness,
the faggotry,
the perverseness
from their midst.
They will not come
clothed in brown,
and swastikas, or
bearing chest heavy with
gleaming crosses.
The time and need
for ruses are over.

They will come
in business suits
to buy your homes
and bring bodies to
fill your jobs.
They will come in robes
to rehabilitate
and white coats
to subjugate
and where will you be
when they come?

Where will we *all* be
when they come?
And they will come—

they will come
because we are
defined as opposite—
perverse
and we are perverse.

Everytime we watched
a queer hassled in the
streets and said nothing—
It was an act of perversion.

Everytime we lied about
the boyfriend or girlfriend
at coffee break—
It was an act of perversion.

Everytime we heard,
"I don't mind gays
but why must they
be blatant?" and said nothing—
It was an act of perversion.

Everytime we let a lesbian mother
lose her child and did not fill
the courtrooms—
It was an act of perversion.

Everytime we let straights
make out in bars while
we couldn't touch because
of laws—
It was an act of perversion.

Everytime we put on the proper
clothes to go to a family
wedding and left our lovers
at home—
It was an act of perversion.

Everytime we heard
"Who I go to bed with
is my personal choice—
It's personal not political"
and said nothing—
It was an act of perversion.

Everytime we let straight relatives
bury our dead and push our
lovers away—
It was an act of perversion.

And they will come.
They will come for
the perverts

& it won't matter
if you're
        homosexual, not a faggot
        lesbian, not a dyke
        gay, not queer
It won't matter
if you
        own your business
        have a good job
        or are on S.S.I.

It won't matter
if you're
        Black
        Chicano
        Native American
        Asian
        or White
It won't matter
if you're from
        New York
        or Los Angeles
        Galveston
        or Sioux Falls
It won't matter
if you're
        Butch, or Fem
        Not into roles
        Monogamous
        Nonmonogamous
It won't matter
if you're
        Catholic
        Baptist
        Atheist
        Jewish
        or M.C.C.

They will come
They will come
to the cities
and to the land
to your front rooms
and in *your* closets.

They will come for
the perverts
and where will
you be
When they come?

CHAPTER

2

VISIBILITY AND BACKLASH

Visibility and Backlash

by Mab Segrest

Here, in the late-twentieth-century United States, the path to our "freedom," to gay and lesbian "liberation," does not seem so direct, so uncomplicated, as we projected in the early, heady days of the movement. Our claims to full humanity, to civil rights and the legal status of citizenship, have met strong and organized resistance. We are, according to even the Reagan Justice Department, the most frequent victims of hate crimes: murders, assaults, robberies, arsons, vandalism, threats, and harassments. AIDS continues to devastate a generation of gay men as the 10th International AIDS Conference recognized bleakly that there is no cure in sight, and the epidemic spreads, leaps country to country, digs its teeth deeper into continents. Some preachers and some senators, out after money, power, and salvation, seize on our successes and our griefs and define us only by their attitudes toward sexuality, that stigmatized category, that eraser of boundaries, blurrer of identities. When as a youth I would sing "Onward, Christian Soldiers" in the First Methodist Church in Tuskegee, Alabama, I hardly imagined they would be marching after me. Twenty-five years after Stonewall, the question of whether we are human or animal is not settled.

Against the rising evidence of violence and entrenched hatred, lesbian and gay activists insist on visibility as both cause and solution of our oppression. Kevin Berrill, who pioneered work against vicious antigay violence with the National Gay and Lesbian Task Force, explains this position eloquently and characteristically:

Over the years, people have asked me, "Doesn't this rising violence mean that the gay and lesbian people are losing ground and that hatred for us is growing?" And I would argue that the increased violence is also a measure of just how much progress we've made. I think we're on a parallel track of increased violence and backlash on the one hand and of increased empowerment and acceptance on the other. The two are not mutually exclusive. . . . What the violence is intended to do is to drive us back into the isolation and self-hatred of the closet.

Kevin continues (emphases mine):

Paradoxically, it often makes us more determined to be visible, *but sometimes it makes us more reluctant to come out, to exercise our right to speak, to associate, and assemble. . . . It is impossible to have a positive gay or lesbian identity in isolation, and the only way that we can feel good about ourselves, the only way that we can organize for equality, is through community. The only way you can have community is through* visibility, *and the greatest threat to* visibility *is violence and discrimination. That is where we come up against the antigay ballot initiatives. This is an effort to increase the price of* visibility—*to make it more dangerous to come out and therefore to diminish our* visibility *and subsequently our ability to create change.*

Overleaf: Lesbian Avengers at the front of the 1994 Dyke March, proceeding down Fifth Avenue. Photo by Carolina Kroon/Impact Visuals.

The second annual Dyke March, when fifteen thousand lesbians took to New York's Fifth Avenue the day before the official Stonewall 25 commemorative march and rally in a manifestation of defiant lesbian pride. Photo by Carolina Kroon/Impact Visuals.

find the dyke in this picture

The controlling metaphor of gay experience and subsequent politics is "the closet," an experience marked by isolation and self-hatred. In Kevin's statement its primary opposite is "visibility." "Coming out" brings progress, empowerment, and acceptance because it allows us to be a community that can then organize for equality. Visibility is the necessary element to community, in Kevin's equation. But violence diminishes visibility and the subsequent ability to create change. For many other lesbian and gay artists and activists I notice that "visibility" sounds like a mantra similar to "creating change."

But I was not "invisible" as a child in my hometown. I felt rather that people could see things about me that I could not see myself, from the way I dressed and carried myself to the ways that longing and resisting longing for other girls and my romantic boredom with boys shaped my physical and emotional self, hands-in-the-pockets constraint and self-consciousness that I carry still. This is encapsulated in one memory from the ninth grade, a bulletin board in an English classroom, a very femme woman looking back over her shoulder in horror at the bottom of her dress: "Your slip is showing," the letters cut out of construction paper proclaimed; it was a poster about the embarrassment of bad grammar. But I felt a rush of shame seeing the display, a flash that people were probably seeing/reading my "gender slips" behind my back.

The problem is not only "*visibility* and backlash." My problem at nine, and thirteen, and twenty, was that I *was* visible. I just wasn't named. Or, the names available carried such lethal stigma. Queer: alone, outside community, outside family, outside love, the only one; something about me, elusive as fog, that people around me acted out of but never explained. When I finally came out at the age

"Find the dyke in this picture," by the New York–based lesbian public-art collective, fierce pussy.

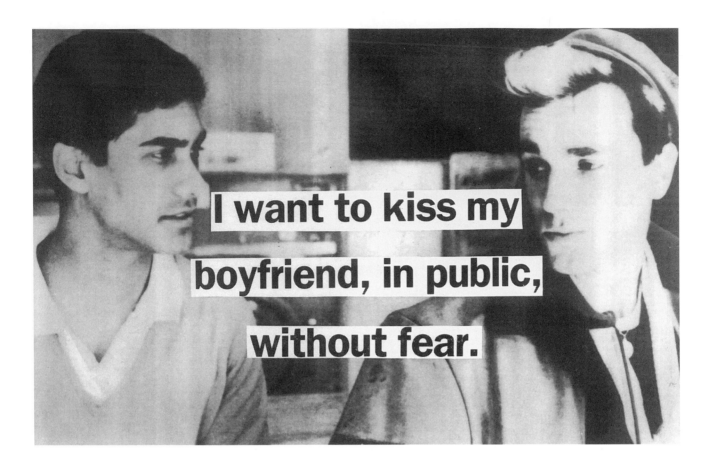

I want to kiss my boyfriend, in public, without fear.

"I want to kiss my boyfriend, in public, without fear." One of a series of posters addressing varieties of street harassment, created by the New York–based collective Cheap Art.

of twenty-four to my mother, she told me, "I have known since you were five by the ways you bossed everybody around, cried when you had to wear a dress to school, and strode across the floor with a pistol on your hip." So much for invisibility. The parade of girlfriends I brought home over the years only confirmed her sighting of me.

And the violence, the homophobia, how can we be sure it has increased in response to our post-Stonewall organizing? It was always already there, when we were alone in our families or in the institutions, public and private, where they sent us to be drugged, electroshocked, restrained. It was always already waiting in the years in the bars when police raided and dragged off the queens, the stone butches, to be humiliated, to be raped and beaten in their cells. It was the violence and our visibility that erupted that evening in Stonewall. Perhaps what *is* visible, named, now is "homophobia," and our naming it has increased our risk, as our moves and movements ride the rough decades that slouch toward a new millennium.

The opposite of *queer* is not *visible*, it is *included, related*. We build community by how we decide to treat one another. But that fragile "we" of the "gay" community is so rent by all the culture's fractures: the racism that sought to annihilate the "Indian," that enslaved the African; the Mexican, the Chinese, brought into the servitude of wage labor; the class schisms, so often running alongside the racial ones; the deep hatred of women's bodies; the tremors of our sexualities, so variously expressed; our terror at our differences, at being identified with one another. Our capital city, like our identities, built on fault lines. And how does "visibility" fare along these divides? It constitutes us in our most "visible" and homogeneous formations only, and in the public eye that cliché, the GAY-WHITE-AFFLUENT-MALE, is much of what the movement seems to be. When we are *visibly* racist toward one another, *visibly* sexist, *visibly* leaning ourselves and our organizations toward a power often brutally manifested in U.S. culture, we destroy community and undermine our claims to equality and fair treatment.

Visibility, what is seen or not seen, is only one aspect of a complex phenomenon, perhaps not even its most important one. When we say *visible*, we really mean much more. Visibility is not the most common element of community. But the claustrophobia of the closet comes more from not being acknowledged than not being seen. The closet puts people not so much out of sight as out of language. The Nazis want us dead: I am clear about that, having organized against white supremacist movements in North Carolina for almost a decade. But folks on the religious right will often allow us our existence as long as we live our lives by their terms, in shame and sexual/intimate starvation (which they think of as "conversion"). In fact, our shame is necessary to constitute their righteousness, their certainty of heaven. Our foes—religious, political, moral, social—are reacting not primarily against the sight of us as against our political presence, our organization, a complex process of our self-definition.

What is there, then, beyond visibility that will allow us to reach our goal of safety and acceptance, which some of us homosexuals have always felt would also necessitate the transformation of the culture?

The Murder of Julio Rivera: Homophobia as Annihilation

The bottom line of the modern assault on lesbians and gay men is violence, and the overkill of our assailants testifies to this impulse to annihilation. One bullet or knife thrust seldom suffices. The effect of these physical attacks spreads far beyond the people actually assaulted (one in four gay men and one in ten lesbians, according to a National Gay and Lesbian Task Force survey), as it is intended to do: surveys show that as many as 80 percent expect to be assaulted or accosted at some time in their lives.

That July evening in 1990, when Julio Rivera, covered with his own blood, stumbled out of the schoolyard onto the street in Jackson Heights, a neighborhood in Queens, New York, his attackers were already fleeing. They figured, no doubt, that they were safe enough from the consequences of their evening's recreation: fag-bashing. After all, six gay men had been murdered in this same vicinity over the past five years. After all, one of the attackers had a brother and a father in the NYPD. After all, Julio was a spic as well as a fag, who would care? Esat Bici, Dan

New York City subway map of Jackson
Heights marking P.S. 69, where Julio
Rivera was murdered.

Doyle, and Eric Brown felt safe enough to brag about the murder to their friends.
These three young white men, two of them with families very well connected,
had anticipated that this case would follow the course of most of the gay-bashings:
victims, if they survived, are too afraid to report the attack to the police; police
make no arrests or plea-bargain for minimal sentences; or if the case comes to
trial, the stigma of the victim often becomes the focus, with acquittals or light
sentences.

Rivera's three attackers had met earlier that evening at Doyle's house at a
party, with other members of the Doc Martens Skins. Neo-Nazi skinheads, taking
their political and cultural identity from British neo-Nazi youth, became the most
visibly violent front of a resurgent white supremacist movement in the mid-1980s.
I had met an earlier manifestation of this resurgent fascism in North Carolina,
when I organized against an active Klan and neo-Nazi movement in the state.
This North Carolina movement was an active part of a revolutionary underground
called The Order, which utilized active-duty military personnel and stolen arma-
ments to prepare for a racist uprising that would eliminate all "non-Aryan" people
from the face of the globe (queers and race traitors included). The White Patriot
Party would march through little Carolina towns, 350 men with arms upraised in
the Nazi salute, to loudspeakers blaring from the back of a pickup truck such tunes
as "Dixie," "Tomorrow Belongs to Me" (a song sung by Nazi youth from the
musical *Cabaret*, ironically by two gay men, Kander and Ebb, and based on the
work of another gay man, Christopher Isherwood), "The Ride of the Valkyries,"
and "Old Rugged Cross." I knew we were in trouble. A couple of years later,
two White Patriot members were indicted for the murder of three guys in an
adult bookstore, reportedly because the fascists wanted to "avenge Yahweh on
homosexuals." When the feds busted The Order, including White Patriot leader
Glenn Miller (largely because its members targeted federal judges, law enforcement, and the president), skinheads emerged as the next violent edge of the white
supremacist movement.

The Doc Martens Skins were only one of the many urban youth gangs,
neo-Nazi or otherwise, into which alienated young people in the United States
flood looking for community from mostly heterosexual families disrupted by abuse
and violence, drugs, neglect. As a child, Esat Bici had heard his father murder his
mother and later was present again when the contract killer sent after his father by
her family mistakenly killed his uncle instead. The most hard core of the three,
Bici was considered a "pussy" by the other skins. Some gay activists would later
say another of the assailants was himself gay. Whatever their sexualities, all three
were prototypical gay-bashers: white, male, eighteen to twenty-one, out to shore
up an inherently unstable masculinity.

At some point in the increasingly drunken evening, the three young men
decided to buy their belonging with another man's blood. Doyle and Bici shaved

their heads in preparation, razor sharp against their vulnerable pink hide. Courage was hardly a consideration in the evening's violent ritual. They first went in search of a homeless person, burning an uninhabited hut. Then they headed over to Jackson Heights, a known cruising area. Once there, they passed up a pair of gay men, figuring three on two wasn't good enough odds.

Then they spotted the twenty-nine-year-old Rivera. Brown served as decoy, apparently offering Rivera sex or drugs to lure him into the alcove, while Bici and Doyle hid behind a Dumpster. The two emerged and Bici hit Rivera over the head with a beer bottle, then laid into him with the claw hammer brought from Doyle's. When Rivera realized the odds were three to one, he fought back furiously, ducking and weaving as Bici beat him over the head and torso. When he refused to go down, Doyle stabbed him in the back with a kitchen knife. "It felt like sticking a knife into a watermelon," Doyle would later testify.

Julio staggered onto the street, aware of the fatal damage. "They've killed me," an onlooker heard him scream. "They've killed me." The first man who saw Rivera was Alan Sack, a friend and former lover, who cradled his battered body, then rode with him in the ambulance to the hospital, where Rivera died.

In the following hours and days, word spread quickly on the streets and through the gay bars of Queens, along with rumors and theories and attitudes. Many people didn't buy the cops' story that is was drug related: the attack had been too brutal, involved too much of the overkill characteristic of hate crimes. But Rivera had been an addict and was known to turn tricks. Some thought, could he have expected another fate?

At the time of the murder, the Queens gay community was second in size only to the Village. Eight gay bars were in an eight-block radius from Seventy-fourth to Seventy-seventh Streets and from Thirty-seventh Road to Thirty-seventh Avenue. The cruising strip where Julio was attacked was famous all over the city as "Vaseline Alley," although AIDS had closed down much of the activity there. The gay residents of Queens were more working class, older, many of them Latino. Julio Rivera's Queens neighborhood was very different from the Manhattan culture of the Village that produced ACT UP and Queer Nation. The neighborhood had changed a lot in recent years, more drug dealers, prostitutes, more violence.

Gay culture, almost by definition, has been an urban phenomenon. The "homosexual," according to gay French philosopher/historian Michel Foucault, emerged in the modern West at the moment in the nineteenth century that industrial capitalism drew people into burgeoning cities and gave them incomes and social structures independent of family networks. Gay life became articulated in the United States in places like Greenwich Village in the 1920s and in San Francisco after World War II, where soldiers and sailors (both those who had served active duty and those who had been discharged for homosexual tendencies)

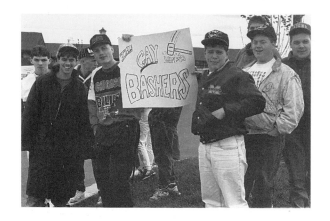

When gay activists in Belleville, Michigan, protested the discriminatory hiring practices of the Cracker Barrel restaurant chain, these high school students held a demonstration of their own. Photo by Jim West/Impact Visuals.

congregated, free of the constraints of home and family networks. So many queers leave their small towns for small cities, their small cities for larger cities, their large cities for New York, Washington, San Francisco, Chicago, Los Angeles, gay and lesbian enclaves made up in part of émigrés from the constraints of family and small town, acting in ways they never could have at home, sometimes acting those ways in the city *because* they could not have at home.

According to gay historian of the Middle Ages John Boswell, the relative freedom of the cities also incubated more tolerance of homosexuality in medieval Europe. Boswell's *Christianity, Social Tolerance, and Homosexuality* explains the difference between rural and urban cultures. Rural cultures structure their social organization principally around extended-family units, where political loyalty is based on blood relations and where kinship structures maintain order and provide social services. Because these more rural cultures are organized by sexual relationships, deviance from the sexual norm is highly threatening and highly punished, just as heresy is punished in theologically organized societies and political dissidence is punished in politically organized societies. Urban societies, on the other hand, are organized "in political units which transcend kinship ties," and the more sophisticated social organization "removes from the family unit much of the burden of social welfare and organization." Urban moral codes emphasize more civic or abstract concepts of right and wrong rather than private considerations like family loyalty. In cities, "most sexual matters are considered outside the proper purview of the state."

Of course, Boswell's distinctions between urban and rural are not absolute for our own time (many gay people in cities grew up there and live in close relationship with blood kin), but they do seem to apply at each remove, demarcating as much the distance from Buies Creek, North Carolina, to Durham as from Durham to Queens, or Queens to Manhattan.

"When they killed Julio, they came up against the wrong people," Tommy, a Queens bartender, one of the core of people who organized in response to Rivera's murder, explained. "We may be quiet and laid-back in Queens, but we organized ourselves." Tommy was quick to distinguish the gay scene in Queens from the queer scene in Manhattan. "Most of the people [here] blend in with the community. There aren't too many activists, and if they do any gay activist activities, it's basically all in Manhattan. . . . Being gay to me doesn't mean I have to shove it in everybody's face. Either you're going to accept me as a person or you're not. . . . It's not necessary to be so out of the closet that you're insulting the person who's living next door to you."

The major battlefronts in the struggle against homophobia have moved out of the urban gay meccas to places like Oregon, Colorado, Maine, and Ohio, where the religious right is introducing a series of homophobic ballot initiatives. Big-city gay strategists, I have observed, can be clueless on this terrain. Their main approach is often to view what happens outside the major cities as merely a "trickle down" from New York or San Francisco or Boston. The emergence of gay and lesbian culture and politics in midsize and smaller cities is influenced by urban developments, but it is not totally determined by them.

I recall a Yankee activist who came South on a self-styled "freedom ride" in the mid-1980s. He jumped off the Greyhound in Wilmington, North Carolina, just long enough to issue a press release about the dangers of the Klan, then he hopped back on his bus and was off to liberate the next town. This was during the period when I was organizing against groups like the White Patriot Party as an open lesbian. I just rolled my eyes. About the same time, ACT UP/New York sent five folks to the Research Triangle Park to take over an office at Burroughs Wellcome to protest the cost of AZT. They refused to coordinate the action with any local lesbians or gay men, explaining to the national gay press that local people were inherently co-opted. They got their fifteen minutes of airtime, and we never heard from them again. We just ground our teeth and kept on working.

We need to acknowledge that a different dynamic is occurring in these more rural places to which we all need to tend: what does it mean when queers don't leave home? Is there more of a tendency for working-class queers and queers of color to remain embedded in their various communities, not so much "coming out," as historian Allen Berube suggests, as "fitting in"? Julio Rivera had tried to do both, at home.

Alan Sack called Julio's family from the hospital soon after Julio died. Peg Rivera, his sister-in-law, answered the phone. The Rivera family was another force on whom neither the killers nor seasoned urban activists had reckoned. Rivera's killers would not be allowed to escape punishment for his annihilation— he would be claimed by his family and his community. "We always knew Julio was homosexual," Peg explained. "He enjoyed bringing his friends to our home. He was always very proud of us and we were very proud of him." Julio would bring the latest dances, bopping around the house in his headphones to "Superfreak" and "Whip It." Peg and his brother Ted loved his style, his aesthetics: "How to present a room, where to put an ashtray, where to hang a picture," Peg explained, talents that Ted and Julio shared.

Julio's sister Josie told the *New York Times* that her brother was "never a really happy person." He had grown up in poverty in the South Bronx. He never recovered from the day when he was fourteen when his mother died in his arms in a taxi on the way to the hospital, or from his uncles and

Drag queens Glennda Orgasm and Hedda Lettuce created a fierce presence in a Queer Nation antiviolence march. Photo by T. L. Litt/Impact Visuals.

The Pink Panthers, a New York City community patrol formed in the wake of increasing bias-related violence against lesbians and gay men. Photo by T. L. Litt/Impact Visuals.

aunts' disapproval of his sexuality. He started hustling soon after his mother's death, learning to project a macho exterior.

But Julio was loved. At his wake on July 4, Julio's gay family came together with his blood relations. His queer friends gathered in the back of the room and came forward one by one to place flowers on the coffin. "When they were finished," Peg remembers, "we rose as a family to speak with them. They kept vigil at the coffin. It was very touching. We had the opportunity to meet quite a few people." In the crucible of grief, new relationships began to form. Within two weeks of the murder, Alan invited Ted and Peg to a meeting of the Julio Rivera Anti-Violence Committee in the basement of a local gay bar. "I had never been into a gay bar, but we said, 'Fine, we'll be there.'" Matt Foreman from the New York City Gay and Lesbian Anti-Violence Project came, and they all began planning a strategy to bring pressure on the police and the DA to find the culprits and bring them to justice.

The Queens response to Rivera's murder now intersected with a peak of gay anger and activism in New York City; the combination led to the city's first gay-bashing trial. In 1986, Local Law Two, the gay civil rights bill, had finally passed, seventeen years after it was first introduced. ACT UP formed the next year; organizations like the Gay Men's Health Crisis were unwilling to respond more militantly to the burgeoning AIDS epidemic. Donna Minkowitz, who covered the Rivera case for the *Village Voice*, said:

In the late eighties the gay and lesbian movement really erupted, especially in New York. In ACT UP, lesbians and gay men came together and each brought different things to that exchange. . . . It was very much about gay and lesbian liberation, about sexual issues, because so much of what had exacerbated the AIDS crisis was the government's unwillingness to talk explicitly about sex, to tell people how to protect themselves. . . . Lesbians were much more ready to deal with sexual issues than they had been before. Queer Nation was founded several years later because ACT UP had decided to stick just to AIDS and not work on gay liberation issues. . . . Daring to be out and celebrating difference, people were saying, "We're queer and that means we celebrate the part of us that's different from society and that may challenge gender roles and ways of living and power.". . . We were willing to be there and to confront people in that way, feeling the federal government hates us, is ignoring us, and doesn't care whether we live or die. That sense of deep outrage wasn't there until the late eighties or early nineties.

All over the city and the country, there was a rising tide of violence against lesbians and gay men. ACT UP activist Gerri Wells explains:

The summer of 1990 was a hot summer in more ways than one. The temperature was hot and gay-bashing seemed to peak. It became like the hip thing to do. You know, people from New Jersey or Connecticut saying, "Let's get a car and go to the Village and beat up on some dykes and fags." It was very scary. You walk down the street and people would yell out of cars or deliberately bump into you on the street.

The Rivera case also intersected with the growing visibility of gay and lesbian people of color in the city. Gay Latino Men had organized earlier in 1990. Their intent was social but soon became political, and they mobilized. Robert Vásquez-Pacheco, then coordinator of education at the Anti-Violence Project, remembers:

When the verdict came down and made the cover of Newsday, *there were members of Latino Gay Men standing in front of the courthouse. . . . This is a community that you rarely saw. Everyone's impression of the gay community in New York is white, gay male, and middle class. Here was an opportunity to see people who are not used to putting themselves on the line for something political. . . . No one in the mainstream of the gay and lesbian movement wanted to discuss race in looking at the Rivera case, although race was one of the most blatant things in it. On a lot of levels, the gay main-stream is still not willing to grapple with all of the issues involved. . . . I think that*

The late David Wojnarowicz, artist and AIDS activist, who participated in many ACT UP demonstrations, including this civil disobedience at the 1989 protest "Target City Hall." Photo by Eli Reed/ Magnum Photos.

one of the reasons it's such a struggle to involve people of color is that people of color do not focus our identity on our sexuality. We identify ourselves not just in terms of our sexuality but in terms of our ethnicity and the culture that comes with it. Our reality is much more complex. For us to do political work we cannot work solely on sexuality. We say, "Look, I don't have the time to do that because you're not addressing everything that's happening to me." You have to have a movement that understands that.

The Queens gays had similar community-based concerns when they carefully negotiated their relationship with the Manhattan queer activists. According to Tommy:

We didn't want people shouting out in the streets because we'd have to walk here the next day by ourselves. We didn't know how the straight majority community was going to handle it, where in Manhattan you do a march down Fifth Avenue, you do a march down Christopher Street—what's the big deal? If you go down Christopher Street, everybody there is gay anyhow. You march down Fifth Avenue and you're protesting and you're demonstrating and you're loud and you're obnoxious and you're getting in people's faces—who

cares? They're not going to see you tomorrow. Here we have to live in the community so we had to put some limitations on what ACT UP and Queer Nation could do. Their organizations agreed. They understood our fears that we still have to shop and walk in these streets. Without their cooperation I don't think we could have gotten anything done.

The Rivera case is unusual in that these often contending forces managed to find a way to work together. Vásquez observed, "On the good side, you could see a variety of groups coming together. It was truly coalition work. It was wonderful to see, and what it taught us is that when we work together, we actually can get something done."

The coalition of groups pressured the DA's office into reclassifying the case as a hate crime, which meant that it would get extra law enforcement resources. Marches, vigils, and demonstrations followed. With Sack's help, police identified the assailants. They were charged in November 1990. Doyle, who the autopsy showed had actually struck the fatal blow, plea-bargained for manslaughter in exchange for testimony against his two buddies on second-degree-murder charges.

When Bici and Brown came to trial in October of 1991, Ted and Peg, other members of Julio's family, and lesbian and gay activists were constantly harassed by skins in corridors and in the courtroom. Peg Rivera remembered:

I entered the courtroom enraged after finding myself alone with Eric Brown in the ante-room. I began looking around and I recognized some members of the Pink Panthers and I asked them, "Please, the next time that I walk through that chamber, would one of you accompany me?" and they said, "No problem." There were several people there from the gay bars in Queens where Julio had worked. They were also ready if we needed any help. Members of Queens Gays and Lesbians United, which emerged as a result of all of the efforts to unite against the violence, were there and said, "Don't worry, we'll make sure you're not alone when you walk through that chamber." . . . But once we stepped outside of that courthouse, we were extremely vulnerable going to our cars or going to a train station, and I know that many members of the gay community risked bodily harm and were followed on some occasions by members of the gang, especially those going back to Manhattan. We were never alone.

Peg added:

I became aware of how important the support of family was through this process of attending demonstrations and the trial. Eventually people began to recognize us as Julio's brother and sister and would approach us, and on many occasions they thanked us. You know, "My mother and father don't know I'm gay and it really means a lot that you come here and offer your support." I had heterosexual people come up to me and say that a gay member of their family was killed and they never went to the trial because they were too embarrassed, and they were glad to see us do what we did because they regretted it very much.

At the end of the trial and jury deliberations, the jury found Bici and Brown not guilty of premeditation but found them guilty of "depraved indifference to human life." The judge giving the three the maximum sentences allowed: Doyle got eight and a half to twenty-five years, Bici and Brown fifteen years to life. The Riveras and New York and Queens gay and lesbian activists marched jubilantly the night after the conviction. Ted Rivera told the crowd, "I feel honored to be here—you honor us with your presence. I know to Julio you were his family, and you have become my family."

Because of my friend Fred, I have recently pondered a great deal the issue of how homosexuality configures itself outside of cities. Fred was my best friend twenty years ago, when we were both undergrads. We were briefly lovers right before we graduated. He was on his way back home to a small Alabama town not so far from where he grew up, another small community—just a wide place in the road. Fred figured he was at least bisexual, and that he could explore that aspect of his sexuality with me. We fantasized getting married. We would have gay relationships on the side, in some little Alabama town. It took about five days for this plan to fall apart completely. It was a real turning point, when I realized that the happiest part of my fantasies of "getting married" had been imagining telling my family. I saw that I should make my life decisions for myself, not on the basis of what I thought other people wanted.

Fred and I kept up during the years when I moved up to Durham to go to Duke graduate school. Soon, I was in my first lesbian relationship with a woman who by that time was clearly not thrilled with being identified as gay. When my partner left me for a man, I erupted into the lesbian feminist community that had been building in Durham in the early 1970s.

Fred did not take the same lessons. Back home, several years later he got married to an attractive and intelligent heterosexual woman. They had children. But Fred also had sexual liaisons with men on the side, on trips to places like Washington, D.C., or just bigger cities closer to home. He vacillated between killing extremes: the good Christian family man in the small Southern town and the seeker after sexual adventures in the anonymity of the big-city bathhouse. He was miserable much of the time, feeling trapped in a cage the door to which was always open. Ten years ago, he found he was infected with HIV.

For a while, I was over men entirely, then I was too aggravated at Fred that he didn't come out, that he didn't take more control of his life, that he was so duplicitous. A couple of years ago, a mutual friend let me know Fred was dying, and I finally called him up. And it came back to me all the things I had loved and enjoyed about him: how easy he was to have fun with, how in the moment, how the deep conflicts he tried to resolve made him open up to other people's pain and confusions. I realized that I had been concentrating on all the things I thought he had lost by not coming out—and they were substantial: intimacy, freedom, self-definition. I found on his bedside table in the front of one of his books: "How does the caged bird sing? Tell me, Maya?" During his last days and months in the hospital, no one knew where he was, and he was not even listed on the hospital registry.

What I came to see in connecting with Fred again was all the things I had lost when I came out, which I felt I couldn't do too near to home: certain cadences in people's voices including my own, the people themselves, whom I left because I didn't think they could understand me or knew that I couldn't understand myself with them looking on, people very similar to the folks Fred greeted each day, each week, on the streets of his town, or in its churches and community meetings.

At Fred's bedside, saying good-bye, I realized that our gay "freedom" is also constituted by all the things we have to jettison.

The Culture Wars: Homophobia and Representation

"The hour is late," warned right-wing columnist Pat Buchanan at the Republican National Convention in 1992. "America needs a cultural revolution in the nineties as sweeping as its political revolution in the eighties." In May 1989, Sen. Alphonse D'Amato had fired an opening salvo on the floor of the Senate when he ripped up a copy of photographer Andres Serrano's *Piss Christ*, which showed a plastic crucifix submerged in the artist's urine. The previous month, American Family Association executive director Donald Wildmon had railed against NEA-funded Serrano's photograph in a fund-raising letter to his constituents. (That Serrano intended the image to comment on the cheap commodification of religion so characteristic of the television preachers was lost on them.)

A Robert Mapplethorpe nude was projected onto the Corcoran Gallery in Washington, D.C., during a 1989 anticensorship demonstration that followed the Corcoran's last-minute cancellation of the retrospective "Robert Mapplethorpe: The Perfect Moment" because of right-wing attacks on the National Endowment for the Arts. Photo by Frank Herrera.

Soon the religious right's culture scouts had brought the work of Robert Mapplethorpe, David Wojnarowicz, and Karen Finley into the fray, focusing on the upcoming congressional reauthorization of the National Endowment for the Arts. In this heated environment, Washington, D.C.'s prestigious Corcoran Gallery of Art canceled the exhibit "Robert Mapplethorpe: The Perfect Moment," fearing it would endanger both their own funding and the NEA. When the Washington Project for the Arts picked up the exhibit, record crowds came to see Mapplethorpe's work, including the controversial X Portfolio, which included a self-portrait of Mapplethorpe as the devil with a bullwhip up his ass for a tail. Sen. Jesse Helms attached a rider to the NEA appropriations bill, requiring that the Endowment deny money to any art containing not only homoeroticism, S/M, sex with children, or the denigration of religion, but the sex act itself. Helms was also encoding this prohibition on the depiction of sexuality into federal efforts at AIDS education—to literally murderous effect. Public Law 101–121 passed a diluted version of the Helms amendment, and the NEA required grantees to sign a pledge that they would not use government money to produce obscene art.

That year three lesbian poets, Audre Lorde, Chrystos, and Minnie Bruce Pratt, received NEA grants, and congressmen railed against their writing from the floor of the Senate in a new wave of hysteria. "I thought I was out to everybody," Minnie Bruce, an old friend from our days together in Durham as lesbian literati (or cliterati, as someone suggested), commented to me over the phone from her home in D.C. "I didn't realize I wasn't out to Congress." Courts soon overturned the NEA antiobscenity pledge.

Never one to abandon a hot issue, in 1990 activists of the religious right turned their attention to gay programming on public television, targeting African-American videographer Marlon Riggs's *Tongues Untied* and later, in 1994, gay novelist Armistead Maupin's *Tales of the City*. The PBS series *POV (Point of View)* picked up *Tongues Untied* for national showing, then thirty-two out of fifty stations decided not to air it, and the others ran it very late in the evening fearing attack by Christian rightists who were terrorizing nonprofit cultural entities around the country. Pat Buchanan used sexually explicit clips from *Tongues Untied* in an attack ad against George Bush in the Georgia Republican presidential primary, this after Buchanan won 31 percent of the vote in New Hampshire, citing federal funding of such "obscene material" as one of Bush's flaws. George Bush immediately moved to dump NEA director John Frohnmayer. Frohnmayer explains his firing:

Sam Skinner [Bush's chief of staff] called me and said, "Things are getting too hot. We're going to throw you off the sleigh as a sop to the political right." That's basically what happened. I was fired, and what happened to the Bush campaign was exactly what it deserved. Because of this craven caving in to the institutionalized hate of Pat Buchanan and the radical right, many moderate Republicans saw that manifested at the

Republican convention and said, "I don't want any part of this." That was exactly the way I, as a Republican, felt about the Bush campaign. I didn't want any part of it. Not because they had fired me, but because they had so little courage to stand up to the kind of moral midgetry that Pat Buchanan exhibited.

In Riggs's work, we can see the move from "visibility" to "representation." (Representation: *re*-presentation as depiction or portrayal; to present *again*, building on the impulse to interpret ourselves and our world: reflexivity, consciousness of consciousness, the mark of our humanity. Re-presentation already implies abstraction, contextualization.) Armistead Maupin comments:

We always want everyone represented. . . . I think as human beings we should be demanding this kind of variety [in which a range of gay/lesbian characters are shown] on television. Not as black people, not as gays and lesbians, not as Jews, but as human beings we must say we want everyone represented, *and that means there has to be an alliance. That's the great pitfall of liberalism, because so many liberals tend to put people in boxes and keep them there, and that doesn't make for the eventual liberation we want [emphasis mine].*

Of course, the danger, as Maupin knows, is that many of the abstracting categories we use to describe people are toxic, contaminated with projections, hatred, and fear. If we have "blacks" or "Jews" or "gays," we have "niggers," "kikes," "faggots." The battle over which words apply is at the heart of the culture wars. Representation of our own lives in their complexities (the ways we have been shaped by social forces, the ways we work to reshape these forces or boxes, and the particularities that also make our personalities unique) counteracts the homophobia of annihilation, the isolation that can make us question our existence, our connections to other people.

Riggs's project began as a video anthology of black gay male poetry; a "work about [black gay] poets, in a somewhat rather conventional documentary form," it soon expanded, because he found that he needed a link between people working in "discrete places all across the country." This attempt to create mutual context for gay black poets required that he offer his audience a relationship with himself, "that I step into the breach, and that I become in many ways a transition, the link, the chain between poems and between experiences. For me, that wasn't an easy decision at all." Riggs, like Maupin, is out not just to represent but to create through representation a fuller humanity for gay people. For Riggs, humanity occurs within community. He sees himself "speaking directly to the experiences of people trying to find identity and find community when the world was telling them that they had none." Marlon's representation of his own life, to achieve great resonance for an emerging community of black gay men, drew on the example of their black lesbian sisters such as Lorde and the women in the Combahee River Collective and Salsa Soul Sisters. He said:

I'm trained as someone who documents the lives and the experiences of people by in some ways effacing myself as much as possible and allowing them to speak, and I think that's in many ways a noble tradition. . . . It was the first time for me that I was directly owning the experiences that I was trying to communicate through the work, that I wasn't relying solely on other people to vicariously tell my life, you know, and to explore my issues. . . . So for me to step out and to affirm and to declare who I was without shame, without apology, in the most vocal, affirming, powerful way that I could, for me . . . was not only a breach of everything that I had done before, but also a way of really claiming my own humanity. And also, I think, claiming the humanity of a larger community, which had also been silenced in our culture. . . . So much of being black in this country and being gay in this country is effacing who you are, so that you can assimilate, so that you can be a part of the larger culture, and nobody will notice you, so that you can be invisible, because once you become visible, as a black person, that becomes a problem in other people's minds. Once you become visible as a gay person, that becomes a problem, and you become a target for attack [emphasis mine].

Invisibility here is not so much that the queer is unmarked, it is that those markings go deliberately *unnoticed*.

Riggs shows that perhaps "representation" has more to do with articulation and language than visibility, more to do with the trope of "voice" than "vision," or sight per se. Voice is more familiar to me, hearing again what I heard from the audience of the Chicago Modern Languages Association Convention in 1977 when black lesbian poet and essayist Audre Lorde, fresh from her first breast surgery, informed us, "Your silences will not protect you. My silences have not protected me." She would live with cancer another fifteen years, pushing the limits of life, approaching mythic dimensions in the minds of the many women who looked to her as a model of self-realization, self-articulation, self-determination. "We can learn to work

In a still from Marlon Riggs's *Tongues Untied* (1989), members of the Minority Task Force on AIDS affirm the solidarity of black gay men.

and speak when we are afraid in the same way we have learned to work and speak when we are tired," she counseled. "For we have been socialized to respect fear more than our own needs for language and definition, and while we wait in silence for that final luxury of fearlessness, the weight of that silence will choke us." Years later, Audre's insight reemerged in the most resonant slogan of AIDS activism: "Silence=Death."

Invisibility has the potential even to reverse self-representation. Pat Buchanan's "attack ad" people took one portion of Riggs's video that speaks explicitly to the racism within the lesbian and gay community, a shot of gay white men's bare buns on Castro Street, over which Riggs describes the "sea of vanilla," the racism with which he and his gay brothers of color must contend. The visual images in this segment were presented as one more image of the (white) gay sexuality that the religious right has constructed as "the gay agenda," creating the impression that *Tongues Untied* is about white gay men and reinforcing the idea (which the same strategists cultivate later) that gay people are only white.

Buchanan's exploitation of images in *Tongues Untied* was but one skirmish in "the culture wars," a far-reaching attack on gay and lesbian artists that began in the late 1980s. The forces of the religious right who so used and distorted Marlon Riggs's life work had been perfecting such strategies for quite some time. Historians trace the beginnings of the New Right back to Barry Goldwater's landslide defeat at the hands of Lyndon Johnson in 1964 as the Republican right-wing's first attempt to organize independently. The effort netted a greater number of small donations than any other candidate had received to that time, the beginning of the modern political mailing list. I remember this campaign and my family's vehement support for Goldwater, including my appearance as one of a football field full of flowers of Southern maidenhood in white dresses carrying red roses at a Goldwater rally in Montgomery. Alabama segregationist George Wallace launched an overtly racist third-party campaign for the presidency in 1968, railing against integration and the Washington establishment of "pointy-headed intellectuals." By then, though, I had switched allegiances, casting my vote for Hubert Humphrey. Nixon's slim victory brought me to the sinking realization that the rest of the nation had stopped chastising the South for our overt racism and had swung behind us. Republican strategists saw the appeal of the Wallace oratory, a chance to add a populist base to a party identified in much of the country's mind with country clubs and ruling elites. In 1969, Kevin Phillips in *The Emerging Republican Majority* explained the formula for forging a right-wing populism based on a racist backlash to issues such as busing and affirmative action. The culture wars I speak of are a direct result of Richard Nixon's 1972 "Southern strategy," which built upon what Phillips had written.

Four African-American gay men gathered on Christopher Street during the 1989 Lesbian & Gay Pride March in New York City. Photo by JEB (Joan E. Biren).

Richard Viguerie pioneered in direct mail, raising money through appeals to Goldwater's and Wallace's campaign contributors. Viguerie and people like Paul Weyrich quickly moved to establish a network of institutions to provide the emerging New Right movement with an infrastructure: the Heritage Foundation, the Conservative Caucus, the National Conservative Political Action Committee, Jesse Helms's Congressional Club. Weyrich recruited the then not particularly political televangelists Jerry Falwell and Pat Robertson to fashion an ultraconservative religious response that quickly positioned itself as a "moral majority" in opposition to the rapidly emerging feminist movement and gay liberation struggles,

Meet the New Willie Horton

A scene from "Tongues Untied," the film used by Patrick Buchanan in his ad campaign against President Bush.

By Marlon T. Riggs

BERKELEY, Calif.
Patrick Buchanan's most controversial campaign ad has given politics a new cast of characters to demonize, then scapegoat. The specter of Willie Horton has returned, but this time, at least in Mr. Buchanan's distorted view, he is a leather-clad bare-chested, sadomasochistic homosexual dancing shamelessly in the street.

As the author of the so-called pornographic images (not *quite* too shocking to show) now so grossly butchered in Mr. Buchanan's anti-Bush, anti-National Endowment for the Arts ad, I've witnessed with rising horror a perversion of a different order now on the rise in politics: the ruthless exploitation of race and sexuality to win high public office.

Mr. Buchanan, of course, is not alone in manipulating the divisive politics of fear and enmity. The Bush campaign of 1988 proved as adept in

Marlon T. Riggs, director of "Tongues Untied," teaches at the Graduate School of Journalism at the University of California at Berkeley.

tarring Michael Dukakis with responsibility for the release of Mr. Horton, a black convict, and his subsequent rape of a white women.

In that single ad, old racial taboos and racist anxieties found renewed expression and public resonance. Since neither the President nor his campaign managers have ever acknowledged how deeply their strategy offended millions of African Americans (or millions of others sensitive to America's shameful history of psychosexual myths about black men), I can't help but feel a certain cool delight in Mr. Buchanan's ironic reversal of the smear tactic against George Bush himself.

But my satisfaction is cut short by the realization that my work and life, and more important, the multiple communities of which I am a part, are being grossly maligned in the process. In this mud-slinging match, I along with other gay and lesbian Americans, particularly those of color, have again become the mud.

Because my film, "Tongues Untied," affirms the lives and dignity of black gay men, conservatives have found it a convenient target, despite the awards and popular and critical acclaim it received after its broadcast last summer on public television.

Buchanan adds anti-gay bigotry to race-baiting.

On Wednesday, Jesse Helms, Republican of North Carolina, denounced the film during Senate debate over a now delayed bill to provide financing for the Corporation for Public Broadcasting.

Last fall, the Christian Coalition collapsed the 55-minute documentary into seven, disjointed, highly sensationalized minutes, then sent hundreds of copies to members of the House of Representatives in an unsuccessful effort to force new content restrictions on the N.E.A. Of the total cost of the film, only $5,000 was N.E.A. money. And that came from an indirect source.

Mr. Buchanan's television ads, of course, have upped the ante. His antiquota race-baiting has now fused with a brazen display of anti-gay bigotry. Presidential politics have thus been injected with a new poison: the persecution of racial and sexual difference

is fast becoming the litmus test of true Republican leadership

Sadly, Mr. Buchanan's strong showing in Tuesday's Georgia primary will likely encourage these tactics, though his campaign claims that the ad will not be repeated in Texas, Tennessee, Florida, Louisiana and Mississippi, all of which have primaries next week. We can nonetheless expect a steady spew of words, "facts" and images that have been ripped out of context, then deflated and distorted into vicious, provocative caricatures.

Willie Horton, in other words, will continue his metamorphosis into a militant, Jesus-blaspheming, psychopathic homosexual. What kind of monster will he become next?

Needless to say, the insult in this brand of politics extends not just to blacks and gays, the majority of whom are taxpayers, and would therefore seem entitled to some measure of representation in publicly financed art.

The insult confronts all who now witness and are profoundly outraged by the quality of political — one hesitates to say Presidential — debate. The vilest form of obscenity these days is in our nation's leadership. □

against abortion, and for prayer in the schools, which they first subsumed under the bogeyman of "secular humanism." In 1972, Jesse Helms won his first race for the Senate. Who was he? A rabidly racist news commentator now running against desegregation in the South.

My own family was conservative without being fundamentalist; our blessing was to be Methodists rather than Baptists. My mother passed on the insights of the "higher criticism" she had learned in college: that the power of biblical texts was in their stories, their symbols, which we had the responsibility of interpreting. I am still indebted to my parents' intelligent approach to Scriptures, which made it easier (though not easy) to come out to them.

By the early 1980s, as Jonathan Mozzochi from Portland's Coalition for Human Dignity points out, the New Right had begun to reframe its debate, subtly but effectively. "Antiabortion" became "pro-life"; "antifeminism" and "antigay" became "pro-family." The "moral majority" had found a way to co-opt and subvert the language of civil rights, repositioning itself as an oppressed minority against special interest groups that had won "special rights."

This code language tapped into a growing climate of economic crisis and widespread resentment. In the early 1970s, at the same moment when the New Right emerged, the corporate sector of the "old right" began to restructure the economic life of the United States. Corporate profits from the postwar boom peaked, then began to decline, squeezed by increased foreign competition from both established and newly industrialized countries. Rather than retool our basic industries, corporate decision makers cut labor costs by attacking unions and finding labor in Third World countries, where people work for one-tenth the wages. The deindustrialization of the United States over the last thirty years has left us a service economy with lower paying jobs and a "feminized" workforce drained of the unionized, higher salaried white men's jobs that had formed the backbone of the U.S. economy. The United States has consequently lost 2.6 million manufacturing jobs since 1978 to offshore operations or to automation.

Under Reagan, the restructuring of federal tax policy cut the percentage of corporate taxes that foot the bill for the federal budget from 23.4 percent to 9.7 percent. Many Fortune 500 companies stopped paying taxes altogether and even got money back from previous years. The massive corruption that led to the Savings and Loan scandal will cost taxpayers $100 billion a year. And with a platform of "balancing the budget," Presidents Reagan and Bush pumped up the national debt from $1 trillion to $4 trillion, with increased military spending and slashed social services, all in the name of "deficit reduction."

Jerry Falwell, the homophobic fundamentalist who was instrumental in recruiting evangelical ministers to the New Right in the 1970s, seen here with his wife at their home in Lynchburg, Virginia. Photo by Steve McCurry/Magnum Photos.

The economic history of the last thirty years is inextricably tied, in the rhetoric of various sectors of the religious right, with the message to white workers that the problem with the country was the minority "special interest groups" and a decline in "family values," that the disappearing jobs had to do with affirmative action rather than tax policy, and that the general decline in economic health was related to the "lower" productivity of these nonwhite workers. The preachers and senators, for example, who led the attack on the NEA did so in the name of the "taxpayers' revolt," another way in which the right wing was able to cut funds available for governing and to direct people's anger away from corporations. "This is a question of abuse of taxpayers' money," Senator D'Amato railed on the Senate floor. Jesse Helms echoed, "The Constitution may prevent the government from prohibiting this Serrano fellow's—laughably, I will describe it—'artistic expression.' It certainly does not require the American taxpayers or the federal government to fund, promote, honor, approve, or condone it."

In this climate of rapid economic displacement, there are unforeseen effects of a "visibility" uncomplicated by its other associations becoming the main strategy and goal of our freedom. If we think that visibility alone is the mark of queer freedom, then the more visible, the more extravagant, the more outlandish, the better. We push ourselves toward spectacle in response to the straight gaze. And when we do, who is it we imagine is watching?

The Gay Agenda is a video that draws heavily on footage shot by roving conservative cameramen at gay rights marches in San Francisco. Thousands of copies have been distributed, free, to churches, legislators, every member of Congress, Pentagon generals. It significantly influenced the congressional debate on gays in the military, and recent assaults on municipal and state statutes protecting the civil rights of lesbians and gay men.

The Gay Agenda uses a common tactic of bigotry: it identifies the stigmatized class with its most outrageous behavior, and the dominant class with the most normal behavior. There are straight and gay practitioners of S/M, straight and gay exhibitionists, and straight people and gay people kiss in public (straight people far more frequently than queers). There are homosexual and heterosexual child molesters. In fact, the last ten years have witnessed an explosion of cases of reported sexual abuse, as survivors reexperience their terrors and come to terms with their memories. But the molester is not most often the "queer pedophile down the street," but a father or brother or uncle or cousin. Stereotypes promoted in *The Gay Agenda* say gay men are child molesters, and lesbians are the result of molestation. But they never ask the lesbians who, like many heterosexual women, were ravaged in their childhoods and whose testimony would show that the rape of children is a largely heterosexual affair. Likewise, straight viewers of *The Gay Agenda* would think that "man/boy love" is the most characteristic element of lesbian and gay sexuality, not its most hotly debated. The vehemence of the portrayal of the gay pedophile is in direct proportion to the burgeoning evidence of "dysfunction" and abuse in the heterosexual family.

Boosters of Oregon's Measure 9, making antigay bigotry a family affair. Photo by Donna Binder/Impact Visuals.

Once you separate same-sex attraction and activity from the most inflammatory set of behaviors (which *The Gay Agenda* works overtime to conflate), issues become clearer. Heterosexuals as a group are not denied jobs, housing, safety, custody of their children, because some minority of them have sexual practices to which the majority objects. Forty-second Street and Ft. Lauderdale on spring break; O. J. Simpson and Nicole; Lorena Bobbitt; the legions of women who seek safety in battered-women's shelters: these are not used as evidence of the essential depravity of heterosexual sex. Mere "homophobia" does not describe this phenomenon, this arrogant heterosexual supremacy.

But I also ask myself: the video brigades of the religious right and the more flamboyant folks in pride parades that they capture on film, have they somehow created one another—the voyeur and the exhibitionist? I get down a little book, *History of Sexuality*, in which Michel Foucault questions the accuracy of the repression theory of sexuality, finding the more prevalent pattern since the seventeenth century to be an incitement to discussion about sexuality, a proliferating sexual "discourse" that serves the interests of social systems bound on bringing their citizens under increasing surveillance and control.

Many lesbian and gay activists understand queer struggles as a battle, primarily, against sexual repression as Foucault explains it: "Repression involves a sentence to disappear, an injunction to silence, an affirmation of non-existence, against which we can free ourselves only by transgressing laws, lifting prohibitions, reinstating pleasure." Under this scenario, queer artists and cultural workers are heroic protagonists in an epic battle. I agree. And yet, a suspicion lurks that we depend somehow on what represses us as much as it depends on us for identity and continuity.

I have observed, close hand, for a good many years my own senator from North Carolina, Jesse Helms, and how he invoked "the powerful gay lobby" in North Carolina, which only came into being once he began attacking it. We had our first pride march in 1981—straight youth jumped men at a "gay" swimming hole and beat one of them to death. There must have been four hundred of us that summer day in 1981 who marched around downtown Durham on "Our Day Out." Soon we showed up in Helms's fund-raising materials as evidence of "the powerful gay lobby" that controlled the country. By 1984, Helms concocted a whole panoply of gay demons that he used in his race against Democratic governor Jim Hunt. Many of us who had avoided becoming involved in a political landscape that didn't seem to offer any real choice between candidates or party, between "Tweedledum and Tweedledee," began organizing in self-defense when, in the person of Helms, Tweedledum began to goose-step. By 1990, we had our own gay-led PAC, Senate Vote 90, and were an organized, vocal, visible presence in black architect Harvey Gantt's strong but unsuccessful race to unseat Helms. A gay movement in North Carolina did not really exist in the early 1980s, but it was necessary for Helms to create one, and we obliged.

We know they get off on us. We know that in the name of "repression" they proliferate our images, if not our representation, to coalesce their political power. They cannot ignore what repulses, fascinates them so, staring so fixedly at images of our sexuality. As one of the myriad viewers who flocked to see Mapplethorpe's X Portfolio at the WPA after the Corcoran canceled the exhibit exclaimed, "I've been here four times already and this show disgusts me each time I see it." Former National Endowment for the Arts chair John Frohnmayer remembers an encounter on Christian television with Pat Robertson: "He went into the kind of litany that he seems to enjoy, which was to describe in graphic detail some of the Mapplethorpe photos. It was almost as if he got some

Marion "Pat" Robertson, head of a multimillion-dollar religious broadcasting empire, created the Christian Coalition out of the donor base from his failed 1988 presidential bid, thereby reinvigorating the religious right. AP/Wide World Photos.

kind of pleasure out of these descriptions, and then after he hopes that he has horrified his audience, he turns to me and says, 'How can that be art?' "

Or, hear Donald Wildmon on *Tongues Untied*: "This is our opportunity. You can see for yourself how awful this stuff really is, so watch it."

Do we also get off on them? Fundamentalist videographers find most useful the scenes from various pride parades and marches that capture the scandalous spectacle in response to the puritan's gaze. Part of what propaganda such as *The Gay Agenda* does is translate and transmit scenes of urban sexuality, of carnival, to rural terrain, with ominous warnings that this homosexual menace is encroaching on small-town America. As one opponent of Measure 9 in Oregon observed, "Why didn't [these films] show pictures of the gay pride parade in Portland? Why did they have to go to New York and San Francisco? Because the gay pride in Portland reflects Portland life and is tame by those standards." In reality, the dykes and faggots who parade bare-breasted and in chains down the streets of New York or Washington, D.C., are hardly headed back to the constraints of small towns in the same getups, because it takes the anonymity of the big cities for them to act out the taboos of their childhood.

I come to a sobering thought: when our whole politic of "visibility" asserts itself to resist repression, distinctions about sexual practices in terms of either ethics or strategy are read only as "censorship," as "more repression." In the 1980s, the religious right shifted its strategy. Talk of Bible and sin was turning people off, as was the rigid version of heaven-on-earth. They chose to be more secular in their campaigns, to highlight "special rights" and the evil of our social menace rather than our sins. They shifted to psychological, medical, and legal arguments. Mind you, I am not saying we should throw anyone who does not look or act straight to the wolves. But is it impossible for us on public occasions to choose to be more, well, mundane?

This incitement to discourse about sex, which Foucault sees as working with and against Calvinism over the past several centuries to tighten social and physical controls, seems every bit as accurate a description of the homophobic propaganda of the religious right as a theory of repression only. Fundamentalists have duplicated and reduplicated these videos of gay men kissing, lesbians lying on top of each other in the D.C. sun, queer rage from podiums and demos. It is they, not us, who take these scenes into thousands of church basements and middle-American living rooms. They are proliferating our images, our visibility, a hell of a lot faster than we are.

Bondage queens in a lesbian and gay pride march in New York. Photo by Philip Jones Griffiths/Magnum Photos.

Facing page: "Sharp." Throughout the 1980s and 1990s, lesbian and gay activists such as Dyke Action Machine have strategically appropriated the conventions of mainstream advertising to bring their messages to popular consciousness.

Check out the channels from your satellite dish on morning TV, as the talk-show hosts explore an amazing variety of sexual identities and activities for the few American housewives who are still at home.

This three-centuries-old compulsion to discuss sex converges with post-industrial capitalism that locates our heavy industries overseas for the "comparative advantage" of cheap labor, detaches surfaces from meanings, and commodifies identities and movements. Lesbian writer and activist Jewelle Gomez gets to some part of the dynamic:

I think lesbians and gays are going into an interesting period in that the large segments of the society are very angry that lesbians and gays are more visible and that's why we have so much more violence. That's why we have such a highly motivated, well-organized Christian Right moving against us. That Puritan anger is because lesbians and gays are actually being noticed and in some cases accepted. There's this parallel. On the one side, the Christian Right is fanning the flames of hatred, while the media on the other side is trying to cash in on us. The media is saying, "Well, you know there is that market out there, and we know they have that disposable income so we better target them." . . . There's a very weird parallel action happening, with the backlash and almost the promotion of homosexual life in magazines or on television, which is very odd but I think that's the nature of the conflict of Puritanism and capitalism.

Evidence of the degree of proliferation of queer images is the phenomenon by which lesbians have become fashionable, chic. What about Madonna? Well, dykes float through her videos, as in the film *Truth or Dare*, along with similarly chic black gay men who surround her in bed. We get chic lipstick killer lesbians like Sharon Stone in the movie *Basic Instinct*. Roseanne's ratings beat out the Grammys the night of her much publicized kiss with Mariel Hemingway. This phenomenal growth of lesbians as a commodity in the mainstream comes simultaneously with the maturation of lesbian artists who have honed their voices and their visions in a twenty-year-old movement of lesbian culture: small presses and little magazines, and lesbian music festivals where women tote into the wilds enough port-a-Janes and pasta and tofu and tarps and crafts and generators and sound systems to produce sophisticated concerts and community in the middle of cow pastures for throngs of lesbians who have driven across several states to sit through a hurricane and listen. Dorothy Allison's *Bastard Out of Carolina* got rave reviews in the *New York Times* and a nomination for a National Book Award. Minnie Bruce Pratt's *Crime Against Nature* won the American Academy of Poets' Lamont Prize. Comedian Lea Delaria's bellows about DYYYKKES were heard in Provincetown and on music festival stages and now sound on late-night TV, *Arsenio*, and even come at me from Top 40 radio at 9 A.M. in Durham. Dyke gender-bending is finally becoming marketable (faggot gender-bending has had a wide and well-paid audience for a good while). Cruising channels one Saturday

Anti-violence whistle as blown by
SAMANTHA, Pink Panther.
Photographed by
GIRL RAY.

SHARP.

DAM!

night I first saw singer k.d. lang romping around the stage in her buzz haircut, cut-off boots, and camouflage skirt on the country-western show *Austin City Limits*. I knew something big was shifting in popular culture. "Elvis is alive," Madonna crooned of k.d., "and she's beautiful." More recently, post–coming out, lang adorned the cover of *Vanity Fair* all bibbed up to get a shave from supermodel Cindy Crawford, k.d.'s lathered cheek resting blissfully on Cindy's ample bosom, Crawford's razor resting on lang's throat. Inside, Cindy leans over k.d., her parted lips two inches from lang's mouth (with a lather mustache), lang's fingers pressing into Cindy's thighs. "Androgyny is making your sexuality available to everyone, using the power of both male and female," lang explains, adding, "I have a little bit of penis envy. They're ridiculous, but they're cool."

Only this month at the dentist's office, I ran across a *People* magazine story about lesbian rock star Melissa Ethridge and her new woman lover, shown at home in their well-appointed kitchen, looking as sexy and happy as a million dollars ever seemed to make straight celebrities.

The Question of Equality itself, the four-part public television series and the book I'm even now helping to write, are a part of this phenomenon.

But what does it mean that our images are suddenly proliferating now? Gay politics and culture are so largely an urban phenomenon, yet this is an age when politicians, corporate elites, and white people have abandoned our cities (fleeing to places like Oregon), leaving visible gay minorities with people of color in inner cities with rotting infrastructures, so that we become synonymous for the country at large with urban blight and decay, which religious moralists turn so quickly into metaphors for spiritual decay, into Sodom and Gomorrah. The gay/lesbian liberation movement consolidates its push for civil rights in an era of economic crisis and decline when Reagan and Bush have spent much of our "discretionary income" on bombs or let it be stolen or given it away to the multinationals. Our images proliferate in the same electron flow that turns money into electronic impulse, restructuring the global assembly line so that production previously done in the United States is dispersed to a host of Third World countries, where people work for one-tenth the wage, and the Clinton administration anticipates an era in the not-so-distant future when half the wages in the United States are poverty wages. Proliferating images serve to mark us in the public mind as cause and symptom of national decline. Our visibility, our images alone, will not necessarily save us. We could win the culture battle and lose the war.

Kevin Tebedo, director of Colorado for Family Values, sponsors of Amendment 2, which a majority of voters in Colorado adopted in 1992 to repeal and prohibit gay rights legislation. Photo by Dana E. Olsen/*The Oregonian*.

Oregon and Colorado: Gay Rights, Special Rights, or Human Rights?

In 1992, Pat Buchanan set the tone for local and state cadres of the religious right, who experimented with homophobia as a wedge strategy to advance a broadly regressive agenda in Oregon, Tampa (Florida), Portland (Maine), and Colorado. **Colorado's Amendment 2** laid out a political homophobia around a theme of "no special rights" that proscribes gay and lesbian citizens from having redress of grievances.

Oregon's Measure 9 was primeval, less restrained, urging that the voters change Oregon's constitution to declare homosexuality "abnormal, wrong, unnatural, and perverse." It would force state and local governments to discriminate proactively against gays and lesbians and our allies. The homophobia of Measure 9 sought to lock homosexuality into the signifying chain of crimes and perversions in the statewide ballot initiative and three local efforts. Its homophobia is what philosophers would call ontological, aiming to erode the ground of our being as humans. It is a homophobia of annihilation.

A huge "No on 9" campaign in Oregon managed to hold it to 43 percent of the vote, but in Colorado, Amendment 2 passed with 54 percent of the vote, immediately becoming the model for similar initiatives in twelve states, including local initiatives throughout Oregon. The struggles in Oregon and Colorado, won or lost, demonstrate how easily our right to exist as constituents of a democratic society can be challenged. Beneath Colorado's Amendment 2, You have no [political] rights, lies Oregon's Measure 9, You have no right to exist. As Marlon Riggs explains to a Minnesota audience complaining about the use of taxpayers' money: "Aren't we [taxpaying lesbians, gays, and bisexuals] therefore entitled to some representation? . . . Aren't we entitled to separate self-representation in a so-called pluralistic democratic society?" Questions of

"Neither the State of Colorado, through any of its branches or departments, nor any of its agencies, political subdivisions, municipalities or school districts, shall enact, adopt or enforce any statute, regulation, ordinance or policy whereby homosexual, lesbian, or bisexual orientation, conduct, practices or relationships shall constitute or otherwise be the basis of or entitle any person or class of persons to have or claim any minority status, quota preference, protected status or claim of discrimination."
—Colorado's Amendment 2

"State, regional and local governments and their departments, agencies and other entities, including specifically the State Department of Higher Education and the public schools, shall assist in setting a standard for Oregon's youth that recognizes homosexuality, pedophilia, sadism and masochism as abnormal, wrong, unnatural, and perverse and that these behaviors are to be discouraged and avoided."
—Oregon's Measure 9

cultural representation easily slide into the political realm.

Questions about our basic existence as humans sound again and again as lesbians and gay men speak poignantly of our need for affirmation, for "self-esteem":

. . . I need to know I am not alone.

. . . It's okay for us to love each other.

. . . The truth about me.

Donna Red Wing explained how this played in Oregon: "I see a televangelist, a neo-Nazi, I cross the street. But when they look like our great-aunt or my favorite cousin, when they're the people we deal with every day, that's really frightening." In the background, powerful organizations and forces such as Coors, the Rutherford Institute, and the Heritage Foundation were pulling the strings, Red Wing said, "but that's not what Oregon saw."

When our neighbors and fellow citizens mount a campaign that links us with bestiality (literally, having intercourse with beasts, with, implicitly, being beasts) in the name of family and God, the effect is profound. Oregon organizer Scot Seibert recalled the effect of the emotional violence in 1992, of the continual inundation of annihilating messages: "You walk past a building that somebody's spray-painted 'Fags die' on it. It takes a part of you to shut it off and just not let it affect you. I left the campaign, and . . . I've built that wall so high so that I wouldn't hear all the nasty things people said that I couldn't even hear the nice things people said. The doors [that homophobes twice tore off my house] were easy. I just put new ones on. But your soul is different."

"Jesus called us to love everyone, to love our neighbor, to love our enemies. The church clearly holds that homosexuality—the act—is a sin, but the people have to be respected. That nuance is not something a lot of Catholics understand," explains a Catholic priest in Oregon whose church was vandalized during the campaign over Measure 9. That *nuance* is not something I much understand myself. If that was the best religious allies could do, and their own place of worship was branded with swastikas and the epithets "Kill all gays and Catholics" and "Family values," no wonder 43 percent of the population voted the way it did. Kathleen Sadaat, another lesbian active on the No on 9 campaign, explains, "There is a violence in not being able to live your life, and whether you are ever actually *struck* by someone is not the only issue. Anything that pushed you toward being less than human, anything that tells you you are not a part of the human family, is a violent act."

Yet, in the face of rising violence and backlash, many of us have, over the decades and through the

Ralph Reed, executive director of the Christian Coalition, announcing the formation of the coalition's Oregon chapter and its support for Measure 9, the failed Oregon ballot initiative that equated homosexuality with criminality and sought to prohibit the extension of antidiscrimination statutes to lesbians and gay men. At left is Lon Mabon, head of the Oregon Citizens Alliance, Measure 9's sponsor. Photo by Shan Gordon.

A priest delivers a homily in a Roman Catholic church in Hillsboro, Oregon, that was vandalized with homophobic, anti-Semitic, and racist graffiti as the vote on Measure 9 drew near. Photo by Tom Boyd.

power of community and relationships, constructed lives bit by bit out of the teeth of loneliness and despair, through the hard-won love for ourselves and one another and our struggles with our families of origin. Our humanity is not negotiable, cannot be debated. We will not go back.

This past summer, my partner Barbara and I celebrated our fifteenth anniversary. We sent out two hundred invitations to friends and family, and half of them accepted. We planned a big celebration at a city lodge, with a commitment ritual. Barb and I soon ran up against our differing opinions of how we wanted the event to be represented. To her, it was her wedding day, plain and simple. I explained how weddings were heterosexual instruments of exclusion. Besides, we knew too much to be getting married: that was for novices who didn't know what they were getting into. My plans for the ritual included an explication of homophobia and a reading of the U.N. Declaration of the Rights of Women. Barb quickly nipped this in the bud. I felt self-conscious thinking about being so personal in the midst of all the people we had invited, but I recognized this self-consciousness as a very old feeling. I wanted to seize what had heretofore been largely a heterosexual privilege of making a public commitment and getting community support. I knew the danger for me would be to turn the event into a political rally, but if I did that I would not get what I wanted from the day, which was spontaneous emotion and a blessing from my community of our relationships and our family.

We had invited our parents and siblings. My dad declined because he was in the midst of his garden and he couldn't take the three days off from harvesting tomatoes to drive up, attend the event, and drive back to Alabama. Barb's parents explained that they couldn't come because of their deep religious antipathy to our "lifestyle." When I realized that we would have no blood family there, I called Daddy again, my voice quavering, and told him we needed family there. I offered him a frequent flier ticket, so that he could make the trip in a day. "What day is this, again, feller?" he asked, then said, "I think I could do that." When he arrived, I showed him our rings and filled him in on the ceremony, for which he had not been given a speaking part, hoping that he wouldn't be taken by surprise.

That afternoon, our friends gathered on the lawn in front of the rustic lodge under threatening skies. I wanted to move the event inside to avoid what I knew would be a downpour, but Barb vetoed the idea once again. After a simple English country dance, through which we hoped to "cast a circle" of community with the disparate people assembled, we joined the circle with our daughter Annie, her dad David, and his partner and his two children. We began with lesbian poems from the four directions. Then we met in the center, speaking to one another lines from Adrienne Rich. I welcomed and thanked our friends for their support, without which we would not have sustained the relationship, and asked them to form a community for the afternoon through which we could make a blessing together. I said that sometimes we have to live into the life we dream and work for, and invited them to live that afternoon as if homophobia did not exist.

Then we made promises, affirmations really, about how we would live together: "I promise to honor the spirit in you, to protect your freedom as if it were my own, because it is; to seek abandon and play. . . ." We gave one another rings, and we kissed, seeing the beaming circle of faces behind my eyelids as I closed my eyes. Quaker-style, we invited our friends to respond, and they did, generously. "There wasn't a dry eye in the house," our friend Pearl later laughed. "You guys really know how to work a crowd."

At the very end of the ceremony, I thanked my father for coming, and he stood up to speak. Perhaps it was my imagination, but many people around the circle drew in a collective breath, having read about my father's conservative politics in two of my books. "Anything that gives dignity to the human personality is good," he began, and I started to grin. "I haven't heard anything here today that does not give dignity to the human personality." He had pronounced the benediction, and the sun broke out from behind the clouds. We have a video of this event, but don't expect to see it on PBS.

I asked my friend Scot Nakagawa, who worked in the No on 9 campaign after directing Portland's Coalition for Human Dignity, about his take on the urban/rural split. His response was characteristically thoughtful:

When gay and lesbian people rightfully feel betrayed by electoral actions where rural communities do not perform well on our issues, there's a kind of class arrogance that fails to recognize what life is like in a rural community, where working-class folks, regardless of sexual orientation, realize that their histories are intertwined, their lives are interconnected, they share a common destiny. The answer to this problem is not to get in their face and scare them. The urban gay male experience has been shaped by a particular class experience that allows inner-city urban enclaves. The people who maintain the roads, provide us groceries, provide basic services, are part of who we are. Identity politics get shaped by these forces, including our failure to recognize class as a defining force in shaping our lives.

I asked him about the tendency of campaigns against the homophobic ballot measures to take on a vague mission against "discrimination," without much other overt content about homophobia, lesbians and gay men, or other classes that face discrimination. He pointed me to the polls, which indicate that people are concerned about fairness. People don't like discrimination, but they also don't like gay and lesbian people or the programs that protect us. So the strategy must be, "We'll talk about fairness, but not about ourselves." But "fairness" to the people answering the polls does not necessarily mean justice for all people. "Rather than use the poll data to learn where people are in order to move them, campaigns accept the polls as the parameters within which they have to work," Scot explained.

Other factors force the campaigns to focus on short-term goals. The No on 9 campaign cost $2.3 million. This is not a lot to spend on a ballot measure (Portland General Electric spent $5 million to keep the Trojan nuclear facility open), but it is a lot to spend on social justice. Also, in Oregon elected officials and businessmen felt a strong need to oppose the Oregon Citizens Alliance out of fear that the passage of Measure 9 would discourage tourism. The result was a broad group of people with varying interests, not all of which directed their energy to overturning the homophobia underlying the initiative or explaining its links to other kinds of discrimination. Again, we may win the battle and still have to fight the war.

Lou Sheldon, founder and chairman of the Traditional Values Coalition. Photo by Rink Foto.

The various strains of homophobia developed to perfection in the Oregon and Colorado campaigns were amplified in the video *Gay Rights, Special Rights*, which takes the sensational sexual scenes in *The Gay Agenda* and adds an overlay of political

Split-screen stills from *Gay Rights, Special Rights*, produced by the Traditional Values Coalition.

argument taking the question of "gay rights" and of homosexuality itself out of the context of civil rights. If they can strip us of our claims to justice, they can push homosexual experience back into the mire of theological, medical, psychiatric, and criminal discourses and reverse forty years of gay and lesbian activism. The video's proliferation of more bacchanalian scenes of urban gay life contribute to demonizing, pathologizing, and criminalizing lesbians and (especially) gay men. Are we a "legitimate minority," or are we sick, criminal, perverse, and sinful?

To understand the political context of *Gay Rights, Special Rights*, I had to go back to the Bakke case, decided by the U.S. Supreme Court in 1978. In 1973 and 1974, Allan Bakke was a thirty-three-year-old engineer, a white man with a burning desire to become a doctor. He had been turned down by twelve medical schools, probably for the reason that two explained to him: his age. He figured his best chance to get into the University of California at Davis was to sue, not on the basis of age—which is why he was getting turned down—but of race. *Regents of the University of California* v. *Bakke* was the first major test case for affirmative action, the legal precedent around which the idea of reverse discrimination was elaborated. Justice Powell wrote for this majority, saying that Bakke's whiteness should occasion the "strict scrutiny" previously reserved for "discrete and insular" minorities with a past history of discrimination. The no-special-rights strategy initiated in Colorado and elaborated on in *Gay Rights, Special Rights* lifts its language directly out of Judge Powell's concern about converting "a remedy heretofore reserved for violations of legal rights into a privilege that all institutions throughout the Nation could grant at their pleasure to whatever groups are perceived as victims of societal discrimination." Ingeniously, the videographers are able to take all the racist backlash leading to and bolstered by Bakke and dump it onto lesbians and gay men, with the help of African-American spokesmen and women.

"It was pure logic that the Civil Rights Act should protect black people from discrimination," intones the black narrator at the opening of *Gay Rights, Special Rights*. The screen shows grainy black-and-white footage of the 1963 March on Washington, over which King's dream eloquently floated that August afternoon. Then the video jump-cuts to the 1993 March on Washington for Gay & Lesbian Equality; ACT UP founder Larry Kramer is speaking, echoing King, and calling for the day when people are no longer judged by the "content of their desires." For the first third of this hour-long video, various black talking heads, male and female, protest the gay movement's efforts to "hijack the civil rights movement" and take their jobs. "[Gay people] want to be elevated from a behavior-based lifestyle to true minority status that would give them special rights," one speaker explains.

An African-American woman identified only as a "public affairs representative" worries, "This [gay] civil rights act would completely neutralize the Civil Rights Act of 1964. Anyone with any type of sexual orientation [would be included] under this law. This is everyone, so there would be no protection for minorities."

Now the dark faces suddenly disappear and the white "experts" take over, a rogues' gallery of civil rights foes: former attorney general Edwin Meese, whose tenure at the Justice Department gutted civil rights prosecutions; former secretary of education and drug czar William Bennett, arch foe of affirmative action; Mississippi senator Trent Lott, who has voted against every major piece of civil rights legislation in Congress in the past twelve years.

These heroic proponents of civil rights inform us that there are three criteria for minority status. First, "immutable characteristics" define an "insular, discrete group," which needs certain rights to take care of past discrimination. These "immutable" characteristics (such as skin color) are "benign" and have nothing to do with "behavior" (the video shows scenes of sexual abandon from San Francisco, Los Angeles, and New York pride marches to demonstrate the "bad behavior" of homosexuals). Second, minority status requires a "history of discrimination." Now the screen parades statistics collected by slick gay magazines of their gay male subscribers' discretionary income, intended to lure advertisers. (Do only I know that a University of Maryland study shows that gay men and lesbians make less than their heterosexual counterparts?) "Have gay people ever been denied the vote? endured legal segregation? had access to public restaurants denied?" the narrator asks. "Homosexuals are not in conclaves as homeless people under bridges and in food lines waiting for things. These are high-income people who want to push their agenda," Lou Sheldon informs us. Gay people don't need *protection*, the viewer is encouraged to conclude; they must want "special rights."

Third, they tell us, minority status requires political powerlessness. Now across the screen parade the representatives of national gay and lesbian organizations, interviewed at the 1993 March on Washington, eager to brag into this unknown camera about gay power and clout, about our influence on the Clinton administration, our allies in Congress. "Clinton is a friend of ours," a baby-faced young man in drag proclaims to the camera. "He will take care of all gay and lesbian rights. He's going to shake up the country." (Sigh.) By this criterion, any group that actually organized to exert any power to obtain or defend its rights would no longer be deserving of them.

Gay Rights, Special Rights works by a series of deliberate and devious confusions. First, it collapses the idea of "civil rights" with the particular history of African-American struggles. Civil rights are "fundamental rights," which belong

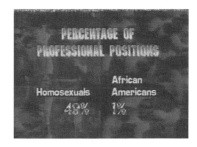

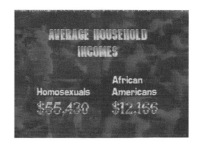

of right to the citizens of all free governments: "protection by the government, with the right to acquire and possess property of every kind, and to pursue and obtain happiness and safety." But the concept of "civil rights" is intimately entwined with the experiences of African-Americans on the North American continent.

The post–Civil War amendments to the Constitution, in addition to the Bill of Rights, have defined the "fundamental liberties" of American democracy, however poorly the United States has often applied these principles. The Thirteenth Amendment outlawed slavery and other forms of involuntary servitude, effecting emancipation after the Southern defeat. The Fourteenth Amendment provided the first definition of citizenship, guaranteeing it to all persons "born or naturalized in the United States." Its "due process" of law and "equal protection" clauses applied many protections of the Bill of Rights (freedom of speech and assembly, religion, fair and speedy trial, against unlawful search and seizure, etc.) to the states, when they had previously been interpreted only as limits of federal power. The Fifteenth Amendment *guaranteed* that citizens could not be denied the vote because of race, color, or previous condition of servitude. (Nowhere in the Constitution, however, are any of us guaranteed the vote.)

Yick Wo v. Hopkins found that the Fourteenth Amendment's provisions "are universal in their application, to all persons within the territorial jurisdiction, without regard to any difference of race, or color, or of nationality." In 1954, the Supreme Court's decision in *Hernandez v. Texas* explained, "Community prejudices are not static, and from time to time other differences from the community norm may define other groups which need the same protection. . . . The Fourteenth Amendment is not directed solely against discrimination . . . based upon differences between 'white' and 'Negro.' "

Less than four decades after hard-won guarantees of the Thirteenth, Fourteenth, and Fifteenth amendments were written into the Constitution, the Southern states reinstituted white supremacy with jim crow laws, which required racial segregation and disenfranchised black voters. Fifty years later, the Civil Rights movement targeted these jim crow institutions, advocating integration and the vote. The Civil Rights Act of 1964, written in the blood spilled at the Edmund Pettus Bridge in Selma, sought once more to affirm equality under the law; it made discrimination illegal in public accommodations, education, federally funded programs, and employment, on the basis of race, color, national origin, sex, or religion. In Title VII, it also made provision for the victims of economic discrimination—primarily people of color and women—to be admitted into "the system" through affirmative-action hiring programs.

The presumption behind the Bakke case was that the Civil Rights Act of 1964 and the Voting Rights Act of 1965 had eliminated racism and established the basis for a "color-blind" society, as if white supremacy were only a matter of jim crow laws and grandfather clauses and poll taxes instituted around the turn of the twentieth century, not arising from five hundred years of slavery and the attempted obliteration of native people. The racism that saw African-Americans defined in the Constitution as something less than fully human is perfectly capable of breeding a succession of racist strategies, most recently the idea that Title VII and the resulting affirmative-action programs bestow "special (and undeserved) rights" on people of color.

Bayard Rustin, the openly gay civil rights leader and close associate of Dr. Martin Luther King Jr., who played a major role in organizing the 1963 March on Washington at which Dr. King delivered his "I Have a Dream" speech. Photo courtesy the Bayard Rustin Fund.

The particular struggles of African-Americans have repeatedly resulted in the codification of civil rights amendments and laws that have extended far beyond the African-American community to other groups. While some of these groups are also economically exploited (such as other people of color and women), people in other "categories" have rights protected without necessarily having a history of economic exploitation or "immutable characteristics" (such as religiously defined groups and the "illegitimate"). Even the most cursory examination of civil rights case law makes this clear and exposes the cheap distortions in *Gay Rights, Special Rights*. If gay people as gay people have not suffered from jim crow segregation, neither have Asians, women, the disabled, etc. . . . The gay rights movement is hardly the first group to have benefited from African-Americans' history of struggle. We are hardly the first group to have taken it for granted. Any group making legal claims for redress of discrimination and protection against violence will inevitably compare itself to African-Americans. But white lesbians and gay men have often played fast and loose with this history and have offended many African-Americans with facile comparisons between the gay movement and the black movement, drawing on its accomplishments without paying back any dues.

Also, too simplistic an application of black strategy to gay experience can result in disaster, as the gays-in-the-military campaign illustrates. President Truman desegregated the armed services in 1948. But Truman issued his executive order because segregation made the United States look bad in the eyes of African nations emerging from colonialism to national independence, and the United States needed Africa's mineral resources to fight the Cold War. The military experience paved the way for a broader acceptance of "race-mixing" in civilian life, which the open integration of lesbian and gay military folks would also do. When gay activists rely too heavily on the race analogy, we neglect to educate potential allies on the particular devastations of what I have called ontological homophobia. Many black

African-American lesbians and gay men at the 1993 March on Washington for Lesbian, Gay and Bi Equal Rights and Liberation. Photo by Jetta Fraser/Impact Visuals.

people object to white people adopting black children because of the racism they will encounter—and the potential erasure of black culture from these children's lives. But almost all gay people are born in straight families and have to navigate many of the same dangers. What if black people, in addition to the brutal visibility of skin pigmentation, also had to worry that their mamas or their church would "discover" they were of African descent and throw them out the door, maybe even wish them dead and then refuse to bury them (as often happens to black lesbians and gay men)? It's a different kind of annihilation.

Clearly, this business of "rights" is not a zero-sum game in which the more you have, the less I have. Rights are not to be competed for. Rather, when we protect the most vulnerable, we are all protected in our vulnerabilities; when we lift the people on the bottom, we all rise. But we live in a society shaped by an economy that fosters competition and thrives on inequality; one person's financial benefit often comes from other people's loss. We should also remind ourselves of the limits of "civil rights," which have never guaranteed economic justice under our Constitution.

"They want to be elevated from a behavior-based lifestyle to true minority status," we hear in the video. Excuse me? *Elevated to minority status?* The words come out of throat after throat and no one gags on the obvious contradiction. Maybe in apartheid South Africa a person would be "elevated" to minority status, but in most other places that elevator goes *down*. Yet *Gay Rights, Special Rights*, with the assistance of African-American spokesmen and -women, collapses the fragile and contested remedial remedies of affirmative action (seen as preferences and privileges) with the whole stigmatized minority status that necessitates them. It was never to "minority status" that Africans aspired, as they mutinied on slave ships and planta-tions, fled north on the Underground Railroad, agitated for abolition, struggled on for freedom. The Civil Rights Act of 1866 gave all people born in the United States the rights of citizenship, which included "full and equal benefits of all laws and proceedings for the security of person and property, *as is enjoyed by white citizens*," with whom they would be subject to "like punishment, pains and penalties." Who wants "minority rights"? The purpose of the Equal Protection clause of the Fourteenth Amendment is to give the disempowered the same legal access as the most powerful have—it's majority rights we want. We would all like to be treated as if we are free, white, and twenty-one—i.e., straight, male, and economically secure. The purpose of *Gay Rights, Special Rights* is to take our eyes off the prize, to get us to fighting over crumbs.

In the fall of 1994, in a victory for lesbians and gay men, an Ohio judge struck down Cincinnati's antigay Initiative 3, ruling that it violated the Equal Protection clause of the **Fourteenth Amendment**, and finding that sexual orientation constitutes a "quasi-suspect class" involving protective judicial scrutiny. Judge Speigel also ruled that sexual orientation is a "deeply rooted, complex combination of factors" that exists "independently of any conduct." The next month, Oregon citizens again defeated the Oregon Citizens' Alliance homophobic ballot initiative, but a national Republican landslide guarantees other battles on "family values" and the continued scapegoating of vulnerable populations, especially immigrants and people on welfare.

You preacher boys, I move we let you know our *real* agenda is "majority sta-tus," for us and every human. What's "equality" without "justice" but the "down-ward humanization" being plotted now in the name of "free markets" in corporate boardrooms from Toronto to Rio: the same low wages, poor work conditions, violated air and water. It's not a question of equality; it's a question of justice.

"All persons born or naturalized in the United States, and subject to the jurisdic-tion thereof, are citizens of the United States and of the State wherein they reside. No State shall make or enforce any law which shall abridge the privi-leges or immunities of citizens of the United States; nor shall any State deprieve any person of life, liberty, or property, without due process of law; nor deny to any person within its jurisdic-tion the equal protection of the laws."
—Section 1, Amendment XIV of
The Constitution of the United States

A final riff on family, out of an impulse to capture the elusive feeling I get sometimes when I hear my daughter's laughter from a distance down the beach, over the muted roar of waves, and I am suddenly back in my own childhood, except that she is me and I am my mother, hearing herself as a child. In the moment, there is generational resonance, harmony, deep happiness. When lesbians and gay men step openly into this cycle, as parents and children, perhaps we threaten heterosexuals who draw on similar moments of memory and identification.

In *Christianity, Social Tolerance, and Homosexuality*, John Boswell observed of sexual nonconformity and rural/kinship cultures: "Only time, familiarity, and education can make room for harmless nonconformity and enable the majority to distinguish between those forms of atypical behavior which actually are destructive of the social order and those which are not."

Peg Rivera, transformed by her experience, became an ambassador of this message. She mused:

Society is very immature about the homosexual community, and when they see someone who accepts it so readily, who embraces and loves it, they learn from that. . . . In particular I'm thinking of my sister and her husband, who attended the trial and heard the summation of Dan McCarthy and were profoundly affected by it. They returned to their community and explained to them what they had seen—the support, the turnout at the courthouse, the obvious hatred on the part of the gang, the difficulty of facing this on a daily basis, the enormity of the crime that had been committed—and they began to voice their acceptance of homosexuals in their community. We were teaching people how to say what they really wanted to say anyway. It's just that certain forces are telling them it's wrong. If those forces—it's the Catholic Church, the conservatives, the "moral majority," individuals who feel that for one reason or another that gays and lesbians are against nature—would just stop that, a lot of people might open up and begin to understand and learn about the community. They don't know gay and lesbian people, because when you come to know someone as we knew Julio, then you love them.

In the eighties, people started talking about AIDS and gays. Groups that historically had already been prejudiced increased the level of the violence that they directed at gay men and lesbians. I was working as the coordinator of education at the New York City Gay and Lesbian Anti-Violence Project on a regular basis. People were phoning our hot lines and telling us about the violence they were experiencing, and by 1990 it had become very frightening. . . . Queer Nation got started that year, and in July they organized a big antibias violence march, which was an incredible and frightening experience because people were attacked all through the march. I was working as a marshal. I don't know how many hundreds of gay men and lesbians were marching down the street, yet there could still be a single straight man who would feel entitled to stand there and fling a bottle at us. What do people like that expect—that we're not going to turn around and do something? The summer of 1990 was a turning point. . . .

The Pink Panthers formed as a group to address antigay and antilesbian violence in Greenwich Village. There had been an influx of African-American and Latino gay men in the streets of the West Village, which, as a place to hang out, had changed. The merchants and people who live in the neighborhood were beginning to respond to this influx of young people of color. They felt it made the neighborhood more dangerous. People started block watches and started calling the cops more. . . . The Pink Panthers entered into that situation. There were incidents where sometimes you would see the Panthers and a group of black and Latino kids. Not every group of black and Latino kids is a wolf pack. Some of them are groups of young drag queens. There could be times when there was friction that was caused by

stereotypes, but the Panthers were really effective. They really helped by demonstrating that we're not going to allow ourselves to be victimized. Just before the Panthers started, I remember being at a bar in the East Village and there were these three straight guys across the street tossing bottles at the bar. There was a group of gay men standing in front of the bar—twenty guys—and they were acting like, "Oh my God, those guys are throwing bottles at us. Call the police." I remember saying, "Why don't we just go across the street and beat the shit out of them? There are twenty of us and three of them. I realize it's a male-aggressive response, but why don't we just go do that." And other people were saying let's not. It showed me how oppressed we are.

I first heard about Julio Rivera's murder in the newspaper. They described a Puerto Rican man who had been killed in a schoolyard, and how the police thought it was drug related. Latinos being

Robert Vázquez-Pacheco is an AIDS activist and poet who worked with the New York City Gay and Lesbian Anti-Violence Project before moving to Washington, D.C., where he is coordinator of HIV prevention at National LLEGO (Latino/a Lesbian and Gay Organization).

killed in New York is not surprising news. But as we started to investigate the case, what was interesting was that people were not sure that it was drug related. As a gay man, I thought, well, if it isn't drug related, and this man was killed in a very well-known cruising area, it must be gay-bashing. We had to fight to get the media and the police to talk about it as a gay-bashing. . . . Groups that had been working separately came together that summer to do a lot of very effective work. The Anti-Violence Project had always been working with the cops and the district attorney. Suddenly, to have a group like Queer Nation come in and apply pressure from the outside was really effective and helped us to get our points across.

One of the most exciting things that came out of the Rivera case was the political activism of Latino gay men. The organization Latino Gay Men had started I think sometime earlier in 1990. It had been torn between being a political and being a social group. But after the murder of Julio Rivera, it was as if the Latino gay community of New York went, "Wait a minute. This is one of us. They're killing us off. We have to do something." And so they approached the Anti-Violence Project where I was working. I also was a member of Latino Gay Men. People mobilized, went to demonstrations, and did phone zaps. And when the verdict came down, there, on the cover of *Newsday*, were members of Latino Gay Men standing in front of the courthouse. This was an incredible experience. Here was a community that you rarely ever see, because everyone's impression of the gay community in New York is of white, middle-class gay men. The picture showed that there are other gay men, gay men of color, who are also politically active and aware. It was a real shot in the arm in terms of visibility for the community; an opportunity to see people who

are not used to doing anything political but who had actually put themselves on the line as if to say, "This is important to me, this is my community, and I'm out here fighting for it." . . .

One of the reasons it's such a struggle to involve people of color [in lesbian and gay political organizations] is that we identify ourselves not just in terms of our sexuality but in terms of our ethnicity and the culture that comes with it. Our reality is much more complex. For us to do political work we cannot work solely on sexuality, because that does not address everything that's happening to me. You have to have a movement that understands that people are complicated. The mainstream gay and lesbian movement has to address issues of race, as well as gender and class. . . . No one wanted to discuss race in relation to the Rivera case, even though race was one of the most blatant things about it. On a lot of levels, the gay mainstream is still not willing to grapple with all of these issues. But in the Rivera case, you could see a variety of groups coming together. It truly was coalition work, including organizations like Latino Gay Men, Queer Nation, and the Anti-Violence Project. It was wonderful to see, and what it taught us is that when we work together, we actually can get something done.

The coverage of the Rivera case was varied in the press. It was covered in depth by the gay, Latino, and mainstream press, which was pretty astounding. The interesting thing was that while the mainstream press focused on it as a gay-bashing, the Latino press treated it as violence against a Latino. . . . It was, however, a very clear incident. There was no way that you could whitewash this case. One of the kids' fathers was a retired police sergeant, which is why the police just sat on the case. There was intrigue, which of course had the media interested. And one of the most incredible effects of the case was its explosion of a stereotype: that gay men and lesbians have nothing to do with their families. Here was a gay man who was connected to his family. Ted and Peg Rivera came to the Anti-Violence Project and said, "We want you to help us. He's part of our family and he was killed as a gay man and we love him, we care about him, and we're not going to let this happen." That message was very different from what people had heard before. In the Latino community a lot of lesbian and gay people are very connected to their families. We don't come out of the closet and then leave. . . .

I think that one of the disservices that the gay and lesbian movement has done is to take gays and lesbians out of the context of general, everyday life, as if we function in a world that's totally separate from everyone else. Now I agree that we are different, but we're still human beings. The gay and lesbian lifestyle still includes things like doing laundry, going to the supermarket, taking a bath . . . . When we focus on identity and concern ourselves with saying, "This is how I am different from you," sometimes the distance we claim makes people unsympathetic. They say, "Okay, you are so different that our rules can't apply to you." . . . And that's where education should come in to show that, yes, we are different, but there are also things that we have in common. Until the lesbian and gay movement moves out and broadens its agenda to include the commonalities, including the fights that other people have, we're going to be isolated and fighting alone. That's one of the things that's happened in Oregon in 1992. . . . We have to show other communities that

we're part of them—because we are— and not just when we need something.

Sometimes I think that our friends are more of a threat than our enemies. They'll say, "Well, I have nothing against lesbians and gay men. I support them, but I don't like them to act lesbian or gay in front of me. I don't need to see their art, their literature, their self-representations. So you can be who you are, but not in front of me or my children or my neighborhood or my church or my place of work." . . . Sometimes the worst oppressor is yourself when you buy into that, which you do partly for survival, because you know the consequences of looking too butch if you're a woman or too feminine if you're a man. Unfortunately, a lot of times the community does not back you up. We victimize ourselves. . . . Look at the arguments about gay pride parades. They're always focused on the butch S/M dykes on motorcycles and the leather queens and the drag queens. It's always, "Well, the rest of us are normal." Hello! The community has got to wake up. None of us is considered normal, and we end up victimizing and marginalizing members of our own community. This is not going to get us anywhere. . . . The Right attacks lesbians and gay men by pulling out the most extreme examples they can find for what lesbians and gay men are. Then, instead of our saying, "Well, yes, these are members of our community and we support them," we back off and go silent. We don't want to claim these people. We're fracturing our community, tossing people aside—and for what? We're living in a system where some people have rights and a lot of people don't. Do we really want to re-create that oppressive system?

The writings of poet, anthologist, and essayist Essex Hemphill have been central to a new blossoming of black gay male literary production. His participation in Isaac Julien's *Looking for Langston* and Marlon Riggs's *Tongues Untied* has been equally important to the emergence of the new black gay male cinema.

Poet and anthologist Essex Hemphill, speaking at the first OutWrite Conference for lesbian and gay writers. Photo by Lynda Koolish.

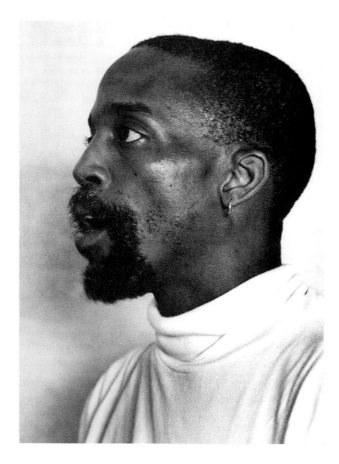

I met Marlon in San Francisco either in 1987 or 1988. I was out doing readings there at the Walt Whitman Bookshop, which is no longer there, and Marlon came by with a friend of his. He was on his way to the airport, so there was luggage out in the car and a bag on his shoulder. My performance partner, Wayson Jones, was in San Francisco with me as well, because at that time I would work my poetry with musicians or other voices just to make it more expansive and accessible. During the break, Marlon introduced himself to me and told me briefly about what would become *Tongues Untied*.

Our friendship evolved out of common interests. I think it deepened not out of necessity, as a result of reactions to *Tongues Untied*, but because there was a sincere concern about one another that ultimately superseded our creative endeavors. It was just a basic friendship that I rather enjoyed. Even after his passing, I don't really treat it as if he's not here. There's so much about him that still is here—not just the film work. Like this little postcard that sits on my desk: it's of Langston Hughes, and Marlon sent it to me inquiring about my health probably six months before he passed. Ours was an ongoing concern. Even when there was silence, there was still concern.

Prior to 1989, when *Tongues Untied* was released, there had been this buildup within black gay communities. Early on in the eighties, I began self-publishing as a response to the homophobia in black publishing circles, and to the racism in white gay publishing circles. That was a development that would occur in Philadelphia, New York, and Oakland as well, because of the list of black gay men who self-published in order to get their work out, knowing that there was a hunger for such representations. With white gay publishing houses, the work is gay, homoerotic; but this black work speaks as well about a certain narrowness that exists among gay publishers about identity. Sometimes they only want part of the story because it works well, but they don't want to know your other issues. Self-publishing was not only an act of independence, it was revolutionary. At the moment when Marlon began formulating *Tongues Untied*, there were documents for him to turn to—not just my own self-published *Earth Life* and *Conditions*, but Joseph Beam's *In the Life* and the journal *Other Countries*. In Oakland, Alan Miller was working on *At the Club*, and there was work going on in D.C. as well. For me, *Looking for Langston*, Isaac Julien's piece, heralded the arrival of *Tongues Untied*. *Looking for Langston* is a sensual document that grounds itself in a particular history—the history of the Harlem Renaissance—and *Tongues Untied* just steps forward from that point. If we look at Marlon as moving with the force of fate, he was right on time.

Tongues Untied is itself so important simply because he grounded it with autobiographical information. Without that you would have been left with a work that represented New York, D.C., California, and other parts of the country. But where would the connection have been? His willingness to tell his personal story was very necessary for that document. Those communities around the country (along with other voices, I represented D.C.)—we were like the Amen Corner. Without us verifying experiences that derived from his autobiographically grounded statements, *Tongues Untied* might have floated without a form. It might have been interpreted as short videos strung together, and that was not the case when he began to reveal his life experiences. . . .

Many of us have been called names on playgrounds, regardless of our race. Maybe we wore glasses, or maybe we were slightly overweight, or maybe we couldn't have the right tennis shoes. People outside of black gay experience found it possible to connect with the basic humanity of what was dispersed throughout *Tongues Untied*. If you were attacked because of whatever you are, you could relate to that. If you're already having trouble with some of the doctrines growing out of Christian fundamentalism, then you found an entrance point. . . . Even though this video was very specific in its target audience, those truths made it a transcendent document. Anything less than the truth, and the reaction would not have been the same—people would not have connected.

If you're a lesbian, gay, or bisexual artist and that's how you've centered your work, then you have to know there's going to be resistance to it. Another thing we need to consider is that some of the work that we're creating isn't good, and we have to say that. Some of it is shocking for the sake of being shocking. Some of it clearly is not art but a throwing up, if you will, a fed-upness. We're quickest to rally around resistance to expression and unwilling to deal with the question of what the merits of any given expression are. Is it really worth it? I don't have any problem fighting for everyone's right to expression. I do have lots of problems when we don't stop and seriously critique what's being made. Because we're hungry, everything has to be put on the table. But you have to be shrewd and wise enough to know that this is going to be good for me, whereas that, which looks so good, may not be.

I come from a very religious family. My father was a minister. My mother was a minister. My brothers are ministers. . . . The church has been important in African-American lives, so when you're raised, you're told that homosexuals go to hell, that it's an abomination. . . . But my black friends, we're "out" with our families. I think that our families are representative of the general black population. When I came out, I got support from my dad, and eventually my mother's absolute support. That prepared the way for me to then say, "I'm HIV-positive.". . . My brother won't sit with a group of his heterosexual male friends and hear "faggot" and "dyke" and all that flying through the air and not challenge it, because my brother, whom I love, is also gay. . . . What you always hope is that your family will resist that sort of thing. My nieces and nephews will resist it because Uncle Essex is gay and he isn't any of those things they hear on the playground. I think that ultimately the black community, by and large, will come to terms and understand that the right wing really has nobody's good intentions in mind. . . .

One message that comes through in *Tongues Untied* is that there is support that can be obtained for the identity you're constructing. There's a network, affirmation, a family you can join. Problematic though that family may be, if you're willing to invest the effort and time, it's family nonetheless and there will be love and support. Previously, there was a hunger that wasn't addressed, so these documents are just being eaten up. How many printings has [Cherríe Moraga and Gloria Anzaldúa's] *This Bridge Called My Back* gone through? It's one of my favorite books and it wasn't even written for me. The truth in those women's voices and experiences transcended that limit and I could connect. I think *Tongues Untied* does that as well. I think we sometimes miss that connectedness in gay, lesbian, and bisexual communities.

The problem that people have with lesbians, gay men, and bisexuals making connections to the civil rights movement is because we haven't made the broader point of connecting our struggles. . . . I think it's largely white gay men and white lesbians who created that problem.

I just can't be free as a black person and oppressed as a gay person. It doesn't work. But the powers that be within the gay community have made a fatal error that's now catching up with them. When they refuse to deal clearly with lesbians, with black people, with Asians and Hispanics, and then they finally reach the point of being conscious of a connection between the civil rights struggle of the sixties and the present struggles of lesbian and gay people, it's almost too late. We're such an insular community. We prioritize AIDS as if it's the only issue that we've ever had to deal with. I know women and men who've had to contend not just with sexuality but with racial and ethnic issues, and with issues around economics as well. I'm sorry that our agenda has not been broad enough to encompass all that. . . . We can't sit here and get upset that there are black folks who feel like you've appropriated something unjustly, because we created that situation with these little gates through which we do not let one another pass. . . . I find it hard to take a side. All I can do is to live my life in its fullness and know that I'm not going to be happy just being free as a black person and oppressed as a gay person. I hope that we will all wake up and understand that our agendas need to be broader.

DONNA RED WING

Donna Red Wing was executive director of the Oregon Lesbian Community Project and cofounder of the Oregon Anti-Violence Project before being named national field director for GLAAD (Gay & Lesbian Alliance Against Defamation).

Measure 8 was the first real victory of the Oregon Citizens Alliance. It rescinded the governor's executive order that would have protected gay and lesbian state employees. They then tried legislation that dealt with abortion and reproductive rights and were defeated, so they

went back to the agenda that in the past brought them money and members— the queer agenda. Look at how Measure 9 affected the average Oregonian. Why would 43 percent of the voters vote against gay and lesbian people? We have to look at the economics, at the fact that there are poor and working-class Oregonians who feel that they're not getting their share. Then you have the religious right telling them that queer folks have more than their share and want even more. The strategy of the religious right in talking about special rights was brilliant. I would walk past the OCA's table and see signs that said, "Should homosexuals have special rights?" and I would say to myself, "Of course not." It was a brilliant strategy that played against the success of gay and lesbian people and into the real fears of regular folks in Oregon who couldn't put food on the table for their kids, who had lost their jobs and whose lives were not what they expected. They handed these people a scapegoat—the gay and lesbian community.

When we look at the members of the religious right, we see people who want things to be the way they were before, people looking back to a time and a place that made sense to them. They're afraid of affirmative action, they're afraid of diversity, they're afraid of things changing, and you juxtapose all of those changes with a bad economy and you get people looking for somebody to blame. . . . I wish I could point to the religious right and say that they are evil people. They're not. They're regular folks and they're afraid and in that fear they're looking for someone to blame. It's that simple. Maybe we need to sit down with the white logger in southern Oregon who doesn't know how he's going to pay his bills, who is looking at a life that is nothing like his father's and granddaddy's. Maybe we have to sit down with him and listen to his fears, because I think that's the essence of the success of the religious right.

The conservative movement is a national one, if not an international one. In the background you can see very wealthy and powerful people pulling the strings. That was evident when Pat Buchanan spoke at the 1992 Republican National Convention. It's evident when we look at Coors, the Rutherford Institute, and the Heritage Foundation. But that's not what Oregon voters saw. We saw an incredibly well put together network, and some of the best grassroots organizing I've seen since the mid-sixties. I wish we understood grassroots organizing as well they do. They understand what resonates with people, so they use simple phrases like, "Should homosexuals have special rights?" We respond with fifteen-minute logical arguments that nobody listens to. When I look at the religious right, I am terrified because I see the national money and power combined with extraordinary grassroots organizing. In Oregon, much of this took place at kitchen-table talks—that's what they called them—where women invited their friends over for coffee and political chitchat. We're not doing that. The religious right has a place of entry for everyone who wants to participate. You don't

Donna Red Wing (right) and Kathleen Sadaat celebrate the defeat of Measure 9 in November 1992. Still from Program Two, *Culture Wars*.

need educational pedigrees, you don't need to be particularly savvy, you don't need to be particularly articulate. All you need is a willingness to work. I look at what's left of the Left and see progressives being a little elitist, not offering an opportunity for people to get involved on the grassroots level.

Early in the campaign, the OCA started to define who gay, lesbian, bisexual, and transgendered people are. One of their first hits was a distribution of pornographic materials on the porches of about a hundred southeast-Portland homes in the middle of the night. Each porch had between twenty-five and fifty photocopies of gay porn. Parents in southeast Portland sent their kid out or went out in their slippers and nighties to pick up the paper on the front porch, and instead of finding just the paper they found these graphic images. Clearly, the OCA did not take responsibility for this, but it happened just a few weeks after they filed the petitions for Measure 9, so I believe someone in their camp was responsible. Then every two or three months, they created broadsides, little newsletters about specific subjects. One was about AIDS being God's punishment for our moral bankruptcy. Through a conservative student group they put out information that talked about gay and lesbian people as predators, pedophiles, and child molesters. That drew a really gruesome picture, taking the stereotypes that a lot of people had and enlarging them into grotesque caricatures. For many Oregonians, that was the only information they had ever had about gay and lesbian people. Then they brought in Dr. Paul Cameron, who had been kicked out of the American Psychological Association in 1983 (he claims he resigned) but still garners more media than most queer activists ever will. He comes into a town and sets up a debate in which he uses his incredibly

flawed studies to claim that the life expectancy of gay men is less than fifty years because of their disease-ridden lifestyle. He puts out the most graphic, obscene misinformation about gay men as scientific truth. He says that lesbians were sexually molested as children and therefore don't like men. As absurd as his information is, for many Oregonians it's all they have ever had.

The gay and lesbian community has got to tell the truth about itself, and about the religious right. When much of a community is closeted, a lot of people are not represented. When you have a campaign that sanitizes itself, that tries to be palatable and mainstream, you're not giving a full and accurate image of gay and lesbian people. In the campaign against Measure 9, there was an effort to heterosexualize the campaign, and I know that was wrong. At one point, the campaign manager stood up and said to the media that this struggle has nothing to do with gay and lesbian people. It has *everything* to do with gay and lesbian people. I understand that the agenda of the religious right is much larger than its queer agenda. But I also understand that when we're dealing with ballot initiatives that call us unnatural, perverse, abnormal, and wrong, that clearly it is about gay and lesbian people. So when we sanitize our campaign, we're sending a message that there is something about us that's embarrassing. When we don't allow anyone to participate unless they fit the straight image, we're doing a real disservice to ourselves. When we take money from the leather community and the drag queens but give them no other point of entry anywhere in the campaign, we're doing something very wrong. I don't think Oregon ever got to really see who we really are. They heard the OCA's holy war against queers. They heard the No on 9 campaign saying that it had nothing to do with queers, and then every queer they looked at looked heterosexual. It was confusing and I don't think we told the truth about ourselves.

Historically, gay and lesbian campaigns have been sanitized. Look at the 1978 campaign against California's Briggs Initiative. After the initiative was defeated, every study said that the reason Californians voted against it was because gay and lesbian schoolteachers went from door to door and said, "I'm your son Johnny's third-grade teacher, and I'm a lesbian." People were able to put a face, a voice, a reality, where previously there had only been the abstraction of homosexuality. But we don't learn. Oregon sanitized its campaign, as did Colorado, Maine, Florida, Missouri, etc. Instead of embracing who we are, whether we're gay, lesbian, bisexual, transgendered, we're hiding it. Americans aren't stupid. They know we're hiding something. We really aren't just like them.

KATHLEEN SADAAT

The threat of violence is a deterrent from action. Random, unpredictable violence affects you, and you have to jump over that fear in order to keep going. . . . This is your country, your state, your city, and you shouldn't have to walk into the Safeway and wonder if the person who is taking your money and checking you out is also going to vote against your existence. . . . There is a violence in not being able to live your life. Whether you are ever actually struck by someone is not the only issue; it's what it does to your heart, your head, and your spirit. Anything that says you are not a part of the human family is a violent act. It can be words, deeds, or legislation. . . .

In the fight against Measure 9, people were absolutely devastated because they were so afraid and it hurt so bad. We were afraid we would lose the election. We were afraid of individuals around us. . . . My most frightening moment was when I could hear my fence being kicked in. I was on the phone with a friend, standing in my bedroom, and I heard the boards give way and the flowerpots in the yard being broken, and

I said to my friend on the phone, "Herb, if I don't call you back in ten minutes, get over here." I hung up and went to the windows and looked down thinking, "Something's wrong, something's wrong." I could see that there were three or four boards out of the fence and I could see through to the building that I shouldn't be able to see. By that time a friend was at my house. She said, "Do you want me to stay?" and I said, "Yes, please do." I guess I slept okay, but I slept with the fire extinguisher next to my bed. This was after Hattie Mae Cohens and Brian Mock had been burned to death in Salem.

When I first heard of the Salem murders, I was terrified and sad. I was concerned about our campaign responding to it, so I called the campaign office and said, "What are we going to say about these murders?" The person who was in charge of the press said, "Nothing." The campaign was not going to say anything about this mentally retarded gay man and this black lesbian who had been burned to death in their home in the capital of our state. I said,

Kathleen Sadaat is a veteran African-American lesbian activist who lives in Portland. Before helping to form African-Americans Voting No on 9, she played a prominent role in the No on 9 campaign.

CHAPTER

3

LAW AND DESIRE

On October 11, 1987, more than a quarter of a million participants assembled in the nation's capital for a March on Washington for Lesbian and Gay Rights. Photo by JEB (Joan E. Biren).

This, despite the fact that I was not among the estimated six hundred men and women who were dragged from the steps of the Supreme Court and arrested by cops in riot gear and rubber gloves for protesting the Court's homophobic ruling in *Bowers* v. *Hardwick*. I only did what I was comfortable doing: I marched with friends as part of ACT UP. There was one seemingly trivial but indelible moment, when I glanced over my shoulder at a place where the flat topography of the city dips almost imperceptibly and was shocked by the vista of tightly massed men and women that extended behind me and my friends to the distant horizon. I felt more a part of a large group during that instant than I ever had and probably ever will. It was an astonishing and stirring experience. Six years later, there I was, at that same dip in the road feeling dispirited. On the drive home, my tired feet told me I'd been on a march, but the rest of me felt I'd never really found one. Where was the impassioned focus of six years before? What had happened to the surging masses of chanting people?

Many of them now are dead.

I cherish the single snapshot I have from October 11, 1987. There was no time to strike a pose. Lynne appeared as if from out of nowhere brandishing a camera. She kissed a greeting, snapped a picture, and just as quickly disappeared. A few days later, the snapshot arrived unaccompanied in the mail. In it my best friend, Bill, is on my right; and Paul, another friend, is on my left. Behind the three of us, arm in arm, banners and other marchers are clearly visible. There is, however, too gleeful an expression on my face, which sets me apart from Bill and Paul, who look more relaxed, more believably happy. Bill's eyes—too deep-set in their sockets— reveal fatigue and the failing health that would take his life less than two years later. To look at Paul—ever the fashion plate in Day-Glo Gaultier camouflage—you'd never guess that he, too, would die in the interim that separates '87 from '93.

The lead banner at the 1987 March on Washington for Lesbian and Gay Rights. Photo by JEB (Joan E. Biren).

It sometimes seems as if an unbridgeable gulf has opened between these two events. It isn't just that Bill and Paul were still alive at the first one; nor even that, implicit in the anger that caused so many lesbians and gay men to demonstrate in Washington that day, there was a measure of hopefulness about ending the AIDS crisis, a hopefulness that since has all but vanished. So clear was the sense of moral purpose about the march of '87 that it assumed physical expression: evident in the tight masses of its many contingents of which none was more raucous, more anarchic in its discipline, than the barely seven-month-old ACT UP. There was, on the other hand, a sprawling dispersal about the march of '93. The aerosol of queer humanity that coated the capital symbolized an absence of urgency, a lack of consensus. There could be no center of gravity to hold it all together because the issues that dominated that event—"gays in the military" and queer "family values"— inspire division, not unity, among lesbians and gay men.

Even less than their straight counterparts, and for different reasons, queer Americans have never united to embrace this country's armed forces, its marriage rituals and nuclear family. Along with the law and religion, it is these institutions that have constructed and maintained the American mainstream as heterosexist. Psychologist Gregory Herek has likened heterosexism to racism and sexism as an "ideology of oppression" that is manifest "both in societal customs and institutions . . . and in individual attitudes and behaviors." It is because these "individual attitudes and behaviors," which range from silent contempt and name-calling to ferocious homicides, are institutionally sanctioned that heterosexism must be classed as a system of oppression. But as an explicitly *ideological* system, heterosexism also exerts more subtle forms of pain and less painful forms of persuasion to compel heterosexuality, despite the bewildering diversity of human sexual desire. Every queer has felt isolation, exclusion, and worthlessness, not least because mainstream culture alternates between rendering us invisible and making us repulsive. Given this situation, it is hardly surprising that some lesbians and gay

The lead banner at the March on Washington for Lesbian, Gay, and Bi Equal Rights and Liberation, April 25, 1993. Photo by Marilyn Humphries.

The federal drug development and approval process has been incapable of keeping pace with the AIDS crisis. In an effort to speed promising alternative or experimental treatments to those who need them, AIDS activists established an underground market, called buyers' clubs, in the 1980s that made unapproved treatments available to people with AIDS. Photo by Jane Rossett.

men respond to the American mainstream with a sweeping dismissal. But it is no less surprising, given the painfulness of being systematically excluded and demonized, that others among us yearn for validation by the very institutions that consign us to the margins. Somewhere between these two extreme, somewhat abstract positions that conventionally have been called "radical" and "assimilationist" reside the bulk of us. We do not particularly want to belong to the mainstream as we know it, yet we demand the rights of first-class citizenship. Like the "liberal" and "conservative" tags that they resemble, "radical" and "assimilationist" are names that increasingly fail to describe the complex, often contradictory, mix of attitudes and outlooks that people cobble together as they navigate through life. To make sense of these configurations and of the way that the political priorities of 1987 were transformed into where we are nearly ten years later, it is necessary to look more closely at the way queers interact with institutions that have defined American culture and society as heterosexist. Perhaps then we would be in a better position to figure out precisely what it is that we would like to assimilate to.

The national mobilization of 1987 marked the attainment of queer critical mass, an explosive consolidation of political consciousness the causes of which are not as simple to reconstruct as one might think. To say that the activist explosion resulted from the galvanizing horrors of the AIDS epidemic would be to recite a truism about something that was far more complexly determined. The immediate catalyst for queer outrage was the Supreme Court's ruling in *Bowers v. Hardwick* less than a year before the 1987 March on Washington. But the significance of that decision—specifically, the way that its meaning was experienced subjectively by gay men and lesbians across the country—depended upon political and personal circumstances that transformed the Court's majority ruling into a document that read like a declaration of war against us.

Even among gay men there had been no mass epiphany about AIDS. As the down-home morality of the Carter administration gave way to the imperial glitz of Reagan's counterrevolution, the realization of the threat AIDS represented only gradually dawned on most gay men and lesbians. My own denial about AIDS was shattered one night early in the winter of 1982, when Bill phoned from the midwestern college town where he then lived and worked to tell me what his doctor in Cleveland had just told him: that he had ARC (AIDS-related complex). I felt his distress but didn't know any words that could help him beyond affirming my love and urging him to get a job in New York so he could live and work here among his closest friends and colleagues. During the previous summer, which we had spent together overseas, Bill had told me about the swollen glands at the base of his neck that wouldn't go away and about the biopsy that his doctor had performed on a single lymph node. But the meaning of that information only became clear after I spoke with him that December night. I had known only one friend before then who had told me he had the mysterious syndrome I knew so little about.

When Bill phoned me, barely a year had passed since the Centers for Disease Control first reported that five gay men in Los Angeles had come down with then-rare *Pneumocystis carinii* pneumonia and postulated an association between this outbreak and "some aspect of homosexual lifestyle." It was not until early 1984 that Luc Montagnier announced the discovery by his team of scientists at the Pasteur Institute in Paris of the virus that would be named HIV. In a press conference to claim the American discovery of the same virus by Dr. Robert Gallo and his associates, Margaret Heckler, Reagan's secretary of Health and Human Services, declared that AIDS had to and would be stopped before it spread to "the general population"—not the last time that people with AIDS in general, and gay men and intravenous drug users in particular, would implicitly be branded as subhuman in the unfolding discourse about this first postmodern plague.

Yet even before Bill's phone call, small groups of gay men with the syndrome that some were calling GRID (gay-related immune disorder) had already been meeting in San Francisco and New York to talk privately about their experiences, and to communicate potentially helpful information through more public venues. For example, San Franciscan Bobbi Campbell, a registered nurse who was diagnosed with AIDS in September 1981, started publishing a column about his experience in a gay community newspaper, *The Sentinel*, early in 1982. This self-help network expanded to other major cities nationwide, giving rise to the movement for PWA (People with AIDS) self-empowerment, which culminated in 1983 when roughly two dozen people with AIDS from around the country traveled to Denver to participate in the Second National AIDS Forum (a conference sponsored by the Lesbian and Gay Health Education Foundation). Anticipating the tactics of AIDS activists later in the decade, the ad hoc group disrupted the conference's closing session to read aloud the manifesto that they called the **Denver Principles.** Their list of demands repudiated the official and popular ways of speaking about AIDS, which consigned HIV-infected individuals to powerlessness and irrevocable decline. The Denver Principles affirmed instead the fundamental dignity and agency of "people living with AIDS," issued a series of recommendations and established in the process many of the central political, theoretical, and practical elements that would inform later manifestations of AIDS activism. Like Project Inform in San Francisco, the Gay Men's Health Crisis in New York, and a host of smaller organizations in cities around the country, the PWA Coalition stepped in to care for a population that, to judge from the inaction of the Reagan administration and the indifference of the media, was widely regarded as disposable.

Using phrases like "the inaction of the Reagan administration and indifference of the media" is not always idle rhetoric. Consider a few facts that date from the year that AIDS consciousness began to dawn on me and so many others.

The Denver Principles
—Statement from the Advisory Committee of People with AIDS

We condemn attempts to label us as "victims," a term which implies defeat, and we are only occasionally "patients," a term which implies passivity, helplessness, and dependence upon the care of others. We are "People with AIDS."

Recommendations for All People
1. Support us in our struggle against those who would fire us from our jobs, evict us from our homes, refuse to touch us, or separate us from our loved ones, our community, or our peers, since available evidence does not support the view that AIDS can be spread by casual, social contact.
2. Not scapegoat people with AIDS, blame us for the epidemic, or generalize about our lifestyles.

Recommendations for People with AIDS
1. Form caucuses to choose their own representatives, to deal with the media, to choose their own agenda, and to plan their own strategies.
2. Be involved at every level of decision-making and specifically serve on the boards of directors of provider organizations.
3. Be included in all AIDS forums with equal credibility as other participants, to share their own experiences and knowledge.
4. Substitute low-risk sexual behaviors for those which could endanger themselves or their partners; we feel that people with AIDS have an ethical responsibility to inform their potential sexual partners of their health status.

Rights of People with AIDS

1. To as full and satisfying sexual and emotional lives as anyone else.
2. To quality medical treatment and quality social service provision without discrimination of any form including sexual orientation, gender, diagnosis, economic status, or race.
3. To full explanations of all medical procedures and risks, to choose or refuse their treatment modalities, to refuse to participate in research without jeopardizing their treatment, and to make informed decisions about their lives.
4. To privacy, to confidentiality of medical records, to human respect, and to choose who their significant others are.
5. To die—and to LIVE—in dignity.

Author, performer, and long-term AIDS survivor Michael Callen, who died in 1994, was an inspiration to thousands of people whose lives have been affected by the AIDS crisis. Callen coauthored the 1983 handbook *How to Have Sex in an Epidemic*, the earliest guidelines for what is now commonly called safer sex. Photo by Ellen B. Neipris/Impact Visuals.

At the beginning of 1982, roughly 400 cases of AIDS had been reported, and 350 people had died, but the Reagan administration recommended that the National Institutes of Health (the federal agency that oversees medical research and health education) *eliminate* one thousand grants. A pitiful $1 million had been assigned for research although a year had passed since health officials had identified the syndrome. Yet within three weeks of the news that seven people had died from cyanide-laced Tylenol capsules, the Centers for Disease Control spent $10 million and assigned a staff of 1,163 people to investigate and solve the mystery. By the time the Tylenol story broke, the *New York Times* had published only three articles about AIDS, but it would publish one story a day for thirty-one days about the Tylenol scare until the crisis ended. The *Wall Street Journal*, however, almost made the *Times* look good, publishing its first article on the epidemic only after twenty-three *straight* men and women were diagnosed with AIDS.

Not only were people with AIDS subjected to the painful effects of obscure, degenerative, opportunistic infections, they were pilloried in the press, fired from jobs, evicted from their homes, shunned by their families, disqualified by medical insurance carriers, denied health care by apprehensive hospital attendants, nurses, and doctors, and refused burial after death. The epidemic was tacitly permitted to become a full-scale national health crisis. Dr. C. Everett Koop, Reagan's surgeon general, said as much in 1989 when addressing the National Commission on AIDS. Summarizing the government's actions up to that date, he said, "I know it, you know it, we all know it. Nothing has happened."

"You rarely hear a thing about it," Dan Rather intoned by way of introducing one of the first nationally broadcast reports on AIDS. "At first it seemed to strike only one segment of the population." Reviving the nineteenth-century equation of homosexuality with sickness and its even more antiquated, but not outmoded, connection with sin and retribution, the media related the spread of the new disease to gay sex in a series of sensational accounts that always began with the same remarkable condensation: stock footage in which a pair of Village/Castro clones are seen from behind, their hands tucked shamelessly inside the snug back pockets of each other's 501s. Just as inevitably, these narratives culminated in a punitive pornography of human suffering in which the "concerned" camera lingers on the emaciated figure of a gay man with AIDS alone in a hospital bed, helplessly awaiting death, his body and face disfigured by Kaposi's sarcoma lesions and otherwise dissolving into the hospital's icy fluorescence. To archconservatives like Pat Buchanan and televangelical opportunists like Rev. Jerry Falwell, the judgments implied by these instant-morality plays were too subtle. "The poor homosexuals," Buchanan offered in May 1983, "they have declared war on Nature and now Nature is exacting an awful retribution." For Falwell, too, AIDS was a godsend: "God's judgment against those who do not live by His rules." To fundamentalist and secular conservative ideologues, AIDS was just the blunt instrument they needed to help spread the gospel of reaction against the anarchic, "permissive" legacy of the sixties.

When the news of Rock Hudson's illness finally broke in 1985, AIDS media coverage quadrupled, making the topic so hot that even President Reagan was compelled to mention AIDS publicly for the first time. However, he would only issue a statement about AIDS in January 1986, when he described the epidemic as "one of the highest public health priorities." There was, however, a catch: public health was itself not a very high priority of his administration. Even as he emoted concern about AIDS for the cameras, the president had proposed to *reduce* spending for AIDS research by an amount that exceeded the cut mandated by the Gramm-Rudman-Hollings Act. In AIDS, as in so many other policy areas, it was necessary to read between as well as behind the lines to get closer to the truth of what Mr. Reagan and his handlers were saying. In a later statement, the president inadvertently affirmed what increasingly frustrated and furious queers already knew about his administration's priorities regarding AIDS: "I have asked the Department of Health and Human Services to determine as soon as possible the extent to which the AIDS virus has penetrated our society." Precisely where in relation to "our society" the president's statement left the roughly forty thousand Americans who had already been diagnosed with AIDS (of whom some twenty-five thousand had already died) had been clarified by the Supreme Court on May 30, 1986. That was the day that the Court announced its ruling in the landmark case of *Bowers* v. *Hardwick*, in which it was decided that the privacy of the bedroom does not extend to homosexual men and women. In roughly half the states, where sodomy was still outlawed, we were habitual criminals—not the types that Reagan was likely to consider part of his society.

Florida-born Atlanta resident Michael Hardwick sued to challenge Georgia's antisodomy statute after having been arrested in 1982 in his bedroom, by a cop who had been harassing him for weeks, for violating the state's sodomy statute. A self-described "party boy," Hardwick was not eager to become national poster boy for a sodomy challenge, and who could blame him? One year before his ordeal began, he had moved to Atlanta from Gatlinburg, Tenneesee, in the Smoky Mountains, where he had gone to clear his mind after a failed relationship and to start up a health-food business that would also fail. After moving to Atlanta, the tall, chiseled blond had no trouble landing a job serving drinks at one of the city's many

The late film historian and AIDS activist Vito Russo, seen here in October 1988 speaking at an AIDS demonstration in front of the U.S. Department of Health and Human Services headquarters in Washington. Photo by Marilyn Humphries.

Michael Hardwick, arrested and charged with violating a Georgia sodomy statute for having sex with another man in the privacy of his own bedroom, challenged the constitutionality of the statute on privacy grounds. The United States Supreme Court upheld the statute, asserting that "the Constitution does not confer a fundamental right upon homosexuals to engage in sodomy." Four years later, Hardwick died of complications due to AIDS.

gay bars. On the night of July 11, he worked so late helping to install new sound insulation that when he left, it was already seven the next morning. Hardwick had decided not to drink the beer that a colleague had given him just before leaving work and claims he tossed the bottle into a trash can just outside the door. That's when he noticed a squad car cruising by. After walking a block or so, Hardwick saw the car turn around, approach him, and pull over. Officer Torick ordered him into the backseat and interrogated him for twenty minutes or so, at which time he ascertained that Hardwick was queer (by learning his place of employment) and fined him for drinking in public. Hardwick had tried to prove that he had done no such thing, but Torick insisted he'd sipped the beer outside the bar.

Whether out of malice, incompetence, or both, Torick filled out the summons for public drinking incorrectly, marking it with two court dates instead of one, each one day apart. Hardwick learned from his roommate that Torick materialized at their door with a warrant for his arrest only two hours after the first date passed. Perhaps it was one of Michael's attorneys who later told him that this would have been the first time in ten years that an Atlanta police officer had personally processed a warrant. "I think," Hardwick surmised, "that he had it out for me." Hardwick's intuitions were confirmed nearly three weeks after he had settled the fine for public drinking. Returning home from work at 6:30 A.M., he found three men in plain clothes waiting for him outside. One approached and said, "Michael," to which Michael answered, "Yes," whereupon the three set upon him, beating and kicking Hardwick so savagely in the face and upper body that all the cartilage was torn from his nose, six of his ribs were cracked, and he was left bleeding and unconscious on the sidewalk.

It happened that Hardwick's mother was up from Florida visiting her son at the time. He has said that it was to avoid upsetting her that he silently dragged himself up the steps after regaining consciousness to pass out in a back bedroom. Unfortunately, he left a trail of blood, which his mother followed to track down her son after she woke up. Aside from wanting to keep her uninvolved and protected, what else can be learned from Hardwick's decision to tell his mother that this beating was only "a fluke accident, [that] these guys were drunk," when he had already presumed that it had to be the homophobic handiwork of Officer Torick? Perhaps he felt shame and the fear that homosexuals are conditioned to feel in heterosexist societies, no matter how loving their families and friends. So long as there are laws on the books that declare the victims of such violent crimes to be criminals themselves, there can be no protection from antigay harassment and violence. No doubt, this is what the legal scholar Kendall Thomas was referring to when he said that the legacy of *Bowers* v. *Hardwick* would be to permit government to "legitimize violence, discrimination, and degradation on the part of one segment of the population toward another."

One day after his beating, at 8:30 on the morning of August 3, 1982, Michael was in his bedroom enjoying oral sex with another man. Something distracted him, which he dismissed as perhaps the wind nudging the door to his room. But when he heard the sound again, this time sensing an alien presence he looked up to find the obsessional Officer Torick staring silently right back at him. Torick stood there staring for a reported thirty-five seconds, then arrested both men for violating Georgia's sodomy statute. Stunned, Michael asked what, for any heterosexual citizen, would have been an obvious and pertinent question: "What are you doing in my bedroom?" Torick watched while the two got dressed, then cuffed them to the floor of his squad car and drove them to the station, where he kept them waiting like that for twenty-five minutes. When Torick threw Hardwick and his companion into the holding cell, and again later when he reassigned them to third-floor facilities reserved for convicted criminals, the cop made sure that every prison guard and convict knew that both men were in for "cocksucking." Hardwick has said that within an hour of being booked someone had arrived to get him out, but that the police managed to keep him behind bars for a full twelve hours. One hour after his release, Hardwick returned

During the 1987 March on Washington for Lesbian and Gay Rights, a massive civil disobedience was staged at the Supreme Court to protest the *Hardwick* decision. Photo by Marilyn Humphries.

to secure the release of his friend, who was understandably "freaked out." While attorneys with the ACLU were able to convince the reluctant Hardwick to sue the state, they had less success with his friend. As a government employee, he was too afraid of the consequences.

The Supreme Court had been asked in *Bowers* v. *Hardwick* to affirm a lower court ruling that would have obliged the State of Georgia to demonstrate a "compelling interest" in keeping the sodomy statute on the books. According to the

The United States Supreme Court justices in 1986, when the *Hardwick* decision was rendered. Seated from left: the late Thurgood Marshall, William Brennan, Warren Burger, Lewis Powell Jr., Harry Blackmun; standing from left: Byron White, John Paul Stevens, William Rehnquist, and Sandra Day O'Connor.

ACLU's then-director of the Lesbian and Gay Rights Project, Nan Hunter, an affirmative ruling would have offered "the first giant step toward dismantling the legal apparatus of homophobia." Hunter continues: "Sodomy laws have functioned as the linchpin for denial of employment, housing, and custody or visitation rights; even when we have proved that there was no nexus between homosexuality and job skills or parenting ability, we have had the courts throw the 'habitual criminal' label at us as a reason to deny relief." Confronted by an already conservative Supreme Court, Hunter and her colleagues reasoned that they could win Hardwick's case. "What brought us within striking distance on this case was the essential conservatism of the claim—a privacy argument based on the intersection of core values of individual identity and a-man's-home-is-his-castle locational sanctity." And with Reagan in the White House, and liberal Justices Blackmun, Brennan, Marshall, and Stevens not getting any younger, this was the only window of opportunity to try to overturn the sodomy statutes, which underwrite so much of the heterosexist apparatus.

The five-to-four majority was even slimmer than the numbers suggest. After he retired in 1987, Justice Lewis Powell Jr. told a group of New York University law students that he had switched his swing vote to determine the majority at the last possible minute, adding, "I think I probably made a mistake in that one." If the tone of this remark suggests a trace of nonchalance, Powell clinched the matter when he calculated the time he'd spent in reflecting on that judgment: "I don't suppose I've devoted half an hour." Powell had concluded that the Hardwick case was "frivolous" because Hardwick was not actually in jeopardy of being imprisoned. In fact, Hardwick had already been incarcerated the day Officer Torick arrested him and his friend. But because the state dropped its sodomy charge against both men, Powell concluded that those who had brought suit could only have done so "just to see what the court would do." Personal suffering and injustice never entered the judge's mind.

If anything, the Supreme Court went out of its way to treat the case as frivolous, assiduously sidestepping any of the constitutional issues it might have raised. Writing for the majority, Byron White refused to have anything to do either with questions of privacy or due process; nor did he concern himself with the possibility —since raised by Kendall Thomas—that *any* imprisonment whatsoever for engaging in consensual sex with an adult constitutes a violation of the Eighth Amendment's proscription against "cruel and unusual punishment." Least of all was the majority prepared to consider the more indirect ideological effects of having sodomy statutes on the books in twenty-four states and the District of Columbia. The majority went along with Georgia attorney general Michael Bowers in dealing with the case as if the only pertinent question was whether or not the Constitution protects "homosexual sodomy." According to ACLU attorney Kathleen Wilde, Bowers's defense was as cynical as it was shrewd. "Every third word in their brief was *homosexual*, and this was not a case about homosexuals. The Georgia statute applies to everybody, even married couples. So for them to make it a homosexual issue was really pandering to the prejudices of the court and the American public."

The majority ruling constituted a classic tautology, a tail-chasing argument in which it is claimed that such statutes must be preserved because they always have been:

Proscriptions against [homosexual sodomy] have ancient roots. Sodomy was a criminal offense at common law and was forbidden by the laws of the original 13 states when they ratified the Bill of Rights. In 1868, when the 14th Amendment was ratified, all but 5 of the 37 states in the Union had criminal sodomy laws.

The *Hardwick* decision recalled the logic that the Supreme Court had employed in two of its most notorious nineteenth-century rulings, both of which helped to maintain the continued oppression of African-Americans well into the twentieth century. In the case of *Dred Scott* v. *Sanford* (1857), the Court justified the continued disqualification of African-Americans from the rights of full citizenship by insisting that, in effect, this disqualification had always existed. The nineteenth-century Court looked to the Declaration of Independence and the Constitution of the United States and insisted that the meaning of these founding documents be limited strictly to the attitudes of their eighteenth-century authors toward the "negro of the African race," who according to the outlook of the Founding Fathers, are subhuman "article(s) of property, and held, and bought and sold as such." Throughout the *Hardwick* decision, the majority opinion returns to the fact that no right to engage in "homosexual sodomy" can be found in the letter of these same documents. Upholding the conservative doctrine of "judicial restraint" that was foreshadowed in cases like *Dred Scott*, the *Hardwick* majority also rejected a more expansive reading of the spirit of these documents. The majority decision in *Hardwick* was similarly foreshadowed when the nineteenth-century Court ruled in the case of *Plessy* v. *Ferguson* (1896) that a Louisiana law prohibiting blacks from riding in railway coaches reserved for whites was constitutional. In *Plessy*, the ruling depended upon the wholly disingenuous idea that "separate but equal" facilities existed for both races; that if blacks considered themselves, or the accommodations to which they were consigned, to be less than equal, then that was their problem. It was an egregious decision that in declaring an unjust situation constitutional perpetuated a two-tiered system and in doing so anticipated the logic and the effects of *Bowers* v. *Hardwick*. Like *Plessy*, for African-Americans, the *Hardwick* decision would have far-reaching consequences on the lives of lesbians and gay men, because it established a justification for a host of prejudicial injustices ranging from discrimination in employment and accommodations to loss of custody over one's child and expulsion from employment in the U.S. military.

In their angry dissent, Justices Blackmun, Brennan, Marshall, and Stevens argued that *Bowers* v. *Hardwick* was "no more about 'a fundamental right to engage in homosexual sodomy' . . . than *Stanley* v. *Georgia* . . . was about a fundamental right to watch obscene movies, or *Katz* v. *United States* . . . was about a fundamental right to place interstate bets from a telephone booth. Rather, this case is about 'the most comprehensive of rights and the right most valued by civilized men,' namely, 'the right to be let alone.' " Neither did the homophobic logic of the majority ruling escape the attention of the dissent. Noting the Court's failure to "comprehend the magnitude of the liberty interests at stake in this case," the majority, it found, had maintained an "almost obsessive focus on homosexual activity [which] is particularly hard to justify in light of the broad language Georgia has used."

Concurring with the majority, Chief Justice Warren Burger revealed how the law and religion reinforce heterosexism (also showing the extent to which the separation of church and state, which is enshrined in the Constitution's First Amendment, remains moot). Burger affirmed the questionable ties that bind American civil law to religious doctrine. Not content with the "ancient roots" of sodomy statutes that Justice White's majority ruling had traced to early American history, Burger bettered his colleague by contending that the "condemnation of those practices" have "*very* ancient roots" (my emphasis), which he traced to "Judeo-Christian moral and ethical standards." That those Judeo-Christian condemnations have been the object of considerable disagreement among Jewish and Christian theologians and religious scholars is clearly not something that the scholars on the Court concerned themselves with.

As if in appreciation for the Court's affirmation in *Hardwick* that American civil law is in fact not wholly independent of Judeo-Christian doctrine, shortly after the ruling was announced the Vatican issued its *Letter to the bishops of the Catholic Church on the pastoral care of homosexual persons.* Among other topics, Cardinal Ratzinger and his Congregation for the Doctrine of the Faith addressed the growing problem of gay-bashing in the age of AIDS. With characteristically misplaced mercy, the document judged gay-bashers . . . well, if not righteous, then at least *understandable*: "When civil legislation is introduced to protect behavior to which no one has any conceivable right, neither the Church nor society at large should be surprised when other distorted notions and practices gain ground, and irrational and violent reactions increase." Had he been consulted, Michael Hardwick could have corrected the cardinal and his righteous cronies: it is the continued existence of laws that *criminalize* homosexuals, not the introduction of laws protecting them, that encourages gay-bashing by sanctioning it. The Vatican also offered the additional comfort to violent homophobes of knowing that, according to Mother Church, homosexual feelings are "ordered toward an intrinsic moral evil."

News of the *Hardwick* decision was enough to awaken the radical in most apolitical queers. The timing had been perfect, in a surreal sort of way. The centennial celebration for the newly restored Statue of Liberty was to reach its kitsch climax on July 4, 1986. Four days earlier, the front pages of every major newspaper in the U.S. trumpeted the Court's ruling, triggering a response among gay men and lesbians that had not been witnessed since the days of Anita Bryant. Spontaneous protests erupted in cities across the country as the news reached communities in which frustration and rage had been mounting over the loss of lovers and friends, the accelerating rate and intensity of bias-related violence, and the unprecedented challenge to queer social identity that the epidemic posed. On the night of Tuesday, July 1, more than one thousand gay men and lesbians returned to the site of the original Stonewall riots to pack Sheridan Square and Seventh Avenue South in the West Village. The demographics of this protest represented a mix of queer humanity that had not been seen in a long time. There, among the disheveled youths, old-time activists, and students were conservative-looking men and women in business attire. Protesters stopped traffic on Seventh Avenue South, the more experienced and fearless among them sitting down in a classic gesture of

In one of the many demonstrations that erupted in cities nationwide as word of the *Hardwick* decision spread, queer New Yorkers protested on July 4, 1986, near the site of the original Stonewall uprising. Still from Program Three, *Hollow Liberty*.

civil disobedience; refusing to oblige the requests of the protest organizers to disperse, the crowd soon migrated east and north to Sixth Avenue, where it blocked traffic again. Who knows who came up with the idea to "Stop the Fourth," but on that Friday a few hundred courageous souls regrouped with every intention of disrupting the nationally televised party for the Statue of Liberty.

Hundreds of thousands of Americans from around the country had converged on lower Manhattan to parade around in foam-rubber liberty crowns as the human backdrop to the media spectacle that was orchestrated by Mr. Smoke-and-Mirrors himself, Chrysler's Lee Iacocca. There were, however, unplanned and dissonant deviations from the upbeat script as revelers responded to the estimated six thousand queer activists in their midst by bloodying a few noses and hurling more verbal abuse. Nonetheless, the protesters persevered and snaked their way downtown from the Village, past a logjam at Trinity Church on Broadway, and proceeding on to the harbor, holding signs aloft that read "Miss Liberty? You bet I do," and chanting untimely slogans such as "Civil rights or civil war!" In the midst of the well-rehearsed festivities for liberty's most famous fetish, lesbian and gay activists risked their lives in order to protest the limits of American liberty. As reported by gay journalist Richard Goldstein in the *Village Voice*, the police did their level best to avoid arresting demonstrators, many of whom were so determined to pick a fight that they came packing first-aid kits and bail money. Intent on maintaining a positive karma at all cost, the police secured a narrow pathway so the protesters could safely reach their destination at the Battery. There, in view of Miss Liberty and her many adoring fans, the demonstrators sang a few doleful choruses of "we shall overcome." The protesters' extreme vulnerability to the taunts and occasional firecrackers that incensed revelers lobbed their way did not prevent them from encircling the hostile celebrants to shout them down with cries of "Bigot go home!" Little or none of this was reported in the mainstream press. But the queer demonstrators had also prevailed in a key way that presaged a renewed radicalism and reinvigoration of the lesbian and gay movement. Recalling this historic juncture, filmmaker and activist Gregg Bordowitz described the protests against the *Hardwick* decision as "catalysts for AIDS activism . . . an opportunity for young activists like myself to meet older activists."

Contending in the conservative political climate of the Reagan era with an epidemic that has had no equal in twentieth-century American history, gay men and lesbians had been noticeably slow to anger—in the opinion of some, too slow. The first attempt to stimulate a less courteous, more forceful queer reaction to the AIDS epidemic occurred in 1983, when novelist and screenwriter Larry Kramer published "1,112 Deaths and Counting" in the *New York Native*. In that article, the future author of *The Normal Heart* and cofounder in 1981 of New York's Gay

Men's Health Crisis (then a grassroots organization of volunteers that provided support services through its buddy program, as well as education, counseling, and legal services) demanded action not just on the part of government officials, scientists, medical insurers, and health-care providers, but also on the part of the gay community.

"Our continued existence," Kramer wrote, "depends on just how angry you can get." Four years later, after the number of officially reported cases of AIDS in the United States was surpassing thirty-two thousand, only ten months after the *Hardwick* decision, a group of mostly gay men who had gathered at New York's Lesbian and Gay Community Services Center to hear Kramer speak were sufficiently enraged and terrified by the events of the previous several years to respond to his inflammatory speech by scheduling a meeting to form a new organization that would go beyond the service orientation and the conventional advocacy methods of GMHC. The roughly three hundred men and women who met on March 12, 1987, formed the AIDS Coalition to Unleash Power, "a diverse, nonpartisan group united in anger and committed to direct action to end the AIDS crisis." Gregg Bordowitz saw this development as an important indication of growing activist self-determination. "What was interesting about the turn from the early *Hardwick* protests to the early ACT UP meetings," he said, "was that we went from a defensive position to an offensive position. Instead of just protesting against repression, we built ourselves up and went forward with our own positive agenda."

As a crucial catalyst in what would become the international AIDS activist movement, ACT UP has played a highly significant role in helping to navigate a safer and more humane course through this crisis. Of course, in the eyes of most people, such as my family back in Canada, who have remained largely oblivious to the effects of this still-selective plague, ACT UP has been synonymous with hecklers, hyperbole, and all manner of ill-mannered theatrics. Without knowing in so many words that I was then a member of ACT UP (New York), my father once said, while we were watching a TV news broadcast together on one of my holiday visits, that such antics would get us precisely nowhere if we were trying to get sympathy from the disengaged or openly hostile "general population." I might have told him that sympathy was not high on ACT UP's agenda.

Through the activities of its general membership and specialized subcommittees, ACT UP has, on the other hand, helped to revolutionize the way that drug research is conducted, to redefine the syndrome more fairly and accurately so that women with AIDS are included in drug trials and receive disability benefits. ACT UP managed to cut through red tape at federal agencies such as the FDA and the

In March 1987, playwright Larry Kramer delivered an incendiary speech at the Lesbian and Gay Community Services Center which helped to spark the formation of ACT UP (AIDS Coalition to Unleash Power). Photo by Jane Rossett.

Overleaf: Contingents of people living with AIDS and AIDS activists at the 1987 March on Washington for Lesbian and Gay Rights. Photo by JEB (Joan E. Biren).

NIH, bringing about the release of nonharmful, potentially promising, but federally unapproved experimental drug treatments in compassionate use programs. Theatrical confrontations have embarrassed more than one pharmaceutical giant into reducing the high cost of drugs that might extend people's lives. By risking arrest and criminal prosecution ACT UP members instituted needle-exchange programs that have since become widely accepted as an effective means of decreasing the rate of HIV infection among intravenous drug users and their sexual partners. A sadly depleted ACT UP struggles on against highly organized and ruthless conservative opponents in local school boards to ensure that safer-sex education is available for students in public high schools so they can make informed choices about how to conduct their sex lives. Subcommittees have been formed to fight for improved health care and living conditions for male and female prisoners with HIV and AIDS; to secure the release of Haitian refugees with HIV and AIDS from American refugee camps in Guantánamo Bay; to secure housing

for homeless people with AIDS in some of this country's largest cities.

The rise of AIDS activism signaled other sea changes in the lesbian and gay movement as well. Since the mid- to late 1980s, queer men and women have been working together in significant numbers for the first time since gay liberation, arguably in more productive ways. Homophobia, AIDS, and other women's health-care issues supplied the initial common ground, but trying to work together in often anxious affiliations has produced a deepening insight into the possibility that political progress does not depend on the misguided belief that the differences dividing men and women either don't exist or should be made to disappear; any more than one can expect or even desire that the varied experiences of queer people from different racial, ethnic, and class backgrounds can be denied when denial may seem politically convenient. It is no longer necessary to aspire as a political movement to the conventionally monolithic exemplar of unity, which in any event, we've never been able to maintain. The key to maintaining a sense of common purpose in the face of so much difference is, of course, a challenge that confronts the burgeoning queer culture: to give meaningful symbolic shape to varied needs, aspirations, and experiences.

The expansion of lesbian and gay political and cultural activities in the age of AIDS has led to developments that are complex and sometimes downright contradictory. Two years ago, my lover and I celebrated our first decade together by exchanging rings. Neither of us likes jewelry, and I don't like shopping. But we went to the used-jewelry counter at Fortunoff and told the elderly Jewish saleswoman that we were looking to buy a pair of wedding bands—for each other. This being New York, she remained as unfazed by our request as she was unenthusiastic. After a little looking, she found a pair of inexpensive bands that were just the right size. "Ten-karat gold," she added, "that's how they made them during the war in England." There was no ceremony. Just a brief negotiation concerning which finger to wear our rings on: ring finger of the *right* hand—to distinguish us from really married people. Soon after, on two separate occasions two friends each commented on my new ring. Rosalind said she couldn't imagine why I was wearing such a thing, adding that for political reasons she hadn't worn her wedding ring in ages. Was this political gesture, I puzzled, a luxury that men and women whom the law and religion don't permit to marry can ill afford? Lynne's reaction was different. She said it was sweet, but then fell into introspection from which she emerged to announce, "Oh. I get it, it's political. For you to wear that ring is socially *resistant*." Is the wedding ring, which still strikes many queers as "assimilationist," also an act of resistance? I don't want to be married; Clay refers to our relationship as the "antimarriage," which suits me fine. I certainly don't want to move any closer to the center of a culture and society that perpetuates so many kinds of injustices. Yet I also wonder, is my reticence regarding the mainstream a little like Rosalind's projection onto me of her feelings about wearing a ring: a political luxury that others can ill afford?

Observers at the mass wedding at the 1993 March on Washington. Photos by Marilyn Humphries.

Straight people, Dr. Herek has observed, are not defined by their sexual orientation the way gay people are: they regularly participate in the rituals and benefit from the privileges that mark them as husbands or wives, fathers or mothers, and this validates them as full citizens and more fully complex human beings. Conversely, lesbians and gay men are defined "in terms of the characteristic [sexual orientation] that relegates them to unequal status and sets them in opposition to the dominant group." Popular representations reinforce this pattern. Film historian and activist Vito Russo long ago referred to Hollywood's narrative tradition of demonizing and punishing queers in the movies as the "celluloid closet." Another thing happens on those still-rare occasions when gay or lesbian characters appear in today's movies and TV shows: the novelty of their sexual orientation often overwhelms whatever other human qualities they might have had. To fill out these cardboard characters and render them more fully three-dimensional would be to risk making it too easy for straight viewers to identify with queers, which would not do in a culture that remains as intractably heterosexist as ours.

There is nothing particularly novel about lesbians and gay men laying claim to social roles forbidden to them by mainstream institutions. Since the formation of the Metropolitan Community Church in October 1968, the Reverend Troy Perry has been offering queers some of the spiritual rewards and sense of community belonging that attracts so many other Americans to organized religion. For just as long, he has also been sanctifying same-sex unions from coast to coast. Since the earliest years of gay liberation, same-sex couples have also applied in vain for marriage licenses and the legal rights that are contingent upon them. In May 1970, librarian Jim McConnell and Jack Baker, a first-year law student at the University of Minnesota, pinpointed a technicality in the Minnesota marriage law that failed to name "opposite sex" as a precondition for marriage, just as state law in California did at the time. Still, it seems to me, and to anyone else who attended the 1993 March on Washington, that marriage has become desirable among more lesbians and gay men during the past half decade than ever before.

Marriage entitles those whom it binds together to scores of legal privileges. To name only a few: shared tax returns, special tax exemptions, deductions, and refunds; coverage of the uninsured under the spouse's medical, disability, and life insurance plans; survivor's benefits from social security and pension plans, inheritance free from taxation even in the absence of a will; next-of-kin status in the case of a medical emergency, mental incapacity, or death. This system of incentives punishes all people—straight or gay—who resist wedlock and helps to reinforce sexist as well as heterosexist injustice.

In 1979, Sharon Kowalski and Karen Thompson exchanged rings and named each other beneficiaries in their life insurance policies in addition to living together as spouses in St. Cloud, Minnesota. On the night of November 13, 1983, everything changed. A drunk driver plowed into the car Sharon was driving, leaving her severely injured—unable to walk, unable to speak more than a few words at a time, and in need of constant care. For reasons that would become obvious over the course of the next seven bitterly litigious years, Sharon had never told her parents that she was a lesbian; never told them that she and Karen were—from their perspective anyway—married. In March of 1984, Sharon's father and Karen Thompson cross-petitioned to become Sharon's guardian. Assuming that Donald Kowalski would not deny her visitation rights, Karen supported his appointment by the court as Sharon's guardian. This was her first big mistake. On July 25, 1985, Sharon's father requested and received court approval to terminate Thompson's visitation rights and relocated his daughter from a nursing home in Duluth to a more remote home in Hibbing. Not until January 1989, almost four years later, was Karen able to convince the courts that her visitation rights should be restored based on Sharon's desire to be with her.

Late in 1988, Sharon's father had informed the court that, due to medical problems of his own, he wanted to be removed as his daughter's guardian. The

Untitled solarized photograph (1979)
by lesbian artist Tee A. Corinne.

witnesses who then testified in favor of Thompson's guardianship were qualitatively and quantitatively overwhelming, but this did not prevent the court from overlooking all the evidence to elect as guardian a "neutral" third party named Karen Tomberlin. Tomberlin, it turned out, was neither neutral nor noticeably interested in Sharon's welfare, as an appeals court would later find. Like Debra Kowalski, Sharon's sister, and Kathy Schroeder, a friend of Sharon's and the Kowalskis', who were the two sole witnesses to testify in Tomberlin's behalf, Tomberlin had rarely visited Sharon at the nursing home in Hibbing and had never once gone to the trouble of taking her on an outing. Despite the ample expert testimony that supported Karen Thompson's guardianship, and despite the fact that no hearing had even been conducted to assess Tomberlin's qualifications, on April 23, 1991, the trial court appointed Tomberlin as Sharon's guardian.

The trial court that blinded itself to reason in order to appoint Tomberlin guardian had also accused Thompson of what it evidently regarded as wildly inappropriate behavior. Thompson was criticized for telling the media and Sharon's health-care providers that they were lovers; for taking Sharon out of the nursing home for occasional trips to lesbian and gay–related social and political events where the couple appeared as featured guests; for soliciting legal defense funds to help pay for seven years of litigation, as if this proved Thompson's intention to capitalize on Sharon's disabilities. Finally, in awarding guardianship, the court was fully aware that Tomberlin intended to move Sharon from the nursing home in Minneapolis that health-care providers had recommended to one in the Iron Range—about as far away from Thompson as it was close to the family that had disregarded Sharon's happiness so insistently.

None of this could have happened had Sharon and Karen's exchange of rings back in 1979 been buttressed by something more legally significant than a pair of life insurance policies. Just like the persistence of sodomy statutes that brand homosexual men and women "habitual criminals," the ineligibility of same-sex couples to receive certification for marriage encouraged judges and juries to deal repeatedly with the guardianship of Sharon Kowalski in flagrantly homophobic miscarriages of justice. These finally ended in 1991 when a Minnesota Appeals Court Judge Davies overturned the previous rulings to award guardianship to Thompson. Thompson would automatically have been appointed her injured spouse's guardian had she and Sharon been legally married, but another point, perhaps obvious but no less important, warrants repetition. There is a reciprocity between the heterosexist structure of America's defining institutions and the homophobic attitudes of individual citizens. The policies of organizations like the ACLU's Lesbian and Gay Project and the Lambda Legal Defense and Education Fund are predicated in part upon the belief that interventions can be made at any weak point in the system where injustice or contradiction seem most extreme, and that the effects of these interventions will eventually ripple out to cause broader changes in terms of not just public policy but also private attitudes. But others may wonder whether this is true.

In the age of AIDS, the need to advance the legal legitimacy of same-sex relationships has become all the more urgent. The limited protections afforded by domestic-partnership legislation have arguably resulted from two sources of concern and contention: first, the long, dismal history of legal battles concerning lesbian mothers who have had to fight to retain custody of their children; second, the rash of horror stories involving gay male survivors of relationships where a lover dies of AIDS. In these situations, elective bonds are often deemed invalid, and commitment is disregarded as lovers discover that they are, in the eyes of the law, less than spouses—and, in the eyes of a dead lover's parents and siblings, much, much less than "family."

On May Day, 1986, an artist friend of mine died very suddenly from complications due to AIDS. Only a few weeks before his death, René had been up in
Canada for a week teaching at the Nova Scotia College of Art. He was up there
with Brad, his lover of four years; this was a treat for them, since lack of money
had not permitted the two much opportunity to travel. It was beginning to look as
though they would be traveling more often, since their financial situation was
improving. René was a gifted, ambitious young artist, and his work was beginning
to sell and to attract the critical attention it deserved. He had come from a wealthy
Puerto Rican family, but his relationship with his parents had always been rocky—

Untitled photograph of artist and AIDS
activist David Wojnarowicz by Peter Hujar.

and never more so than when his father learned that his firstborn son was gay. The news just about drove the man crazy. From that moment, René was financially on his own.

In Nova Scotia, René started running a fever and experiencing shortness of breath. He'd had all kinds of health problems over the years, but never respiratory problems; and he'd never been tested for HIV. By the time he and Brad returned to New York, his fever was high. He went to a doctor, had X-rays taken, and learned he had pneumonia. The pneumonia turned out to be *Pneumocystis carinii*, which in those days, before the therapeutic benefits of aerosol Pentamedine were recognized by foot-dragging bureaucrats, was almost always fatal. Like 40 million other Americans, René had no health insurance; the hospital said it had no beds. For several days, he languished at home while Brad struggled to relieve the high fever and worsening dehydration and to help his lover breathe. Finally, Brad took René back to the hospital, this time to the emergency room.

René had contacted his mother in San Juan, and his parents wasted no time in flying to New York. Brad recalls the frustration and helplessness he felt at not being able to assist his lover. He also speaks ambivalently about the arrival of René's father, about the way this moneyed older man deployed his considerable authority to get his son a hospital room and take over his care. It was with the same quiet authority that he steered Brad down the hall, away from René's room, to say, "You'll have to go away now." Brad returned to his lover's hospital room and said, "Your father just told me to disappear." The repercussions, according to Brad, were swift and noisy. René and his father yelled at each other furiously; when Brad pleaded with them to calm down, René's father snapped, "You're not part of this family!"

Brad's ordeal is linked to that of Michael Hardwick's nameless lover by lack of money, privilege, and the sense of entitlement that often accompanies such birthrights. Just as Hardwick's sexual partner could not join Michael in bringing suit against the state that his livelihood depended on, in this situation Brad was not legally, financially, or emotionally empowered to demand of René's father that he, too, should have a say in decisions pertaining to the care of his dying companion. The law that leads many gay men to accept humiliation in silent anonymity rather than fight is the same law that inscribes the authority of marriage, family, and the "law of the father." It was this system that determined Brad's powerlessness. Conversely, the legal system is itself buttressed by the actions of those whom it protects and represents, be they officers of the law or heads of families.

During a brief spell when René's fever abated, he told Brad to contact a lawyer so that he could draw up a will. Over the years he had given Brad some of his paintings, drawings, and photographs, which they stored in his studio; there were also a number of works by other artists they both admired that they had kept in their apartment. Brad had worked for months on that apartment, using his skills as a designer and craftsman to transform René's tacky, cramped one-room Village apartment into a compact and comfortable home. There were beautiful new shelves and built-in cabinets for the TV and stereo and René's impressive book and record collection. He had worked minor miracles in the kitchen and bathroom to make them pleasing and efficient. René had tried to get the landlord to add Brad's name to the lease, but he refused. The landlord was trying to turn the building into a co-op and was eager to "warehouse" empty apartments—especially nicely renovated ones like René and Brad's.

Soon René's fever was raging again, and his parents had the doctor put René on experimental drugs and steroids. None of this was done with Brad's approval, not even when René ended up tethered to a respirator. The lawyer was never able to see René at the hospital, and so was never able to execute the will. After René died, his parents shipped his body to Puerto Rico for the funeral, to which Brad was not invited. They removed their son's art from his studio and tried to prevent Brad from getting the works René had given him.

Meanwhile, the landlord was interested in removing Brad from the apartment. One day, while Brad was still attempting to recover from the trauma of helping his lover to die, there was a knock on the door. The superintendent's wife was there to ask Brad a question to which, in all likelihood, she already knew the answer. "Where's René?" she asked. "He's dead," Brad replied, slamming the door in her face. Minutes later, the management company phoned to inform Brad that he'd better leave. Papers were served, eviction notices taped to the door. Along with learning for the first time to grieve, dealing with harassment was now part of his life. For three years Brad fought the landlord with the few legal resources left at his disposal. For three years he lived in that familiar, now sorrowful place, not knowing if or when the city marshal might appear.

In 1989 the landlord won the case, and Brad moved away. Brad recalls with sad irony that it was only two weeks later that an appellate court ruling in the case of a New York resident, Miguel Braschi, established that same-sex spouses must be included in the definition of family members who can continue to live in a rent-controlled apartment after the leaseholder has died.

In the debate that has taken place about lesbian and gay access to marriage, some lesbians have been especially clear in articulating their opposition to it. By her own admission, lawyer Paula Ettelbrick has spent a sizable portion of her professional energies advocating for New York City's domestic partnership legislation. Recently, she reflected on this kind of legislation and summed up her feminist argument. "I want our relationship(s) to be respected even if we don't register," she observed. "I think perhaps we've done a disservice in not thinking this new registration system through as a community. It's being used by people now to say that those lesbians who register . . . are the good ones and those who don't are the bad ones." Ettelbrick opposes marriage as a goal of queer politics because she sees it perpetuating social inequality. The many rights and privileges that marriage confers upon those who can and do buy into it are denied to "families and couples or individuals who are not defined by marriage." To Ettelbrick and her lover, Lambda attorney Suzanne Goldberg, gay men and all women should fight institutionalized privilege, not try to benefit from it. For them, the queer drive to gain access to marriage contradicts the revolutionary, liberationist aspirations of the lesbian and gay movement, which they see as the product of late-sixties countercultural, feminist, and postcolonial political philosophies. But a growing contingent of articulate queer conservatives now insist that it is time to move past the movement's liberationist roots, to no longer permit considerations that date from the movement's inception to determine the goals and strategies of contemporary gay and lesbian politics.

Conservative gay writer Bruce Bawer appropriates the rhetoric of "diversity" in order to argue that voices like his have been silenced as left-leaning lesbian and gay leaders have presumed to dictate policy for all those who have been too timid to speak up. Until now. If the words of the old gay-power slogan are true and we are, indeed, "everywhere," then there is reason to believe that the politics of the lesbian and gay majority more nearly reflect the politics of the increasingly conservative American mainstream. Certainly there was ample evidence of that at the 1993 March on Washington. Whether it follows that our political struggle should therefore be shaped by aspirations to mainstream acceptance is by no means certain. In a society that is, if anything, more, not less, homophobic, such aspirations can yield strange results.

Gay *New Republic* editor and Gap model Andrew Sullivan has no problem bestowing rights and privileges on married couples. He merely wants to see them extended to homosexuals and argues for that right with an argument that in every other way is indistinguishable from remarks made by such straight champions of the nuclear family as New York senator Daniel Patrick Moynihan and former vice president Dan Quayle. Sullivan asserts that in the context of "the weakened family's effect upon the poor," to fail to promote marriage is to "invite social disintegration." This situation is no different for gay men and lesbians, he insists, for whom marriage would also foster "social cohesion, emotional security,

Lesbian mom Maxine Wolfe embraces her daughters. Photo by Linda Eber/Impact Visuals.

and economic prudence." In his pitch for gay marriage, Sullivan also notes that it would nurture children; after all, "there's no reason gays should not be allowed to adopt or be foster parents." Hard to say where in Sullivan's considerations one finds the many lesbian moms who have not had to adopt in order to become parents. In light of the 1989 American Bar Association study that estimated 8 to 10 million children are being raised in 3 million queer households, it is a measure of heterosexism's power as an ideological system of oppression that reproduction can still be claimed—even by queers—as a necessarily straight prerogative. Sullivan also attempts to clinch his argument for gay marriage by claiming that in the age of AIDS it would "qualify as a genuine public health measure." Contrary to Sullivan's thoughtless assertion, not all people who marry are virgins when they marry; nor do they all practice monogamy. To read his delusional claim is to understand, however, how marriage, in and of itself, can lull couples into unsafe sexual practices. In short, a marriage license is a poor substitute for a condom.

There are less strictly pragmatic, less partisan, and more personal ways of understanding why so many lesbians and gay men are now pressing for the legal legitimation of same-sex relationships, and why others are celebrating their unions in social or religious rituals that have a public dimension. One spring evening in 1993, I attended not one but two gay commitment ceremonies. A few days later, I read in the *Times* about a more prominent "gay marriage" that took place in a lavish downtown restaurant. None of these ceremonies took place in a church, but the two I attended both featured the central element of any marriage ceremony— two people declaring their love for one another in the presence of others who honor it. I have always presumed that AIDS has had something to do with this phenomenon, but precisely what I hadn't bothered to figure out. Reading what psychologist Walt Whitman Odets has had to say about the effects of the AIDS crisis on gay male *survivors* of the epidemic sheds light on the current determination to legitimize and sanctify lesbian as well as gay primary relationships, and to demonstrate the importance of queer families.

Odets is a pioneer in the clinical care of HIV-negative men, whose often dire psychological condition has until recently been overlooked as limited resources have been spread thin to deal with the urgent needs of people with HIV and AIDS. Odets insists that such thinking is shortsighted and has supported this assertion by focusing attention on the continuing conversion from HIV-negative to HIV-positive of gay men who know the limits of safer sex practice. Odets relates this seroconversion to the emotional toll exacted upon such men as AIDS decimates entire communities and erodes the will to live. Dr. Odets has examined the crippling effects of "survivor guilt" among his gay male patients, insisting that its prevalence and severity cannot fully be understood if one defines this phenomenon literally—as the remorse that is suffered by those who live on in continued good physical health as lovers and friends sicken and die. He concludes that his patients suffer disproportionately from feelings of guilt—an assertion that in all likelihood can be applied to some lesbians as well. To understand the severe depression and despondency of those in his care, Odets has taken a broader view of "survivor guilt," one that encompasses the difficult formative experiences of children who grow up to become gay in a heterosexist society. Being homosexual, Odets notes, contributes to the problem for the survivors, who must live directly "in the shadow of AIDS," because all queers initially experience their sexuality as a guilt-inducing psychological "abandonment" that "occurs in the necessity of emotional separation from the family because of the conflict over sexuality." Abandonment is then made concrete as the "child" leaves home "in order to live homosexually."

Because abandonment of the family may be integral to being homosexual, survival guilt may be too. . . . The homosexual son is often felt to take from his parents the "normal" son that they wanted and expected; and he may be experienced as taking their grand-children and their respectability in their community as well.

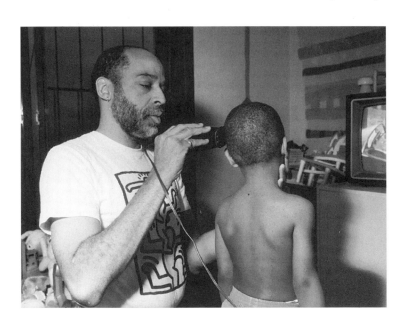

Doug Robinson gives his son a haircut. Photo by Tom McKitterick/Impact Visuals.

This scenario strikes a resonant chord in me, though I count myself among the fortunate few queers in this discouraging day and age who would not feel justified in describing his life in terms of suffering. And yet, among Walt Odets's many humane insights has been his observation that the disfiguring effects of guilt and abandonment among homosexual men and women can be as subtle and nuanced as they are widespread. I was raised in an observant Jewish family in Montreal and remember my father explaining to me one morning in synagogue that Jews do not believe in an after-life—at least not in the Christian sense of that term. According to Conservative Jewish doctrine, eternal life is something that one only

experiences through one's descendants (*"l'dor vador,"* from generation to generation). No children, no eternity. There was good news and bad in my father's lesson. The good news: no fire and brimstone; the bad: a judgment, implicit in his decision to share this Talmudic nugget with his only gay child. I know he meant no conscious harm; he was trying to impress upon me the concreteness of Jewish spirituality, a paradox that has always made him proud of the religious identity he has tried so hard to pass on to me and my siblings. My father's story left me feeling grateful to my older brother and sister for having raised so many children, which relieved me of the guilt I would have had to bear had my parents' desire for grandchildren—for *their* eternal life—depended upon me alone.

When I came out to my parents, separately, nearly twenty years ago, my mother made things much easier on me than my dad—or so I thought. My father responded in extreme agitation, demanding in one of our several screaming fights that I try a little "self-discipline." My mother's less immediately burdensome reaction (eyes glistening: "I only want you to be happy, dear . . . .") now seems less honest, though just as connected with guilt as was my father's rage. Not long before she died of cancer in 1981, my mother insisted that we speak about our feelings for each other. We talked with difficulty about love and about disappointment, but neither she nor I ever brought up the fact that my life must have dissatisfied her in ways that included, but were not limited to, my sexual orientation.

Although my family is about as accepting of and content with my twelve-year relationship with Clay as I can imagine any family being, when I visit them I rarely speak about our life together. Even when they ask, my answers are evasive, pat, and come out fitfully. I tell myself I know the limits of what they really want to know, because when I've crossed that line—as I did when Bill died—their behavior told me so. I don't believe that I'm the one who draws these lines, but I know that they're not wrong to interpret the life I've made away from them as a desire for "privacy." And I also know that it's as convenient for them as it is for me that I should be granted so much of it. Lines like these are older than anyone in my family; they're socially inscribed, and one of their most prodigious products is guilt.

Queers are distanced by our families at least as often as we distance ourselves from them. And even when this does not occur in shattering acts of disassociation, the emotional residue of a more subtle but nevertheless painful abandonment will be felt. Lesbian writer Sarah Schulman said as much in 1992 when she reflected on the failure of her family and straight friends to communicate the slightest concern for her emotional and physical well-being throughout the weeklong outpouring of hatred for lesbians and gay men that accompanied that year's Republican National Convention. As Schulman saw it, such an expression of concern would have required them to "commit [a] cultural violation."

Among the many remarkable stories that Dr. Odets has related from his clinical practice is one heartbreaking account that crystallizes for me what I think many of the gay men and lesbians who now insist on the right to marry, to bear children, and/or to have families are trying to overcome. It concerns a forty-one-year-old man who, six weeks after watching his lover of four years die on their living room couch, decided to spend a weekend with his own mother, his two sisters, and several of their children at a country cabin. Neither his mother nor his sisters— not even the one who was his twin—were able to offer him any meaningful support or sign of emotional understanding. As he sat at a table and cried and cried, his twin sister stopped fussing just long enough to act out a gesture of comfort, but her gesture came out as a denial of his pain and of the magnitude of his loss. "Gary," she asked him, "are you *sure* you're all right?"

In 1980, just months after women were integrated into active duty at sea for the first time, twenty-four women aboard the USS *Norton Sound* were investigated for "lesbian activity" in a witch-hunt. Here five of the defendants wait out the hearings at the Naval Station in Long Beach, California. From left: Chick Fitzmorris, Sharris Meusser, Carole Brock, Barbara Lee Underwood, and Norma Mohl. AP/Wide World Photos.

Odets explains, "The family wishes to deny the grief, for to recognize it would be to acknowledge the relationship for what it was."

Precisely how American youths put distance between themselves and families that don't want them to live as homosexuals, and where they go once they do, are questions that Kate Dyer, then executive assistant to Massachusetts congressman Gerry Studds, addressed in relation to the campaign to lift the military's ban on homosexuals.

I've talked to a lot of [gay] service members from the Midwest who knew no other gay people and needed a way out. Their families didn't have money, and college was not an option. The first bus up the dusty road is going to the military recruiter in the big city.

This is a valid way for many people to get out of unhealthy, potentially violent situations, to get on with their lives and to meet other gay and lesbian people. . . . The military is one of the best options for people who don't have many economic choices. We don't have a "great jobs" program. We don't have free college education. The military is like a trade school that teaches you and pays you while you learn.

We live in a country where a great many people are born into grim disadvantage, their chances of developing a viable future exceedingly slim—and slimmer still if being queer is part of the equation. However one perceives the military—as the nation's largest employer, as an imperialist killing machine, as a patriotic crucible that transforms pimply wimps into "real" men and lost girls into women with "leadership potential"—however you see it, the military too often is a youth's only hope of getting by. As our elected officials prepare to dismantle whatever remains of social welfare programs, some of which date back to the 1930s, a thought comes to mind: to what extent does the military now function as a substitute for that frayed social "safety net" that so many American youths still depend upon to make a life?

The fact that the military may function more than ever as a Faustian substitute for endangered social-welfare programs suggests a less familiar perspective on the human cost of the military's ban on homosexuals. The focal point of this perspective lies beyond the self-ignorance that the military imposes on enlisted youths who may or may not even know what their sexual orientation is; beyond the dissembling, harassment, and humiliation that the ban justifies; beyond the coercion, betrayal, and imprisonment that it imposes upon servicemen and servicewomen who refuse to comply with queer witch-hunts; beyond the refusal of respect in life and honor in death that less worthy soldiers are granted as automatically as their uniforms. It centers on the fact that the military's half-century-old ban on lesbians

Gay veterans towing the Stars and Stripes in the 1993 Lesbian and Gay Pride March in New York. Photo by Stacy Rosenstock/Impact Visuals.

Air Force sergeant Leonard Matlovich, a gay Vietnam veteran whose 1975 challenge to the military's discriminatory policy against lesbians and gay men marked a decisive turning point for the gay movement. In 1987, Matlovich was arrested during an AIDS demonstration at the White House as the Third International Conference on AIDS met in Washington. Here, he is reaching for the return of the U.S. flag he carried before the arrest. Photo by JEB (Joan E. Biren).

and gay men denies an entire class of American citizens the only chance that many of them will ever get to save themselves from the downward spiral that awaits the uneducated, the untrained, and the chronically unemployed in this country. The fate of the literally tens of thousands of women and men who have been forced out of the military highlights a kind of inequity that is unique in American society today.

In February 1990, the Supreme Court decided to let stand lower court rulings that permitted the expulsion of Drill Sgt. Miriam Ben-Shalom and Ens. James Woddard for verbally acknowledging their homosexuality. In explaining the implications of the Court's action, Kenneth W. Starr, then George Bush's solicitor general, indicated that the ruling in *Bowers* v. *Hardwick* made it "implausible to say that those with a proclivity to commit such acts [sodomy] constitute a group that deserves special protection from the courts under the Equal Protection clause." One year before, a similar observation regarding the instrumentality of the *Hardwick* decision in relation to the military's ban had been made by federal judge Stephen Reinhardt—though with diametrically opposing intent. In a soul-searching dissent against a ruling that would have reinstated Sgt. Perry Watkins (who had been discharged only after seventeen years of unblemished military service despite having acknowledged his homosexuality from the start), Reinhardt lamented that until *Hardwick* is overturned, gay men and lesbians in the military can expect little else but such *un*equal justice under law.

In my view, Hardwick *improperly condones official bias and prejudice against homosexuals, and authorizes the criminalization of conduct that is an essential part of the intimate sexual life of our many homosexual citizens, a group that has historically been the victim of unfair and irrational treatment. I believe that history will view* Hardwick *much as it views* Plessy *v.* Ferguson. . . . *And I am confident that, in the long run,* Hardwick, *like* Plessy, *will be overruled by a wiser and more enlightened Court.*

The extent to which Reinhardt wanted to foreground the parallel with *Plessy* is evident even in his choice of words. One passage conspicuously echoes the prophetic statement made by the sole dissenting voice in the nineteenth-century case. "The judgment rendered this day," Justice John Marshall Harlan wrote, "will, in time, prove to be quite as pernicious as the decision made by this tribunal in the *Dred Scott* case."

To the contemporary queer observer, the 1896 ruling in *Plessy* v. *Ferguson* is therefore striking not just because it relied upon the same kind of tautological reasoning that the court would employ ninety years later to justify its decision in *Bowers* v. *Hardwick*. *Plessy* is striking as well because it employed that circular reasoning to rationalize the "separate but equal" treatment, which would only successfully be challenged six decades later in the case of *Brown* v. *Board of Education*. In *Plessy*, white supremacists in the post-Reconstruction South perpetuated a myth of "separate but equal" facilities—from railway cars, restaurants, and drinking fountains to hospital wards and public schools—in order to retain exclusive access to a host of public and private amenities that would at once ensure the historic advantage of "whites only" and guarantee lives of continued poverty and degradation to the vast majority of African-Americans. As the military ban deprives lesbians and gay men of the right to serve their country, it not only denies them access to a social role that Americans look up to as one of the principal measures of full citizenship and complete personhood, it also deprives them of access to an institution that offers increasingly rare opportunities for education, training, and employment in the absence of which it is hard to see how they are supposed to survive, let alone exercise inalienable rights to life, liberty, and the pursuit of happiness.

There was another echo of *Plessy* in the 1980 expulsion of alleged lesbians Alicia Harris and Wendy Williams from the USS *Norton Sound*, one that points to the deep structural links between homophobia, racism, and sexism in American society: both of the discharged were African-American women. Indeed, of the nine black women on the *Norton Sound*, eight were targeted in the initial charges of lesbianism. "It just smelled of racism," Susan McGrievy, ACLU counsel in the case, said of their discharge. "They were convicted because people believe that African-Americans are oversexed." Of the sixty-odd women on board the *Norton Sound* nearly half were named in the initial charges. It was known that there were

Alicia Harris (above) and Wendy Williams, the two *Norton Sound* defendants who were discharged from the Navy, appeared on television in the flood of media coverage that was generated by this witch hunt. Stills from Program Three, *Hollow Liberty*.

gay men on board the *Norton Sound*. One had actively sought to be discharged, but his superiors were more intent on giving the female servicemembers a hard time. No doubt it was more than a coincidence that the *Norton Sound* was part of the "Women at Sea" program, an early test to see whether women and men could serve on ships together and get the job done. The *Norton Sound* had initially attracted the attention of Defense Department investigators because of reports of widespread drug dealing, loan-sharking, and violence, including one unexplained death. Undercover agents assigned to the ship failed to turn up useful evidence of criminal misconduct.

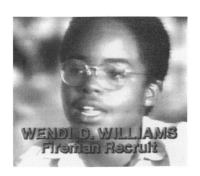

They were more fortunate when a U.S. Naval Investigative Service [NIS] agent questioned Helen Teresa Wilson, a mess specialist third class who had a problem with dykes in general and with black dykes in particular. Wilson obliged with a four-page statement in which she insisted—without a shred of concrete evidence—that half the women on board were lesbians. The NIS promptly turned from its failed investigation into criminal misconduct to search for signs of sexual misconduct among the women of the *Norton Sound*. This was neither the first time, nor would it be the last, that the Navy would "discover" labyrinthine homosexual cabals when it had reason to distract the public's attention away from problems that had little, if anything at all, to do with sex.

Aside from the alleged corruption and incompetence on board the *Norton Sound*, the ship's biggest problem concerned gender and, of course, sexual orientation. The men on board had made it clear from the start that they did not want women sharing their duties and invading their space. Objecting to the presence of women is intimately related to the assurances that military men also seem to need that neither are there men around who desire other men. Queer theorist Eve Kosofsky Sedgwick has explained that, ever since the nineteenth century, as men in patriarchal Western societies have consolidated their privilege, they have invariably found themselves maintaining "intense male bonds" that are not readily distinguishable from homosexual ones. Homosexual panic—the fearful, often violent way in which straight men sometimes respond to the chance of being taken for queer—is endemic in this patriarchal regime to the extent that the acceptable "homosocial" bonds ("male friendship, mentorship, admiring identification, bureaucratic subordination, and heterosexual rivalry") can be misconstrued as the dreaded feminizing homosexual relation. Above all, it is in the armed forces, where "men's manipulability and their potential for violence are at the highest possible premium," Sedgwick notes, that "the *pre*scription of the most intimate male bonding and the *pro*scription of . . . 'homosexuality' are both stronger than in civilian society—are, in fact, close to absolute." Kate Dyer sees part of this situation plainly: "The men who run the military . . . are going to keep gays out rather than ever be perceived of as a sexual object." The flip side of this situation also applies: some men would rather kill than be construed as homosexual *subjects*.

The lengths to which such men will go to annihilate whatever, or whoever, may imply that perhaps they are not straight became horrifyingly evident in late January 1993, when major newspapers across the country picked up the unfolding story of a murder in the Navy. In late October 1992, the Navy had reported the murder in the rest room of a public park in Sasebo, Japan, of twenty-two-year-old radioman Allen R. Schindler. The murder, it claimed, was the result of a "difference of opinion." Shortly after, a pair of gay American entertainers who had been working in that seaside town wrote a letter to the Navy newspaper *Pacific Stars and Stripes* in which they suggested that the Navy was covering up a lethal gay-bashing. Valan Cain, one of the entertainers, later told reporters of the relief that Schindler expressed at meeting him and his friends. "We were his outlet," said Cain. "He attached himself to us every moment he could. . . . He was so hungry to be around people who would understand him." During those late-night conversations, Schindler described life aboard the USS *Belleau Wood* as a living hell. The harassment had gotten so extreme that on September 24, six days before the amphibious assault ship was to arrive in Sasebo, he approached his commanding officer to confess his homosexuality, knowing full well that the result would be his discharge from the Navy. What Schindler did not know was that this information would soon leak out to other men on board, making life even harder for him than it already was. After the *Belleau Wood* docked in Sasebo, some straight sailors on the ship with whom Schindler had maintained cordial ties introduced him to Cain and his friends. Six days later, Schindler was found beaten beyond recognition on the floor of the blood-spattered rest room of a public park.

The house in Chicago Heights, Illinois, where Allen Schindler, a twenty-two-year-old sailor who was bludgeoned to death by his shipmates because they discovered that he was gay, was raised. Photo by Loren Santow/Impact Visuals.

There were conflicting stories about what had happened. Some reported that as many as five sailors took part in the beating. After Schindler's civilian friends blew the whistle on the Navy, throughout the investigation and trial, which extended from the end of January through May 1993, it became apparent that twenty-year-old Airman Apprentice Terry M. Helvey had conspired with at least one other sailor, Airman Apprentice Charles E. Vins, to pulverize Schindler. Helvey was the type of guy who shored up his fragile masculinity in steroid consumption and compulsive bodybuilding. This gave him the imposing physique and formidable strength with which he held Schindler in a side headlock while smashing his head and face with his fist. According to the autopsy report, Helvey also repeatedly rammed Schindler—headfirst—into the porcelain and steel urinals. This would explain how his skull got so completely crushed that he could only be recognized by the tattoos on his arms. The newspapers were less descriptive about explaining how all but two of Schindler's ribs were broken; or how his penis got lacerated. "I had hoped," said Schindler's mother, Dorothy Hajdys, "that when the body got home, I would be able to identify it, and hold it and kiss it good-bye. But I couldn't do that because there was this body . . . but it was so badly destroyed that there was no way of knowing it was my son." Predictably, after Helvey was charged with the murder, he tried to beat the rap with a "homosexual panic" alibi. Lying through his teeth, Helvey claimed that Schindler had approached Helvey from behind—pants open, penis exposed—as Helvey was pissing at a urinal and put a hand on his shoulder. It goes without saying among men like Helvey that had

Overleaf: These posters were created by the queer design firm Bureau and wheat-pasted throughout New York City while the Senate Armed Services hearings on the military ban were televised and the media frenzy over "gays in the military" escalated

TO DIE FOR

RADIOMAN **ALLEN** R. **SCHINDLER**

b. 1971 – 1992 †

THE BAN ON GAYS IN THE MILITARY IS PROFOUND DISCRIMINATION AND PERPETUATES VIOLENCE.

BUREAU DEPLORES ALL VIOLENCE AGAINST GAYS AND LESBIANS.

HELVEY STALKED SCHINDLER INTO A PUBLIC TOILET AND BEAT HIM [TO DEATH] BECAUSE HE WAS A HOMOSEXUAL

N.Y. TIMES 8.27.93

AIRMAN TERRY M. HELVEY
b. 1972

173

Dorothy Hajdys, Allen Schindler's mother, at the 1993 March on Washington for Lesbian, Gay, and Bi Equal Rights and Liberation. Photo by Donna Binder/ Impact Visuals.

Schindler in actuality been insane enough to come on to him, he deserved to die a thousand deaths. How is it that women who respond violently in self-defense to the unwanted advances of men are widely regarded with skepticism, when they are not dismissed as crazy (*Thelma and Louise*; Lorena Bobbitt . . .)? How is it that men who annihilate other men for allegedly coming on to them—or merely for existing in the same spaces as them—expect to be understood and excused for defending their masculinity? This disparity speaks volumes about the relative value ascribed to femininity and masculinity, to women and men, and to gays and straights, in American culture and society. Even after it was exposed that Helvey fabricated this story, he was quoted as saying that Schindler still got what he deserved. "I don't regret it. I'd do it again."

As this story played itself out in the press, the military managed handily to turn it to its advantage. In Senate hearings about the ban against homosexuals, Col. Fred Peck, a prominent Marine, offered dramatic, twisted testimony about his gay son that just about said it all. He would not want his beloved son to serve in the armed forces because his life would be in danger.

In this context, who can forget the shenanigans that Sam Nunn and six other senators staged for the media on May 11, 1993 (two weeks before Helvey was finally sentenced to life in prison), as they dramatized what they considered was at stake in the national debate over "gays in the military." There were the balding, bespectacled chairman of the Senate Armed Services Committee and his stalwart colleagues on national television, ducking among the berths and nosing around the lavatories of eight Norfolk-based Navy warships as they elicited sound bites from sailors who fretted on cue at the thought of sleeping or showering in close quarters with queers. Perhaps some of these guys were flashing back to the more lurid scenes of gay sexual self-display in *The Gay Agenda*, the homosexual-panic-inducing antigay propaganda video that religious right-wing organizations flooded the Pentagon and Congress with immediately after presidential candidate Bill Clinton proposed to lift the ban.

In the midst of the overheated national debate over the military's ban on homosexual service members, Senate Armed Services Committee Chairman Sam Nunn staged a photo opportunity in the berths and lavatories of Navy warships for a battery of newspaper and television cameramen. Still from Program Three, *Hollow Liberty*.

Above all, it was women who had reason to express dismay at all the obsessional talk about showers. Being on the receiving end of what Kate Dyer has called the "roving sexual eye" is hardly unfamiliar to women. The extent to which the national debate concerning the ban was dominated by the expression of exclusively male anxieties was infuriating to female servicemembers for two reasons. First, the majority of the discharges that have resulted from the military's ban have affected women, not men. Second, the Navy had responded with characteristic evasiveness to the charges brought by female servicemembers over sexual harassment at the Tailhook convention. They had charged their male colleagues—young "top guns" of the type that Helvey was supposed to become had he not first murdered Allen Schindler—with molesting them in the hallways of the Las Vegas Hilton hotel and charged commanding officers with turning a blind, not to say vicarious, eye at all this animal-house behavior. The Tailhook scandal together with the Schindler murder exposed the extent to which "troop cohesion and morale" is constructed on the basis of homosocial relations in which young men rival one another in ritual misogyny and homophobia. Few press commentators, and even fewer politicians, bothered to make the obvious connections.

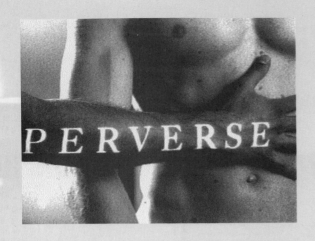

Many of the queers that I know wish that the entire matter of the military ban had never come up. "I never dreamt that my issue would be the military," quipped a lesbian friend of mine, her voice tinged with equal amounts of sarcasm and exasperation as the story played itself out in the media during the winter, through the spring, and into the early summer of 1993. It was not a fight that we had picked. However, we had little choice but to lend our support. Before and after the November election, the adversaries that lesbians and gay men share with Bill and Hillary Clinton worked overtime to embarrass him for making a pledge to the constituency that Republicans had bet their platform was the most unloved in the land. But queers who supported the issue, begrudgingly or not, once Clinton and his advisers had turned it into a federal case felt compelled to do so in large part because of the undeniable fact that lesbians and gay men in the military were (and, as of this writing, still are) being subjected to a kind of institutionally sanctioned abuse that had not been experienced since "sexual perverts" were purged from federal employment in 1950.

It would be hard to envision an issue that is less compatible with the liberationist legacy of the movement that emerged after Stonewall than fighting for the right to join the American armed forces. Robert Vázquez-Pacheco, a Washington-based AIDS educator, has explained his discomfort with the issue in relation to both hemispheric history and personal identity: "I'm Puerto Rican and consequently Latin American. The U.S. military has been riding rampant through Latin America for centuries. Why would I want part of my community to be in the military?" The anti-imperialist and nonviolent orientation of the lesbian and gay movement dates back to its roots in the Vietnam era, but that orientation did not end with the withdrawal of American troops from Southeast Asia in 1973. Gay men and lesbians participated in the nuclear freeze movement in the early eighties, as they did in the national mobilization to stop U.S. intervention in South and Central America in 1984. More recently, historian Barbara Epstein has noted, AIDS activists and queer nationalists were among the most prominent and colorful participants in the short-lived coalition that mounted large protests against the Gulf War in December of 1990 and January of 1991 before and immediately after George Bush sent American troops into combat with Iraq.

Kendall Thomas has addressed in somewhat less sectarian terms the sense of conflict and disillusionment that many of us felt about the campaign to lift the ban.

One of the most utopian and morally compelling aspects of the gay and lesbian movement is that we presented ourselves as an army—yes—but an army of lovers. And increasingly that sense of [the movement as representing] an alternative way of being human, an alternative way of relating to one another as individuals and as members of community, is being lost. I think it fair to say that the campaign to lift the military's ban against gay men and lesbians is an instance of that.

On a more practical level, many people felt that there were just too many other threats and challenges, and too many other demands on our limited resources, to allow this issue to assume the prominence that it did. At a time when most of the first wave of AIDS activists had either died or suffered from burnout, it was as necessary as ever to continue finding ways to keep the pressure on, to draw attention to the plague that most Americans regard as somebody else's problem. We still were being bashed—in fact, more than ever—were still being confronted by homophobic groups who remain intent on finding ways to censor our art and culture; were still having to respond whenever and wherever the religious right decided to open another front in its crusade against our rights. There was also an emotional cost involved in shifting the movement's priorities away from these issues to focus on lifting the military's ban. "As a person with AIDS," said Gregg Bordowitz, "I felt that the shift away from AIDS as the primary issue to a focus on the military was threatening. . . . Many of my peers in the AIDS activist movement felt and feared abandonment by the community. Not only had energy gone from the AIDS activist fight in order to fight the ban in the military, but also money. There was a real fear about resources."

Between the end of the Gulf War and the 1993 March on Washington, quite a few things had happened to determine that shift. Candidate Clinton first broached the subject of lifting the ban in September 1991, at Harvard University's John F. Kennedy School of Government. As president, he said, he would lift the ban because the United States could ill afford to waste the talents of any of its citizens. It took little time for the military and its many champions in Congress to respond, demonstrating how ineffectual such reasonable arguments are in eliminating homophobia from one of the central monuments of institutionalized heterosexism. Clinton and all of us would no doubt have been better off had he satisfied his ethical and political obligation to lesbian and gay voters by issuing an executive order to lift the ban, simply letting the congressional chips fall where they may. By the time of the inauguration, the president's inclination to overthink everything and to negotiate political principles until they disappear had led him to make a deal with the devil in Sam Nunn. This resulted in the "Don't ask, don't tell" policy, a federal statute that by now is widely regarded as representing no progress at all.

In his book *Conduct Unbecoming*, Randy Shilts observed that Bill Clinton's staff started to lose control of the military issue when his promise to overturn the ban prompted more than a few lesbian and gay servicemembers to come out publicly.

Hearings of the Senate Armed Services Committee on lifting the ban on lesbians and gay men in the military, held during the spring of 1993. Photo by Rick Reinhard/Impact Visuals. Inset stills from Program Three, *Hollow Liberty*.

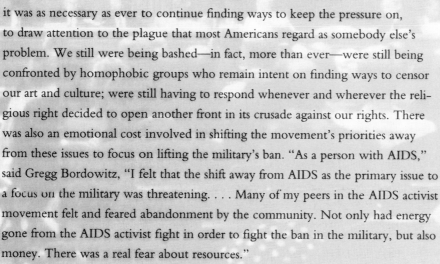

An antimilitarist contingent at the 1993 March on Washington reminded onlookers of the historic role of the United States military in undermining liberation movements in the third world, making their presence felt with such messages as "We Like Our Queers Out of Uniform." Photo by Ellen Shub/Impact Visuals.

Lesbian and gay veterans and servicemembers at the 1993 March on Washington. Photo by Cathy Cade.

Shilts reported that "with each passing month, more lesbian and gay soldiers began stepping forward; for much of 1991 and 1992 it seemed one could not turn on a morning talk show or evening network news broadcast without some new soldier declaring his or her sexual orientation." None of these soldiers had been caught in violation of the Uniform Code of Military Justice, which prohibits servicemembers from engaging in sex—gay or straight—while on military duty. They had merely acknowledged their "nonconforming sexual orientation" as had others before them, including Col. Margarethe Cammermeyer, Sgt. Miriam Ben-Shalom, and Staff Sgt. Perry Watkins. It was at this time that the American public first encountered PO Keith Meinhold, Lt. (j.g.) Tracy Thorne, and other telegenic young servicemen. It was also during this flood of televised forthrightness that legal challenges to the ban were set in motion that would result in rulings like those of federal judge Terry Hatter Jr., who insisted on more than one occasion that the Navy reinstate Keith Meinhold.

When Clinton made his deal with Sam Nunn and his congressional and military allies to wait until July 15 to study further the matter of lifting the ban, the president and his advisers feared with good reason that Congress would write its own version of the military's gay ban into federal law for the first time. Supporters of the ban had already dug in their heels, but promised to stage "free and open" hearings in the Senate that turned out to be neither. It was in this desperate context that David Mixner called for the formation of the Campaign for Military Service (CMS), which he placed under the direction of legal scholar and activist Thomas Stoddard, formerly the head of the Lambda Legal Defense and Education Fund. Mixner and Stoddard had little difficulty raising a great deal of money, which they used to pay largely heterosexual lobbyists

to set in motion a countercampaign to support lifting the ban. CMS stressed "civil liberties" in the abstract—a strategy that never fools homophobes and does little for the self-esteem of lesbians and gay men. The money also went to pay for CMS's centerpiece, the cross-country bus ride called the "Tour of Duty," in which patriotic gay and lesbian war vets could plead their case to middle Americans. The tour attracted pathetically little publicity as the media focused on the sometimes riveting testimony at congressional hearings on the ban, which started late in March and did not finish until May.

Americans got to witness more straight-acting gay men and lesbians than ever before in television history, but this proved powerless in undermining the viability of the homophobic stereotypes that informed the testimony of those who favored the ban. The campaign to lift the ban offered a classic example of what can happen when lesbian and gay people try to outsmart the homophobic mainstream by

PO Keith Meinhold was discharged from the Navy after coming out on national television in 1992. Although reinstated by court order, he was refused entry when he first attempted to return to Moffett Field Naval Air Station. AP/Wide World Photos.

insisting that there is no difference between us and them. Kendall Thomas commented on the harm we do to ourselves when we employ such arguments to gain acceptance to mainstream institutions that, in their present form, will not accommodate queers: "We saw in the media a group of people who were overwhelmingly white and male, and yet the reality is that the discriminatory policies of the military strike disproportionately women—especially women of color. The bottom line is that we lost. . . . For people in the halls of power, the effort to make ourselves look like them finally makes no difference."

Even though we may not *be* all that visibly different from other Americans, lesbians and gay men still *represent* difference in ways that are challenging—and still threatening—to the heterosexual majority. This is why it has remained largely impossible for us to gain access to the law, religion, marriage, family, the military—in fact to any of the institutions that have constructed and maintained American culture and society as heterosexist. Because America's defining institutions cannot accommodate us without themselves being fundamentally transformed, this presents lesbians and gay men with a moral challenge as we continue to debate the desired course of the movement for our civil rights. History has shown that homophobia and heterosexist privilege do not yield easily, when they yield at all, to our demands for first-class citizenship. Perhaps queers need to take the hint. The survival of this movement, and of its claim to moral authority, depends upon our making sure that as we chip away at these glacial structures, we figure out how to shape them (and our own institutions) in ways that more nearly reflect the needs of the many different kinds of people whose interests this movement claims to represent.

The question, then, has never really been "radical or assimilationist?" This way of thinking is fostered by institutions that limit people by defining them as either inside or outside of the social mainstream. When gay men and lesbians identify one another as either radical or assimilationist, we not only perpetuate this dehumanizing situation, we also obscure the radical prospects of alternative, truly queer, ways of being. Consider, for example, the millions of lesbian and gay parents who are raising children despite their disqualification from the legal protections and economic advantages that are reserved exclusively for married people. Queer parents are situated both inside *and* outside of the mainstream; at the center *and* on the periphery of society. Their situations prove that, contrary to conventional thinking, reproduction is not necessarily tied to sexual orientation. Yet reproduction is still widely presumed to be synonymous with heterosexuality—so much so that this myth functions as the linchpin in securing a host of legal and economic inequities. In this context, the lesbian and gay families who marched in Washington in 1993 must be seen as representatives of some of the most traditional *and* subversive (family) values in American life. Queers have always assimilated to something. The question is "Assimilate to what?" There is no fixed answer to that question, only fluid answers that overtake each other like waves; multiple answers, some of which apply to some people but not to others, to some situations but not others. Figuring out what kind of society we want to be a part of requires patience, an appreciation for process, respect for others, and a willingness to listen—not just when someone is speaking, but when they fall silent as well. Each of us has those silences, as parts of us that lie buried in distrust or disbelief or shame and want to be heard but cannot be as a result of having been cast off by a society that should feel more like home but too often still does not.

During a walk in the park in Alexandria,
Virginia, Darquita asks her mother
Denyata about a wildflower.
Photo by JEB (Joan E. Biren).

Kendall Thomas is professor of law at Columbia University in New York, where he teaches courses in constitutional law, communications law, legal philosophy, critical race theory, and law and sexuality. His writings have appeared in the Virginia, Columbia, and University of Southern California law reviews, as well as in *G.L.Q.: A Journal of Lesbian and Gay Studies,* and in *Assemblage: A Critical Journal of Architecture and Design Culture.* He is coeditor of *Critical Race Theory: A Reader,* forthcoming from the New Press.

The mood in the courtroom the day that the oral argument took place on the *Hardwick* case was very solemn. We felt that finally after several years we were going to have an opportunity to present our strongest arguments against the constitutionality of sodomy statutes. And we had one of the best lawyers in the United States, Lawrence Tribe, making those arguments for our side. . . . I think the mood became even more hopeful once we heard the ridiculous arguments that were being made for the State of Georgia. And we were even more encouraged when we heard Lawrence Tribe's arguments, which came again and again to a very simple and—for me—compelling point. Tribe said that a state has to be able to offer a reason for a law such as the Georgia sodomy statute. A law cannot be based simply on the fact that some people find conduct distasteful or that some people find conduct morally objectionable. Ours is a republic of reason. And I was heartened because it seemed to me that in the Supreme Court chambers that day we had reason to believe that the United States was still a republic of reason. . . . Once the oral arguments began and the questions were directed at Professor Tribe, I began to be a little less hopeful. In fact, I was a bit astonished by the obvious lack of engagement with the issues raised in *Hardwick* that was shown by a number of the justices. . . . I remember quite distinctly that Justice Powell asked a question about whether or not the right of privacy would extend to public toilets. The *Hardwick* case had nothing at all to do with public toilets. This man was arrested in the privacy of his bedroom while he was engaged in consensual sexual conduct with another man. The simple fact that a justice of the Supreme Court of the United States could ask that question meant that we were in trouble. It was clear that they

were in the grip of some very damaging misconceptions, myths, and prejudices about gay men and lesbians. . . .

If you read the opinion that Justice White wrote for the Court, there is an almost obsessive focus on this notion of "homosexual sodomy," and the return, again and again, to this notion seems to me the clearest indication that the courts were expressing not only their views about the constitutionality of Georgia's sodomy statute but their views about homosexuals. . . . By linking *homosexual* with *sodomy,* the Court was mesmerizing the reader into thinking that sodomy is conduct that is committed only by homosexuals, which we know is not the case. . . . Quite frankly, I don't think there's any way that a criminal law against private sexual conduct between consenting adults of the same sex can say anything but, "We consider people who engage in this conduct to be second-class citizens." If you look at the actual application of these statutes, you find a historical connection between the presence of criminal laws against homosexual sodomy and violence against gay men and lesbians, or people who are perceived to be gay and lesbian. I don't think there's any way to enforce these statutes without sending the message and actually acting in such a way as to make gay men and lesbians second-class citizens. . . .

All laws are based on morality, but in the United States—at least until the *Hardwick* decision—it has never been the case that a moral judgment by a majority of the people in a particular state could uphold the constitutionality of a law in and of itself. In a secular, liberal democracy—and that's what the United States is—the fact that a group of people find the sexual behavior of another group of people aesthetically distasteful or morally objectionable is not a legitimate basis on which to criminalize that behavior. The tragedy of the *Hardwick* decision is that it refused to recognize that in a liberal democracy we draw the line at the point where some people want to impose their private morality on another group of people by using our common secular criminal law. . . .

Hardwick is a deprivation of the civil rights of gay men and lesbians because it says that government can withdraw the guarantee . . . to protect each and every member of the body politic from invidious, irrational, prejudicial, biased, discriminatory state action. . . . The legacy of *Bowers* v. *Hardwick* is widespread disrespect for the law. Everyone knows that gay men and lesbians, as well as heterosexuals, will continue to engage in the sexual practices prohibited by the Georgia statute and others like it. The legacy of *Bowers* v. *Hardwick* is the death of the notion that the Supreme Court of the United States can be relied upon to protect a weak, powerless, disenfranchised minority from the prejudices and whims of powerful majorities. The legacy of *Bowers* v. *Hardwick* is that government can legitimize violence, discrimination, degradation on the part of one segment of the population toward another. Those are to my mind its shameful legacies.

One of the reasons I think so many gay men and lesbians were ambivalent about the campaign to lift the military ban was because this was the first time the gay and lesbian community had waged a national campaign to bring our issues before the American public. And in the face of all the other struggles that preceded the struggle over the military ban—HIV, AIDS, housing discrimination, employment discrimination, the disastrous results that gay fathers and lesbian mothers had experienced in custody and other parental-related cases—I felt and I know that many other people felt that we had chosen an issue which simply did not speak to the lived experiences of the overwhelming masses of gay men and lesbians in this country today. And for that reason I found it very difficult to bring myself to engage the issue with the energy and the moral anger that so many other of the issues that the community faces can command. . . . However, to say that the campaign to lift the ban was a reflection of assimilationist politics is too simple. In any nation, those citizens who can and are willing to serve and fight and die if necessary for their country ought to be allowed to do so. In many ways it's at the core of what it means to be a citizen. So whatever one thinks about war, about military forces, I think one can fairly say that the question of military service did not necessarily mean that we had abandoned the more militant liberationist agenda of the gay and lesbian movement. . . .

The obsession with showers in the debates over the lifting of the ban represented a real degradation in the public discourse, and a deflection away from what was really at stake. One has to remember that the biggest recent scandals involving sexuality in the armed services were not scandals in which the participants were gay men or lesbians, but heterosexual men. I'm thinking of course of

Tailhook, where at a military convention a number of female members of the armed services were sexually harassed by male members of the armed services. The military has always needed an ideological glue that would bind its mostly male members. And an aggressive macho heterosexuality has served that function. . . . I think that what people who opposed the lifting of the ban were really saying when they talked about the showers was that the recognition of the fact that there were gay men in particular in the military would be a recognition that there were other ways to be men, and other forms of male sexuality that were not necessarily aggressive, violent, and misogynist in the ways that we saw in the Tailhook episode. . . .

The tactics of the people who led the campaign to lift the military ban shows the limits of what have been called "the politics of respectability." We saw in the media a group of people who were overwhelmingly white and male, and yet the reality is that the discriminatory policies of the military strike disproportionately at women—especially women of color. The bottom line is that we lost, and I think the lesson we ought to take from that is that for people in the halls of power, the effort to make ourselves look like them finally makes no difference. We will be demonized all the same. Our great strength is to show to the American people the diversity of gay men and lesbians in this country; that we are literally everyone, and that we are quite literally everywhere; that we are black, that we are white, that we are Asian, that we are men, that we are women, that we are poor, that we are rich, that we are educated, that we are illiterate—that we represent the full spectrum of the American body politic itself.

PAULA ETTELBRICK

Attorney and activist Paula Ettelbrick was legal director for the Lambda Legal Defense and Education Fund between 1986 and 1993. Currently she is legal councel for the Empire State Pride Agenda, a New York State–based lesbian and gay political organization.

There is a tremendous need for affirmation of our relationships, a need to feel like part of a larger body. I loathe the legal aspect of marriage. I think it's fundamentally unjust that married people are able to get so many rights and privileges that families or couples or individuals who are not defined by marriage can't get. It's unjust. But it doesn't appeal to me to think that if only we could get married, we'd be on the inside and get these benefits. It demeans commitments outside of marriage. Marriage is not the only way to form a family, not the only form in which people's commitment to one another should be respected and recognized. . . . All families should be recognized in society. I want to live in a world in which I can choose not to marry and still be able to be respected and have my relationship viewed as a family relationship. I think it's outrageous that any benefit—social security benefits for instance—would be provided to the surviving spouse of somebody who was married for only a year. But if my lover and I are together for thirty years and I die first, she's not able to receive social security benefits. . . .

We've talked about registering as domestic partners. I have spent the better part of my legal career working to create the so-called right to domestic partnership in New York City, which I'm now having second thoughts about. I want our relationship to be respected even if we don't register. I think perhaps we've done a disservice in not thinking this new registration system through as a community. It is being used by people now to say that those lesbians who register with the City of New York are the good ones and those who don't are the bad ones. I also wonder if we haven't taken a path that leads to second-class marriage. It doesn't give you nearly what you would get if you were married. It says, "Okay, your family is legitimate in the City of New York, and others are not." . . .

The lesbian and gay community, so to speak, is not a monolith. Even if you were to distinguish between lesbians and gay men, there remain distinct differences within each category. But the world has responded to us as if somehow we have so much in common simply because I'm a woman in a relationship with another woman; or these men are in relationships with other men. Simply because we are women and men, we are so extraordinarily different from one another that it's amazing we can agree on anything. Certainly the issue of marriage is a prime example of how nonmonolithic our community is. So much about how you relate to the issue of marriage and family depends on your class, gender, and sense of privilege and status in the world.

ROBIN AND FRAN SHAHAR

As Robin and Fran Shahar approached the date they had set for their commitment ceremony, word of this event reached the office of Michael Bowers, attorney general for the State of Georgia. As a law student, Robin had interned for Bowers, who then offered her full employment to begin in 1991. Upon learning of her plans to marry Fran, Bowers revoked this offer. Shahar sued Bowers, and while the district court found that the Shahars' relationship was protected under the Constitution's freedom of intimate association, it ruled in Bowers's favor in 1993. On December 1, 1994, the Eleventh Circuit Court of Appeals in Atlanta heard oral arguments in Robin's appeal of this decision. Fran Shahar is a Ph.D. candidate in psychology who does freelance work in Atlanta. Robin is employed as an attorney by the City of Atlanta's Department of Law where she often works on employment discrimination cases. They have been together for eight years.

FRAN: Lesbians make jokes all the time about being married on the second date. There was that initial coming together and taking ourselves seriously as a couple, but within a year we bought this house together, which was the first step towards a lifetime commitment. Within two or three years we were seriously thinking instead of joking about it. What does it mean to choose somebody and say to the world, "This is it, this is who I consciously choose?"
ROBIN: We knew we wanted to make that commitment within a Jewish context—in front of our families and friends, in a ceremony that was consistent with Jewish tradition. We spoke with Sharon Kleinbaum who was a visiting rabbi at our synagogue and whom we were both very fond of. She agreed to perform the ceremony for us. . . . To stand up in front of this group of people and have the ceremony to make this commitment to each other felt like a very positive shift in our relationship. One process that was very good for us was that we had to write what is called a ketubah, which is a

Jewish wedding contract. There are standard ketubot that Jews use, and they have a lot of language that didn't feel right for us, so we wrote our own, really having to decide what this commitment to each other meant, going through the process and choosing phrases that symbolized what the commitment meant for us.
FRAN: The custom in Judaism is that the ketubah becomes a visible part of your daily existence, a reminder of your highest aspirations as a couple. Having said that, now I don't remember very clearly . . .
ROBIN: I know—we've got to treat each other's families as our own.
FRAN: And we must listen with an open heart and strive to live consciously with each other.
ROBIN: And take each other's needs seriously.
FRAN: Together we work to create a more just and loving world.
ROBIN: And a Jewish home.
FRAN: Right. Create a Jewish home together. I grew up in the Jewish Youth Movement, you know, Camp Ramah and United Synagogue Youth and

Massada, and other Jewish youth groups. There were weekend shabbatot where you go and spend a whole weekend together really getting immersed in the theme of the weekend. There wasn't that seam between the Jewish and non-Jewish aspects of one's experience. The whole weekend was an experience of living Jewishly, from the time you wake up to the time you go to sleep. Our ceremony weekend was not quite like that. It integrated the secular and nonsecular, but it was based on the same kind of idea: that we could create a whole weekend of sacred time together. We consciously planned to pull community together from the very diverse parts of our lives: new friends, old friends, Atlanta friends, New York friends, friends from Israel, friends from Boston, friends from our generation, and friends from my parents' generation and that of Robin's grandmother.

ROBIN: Between my second and third years of law school I worked for Michael Bowers in a summer program. He has ten clerks come and work for him, and I was one of the ten. I wanted to work for him because I was interested in doing public interest law, and a lot of the cases that he handles are very interesting. I was specifically interested in criminal law and was working in the criminal division while I was there, getting a lot of the experience that I had wanted to get during that summer and also when I finished with law school.

FRAN: Initially I was opposed to Robin's working for Mr. Bowers. I remembered very distinctly when the *Bowers v. Hardwick* decision came down. I was living in New York at the time and I remember feeling personally victimized by the decision, and I was pretty horrified that Robin would want to work for him on that ground alone. Also I'm personally opposed to capital punishment, and that's part of

what they do in the criminal division. But Robin had this idea that she wanted to be a prosecutor, that she wanted to get good training, that it would be okay and that she could do it in such a way that it did not feel like a compromise of her integrity.

ROBIN: I'm embarrassed to say I really have no memories of the *Hardwick* decision when it came out. I probably knew of it but I was not out as a lesbian, either to myself or to anyone else, and so it didn't have an impact on me. That doesn't mean that as a lesbian working for Mr. Bowers I wasn't aware of the case. I was very well aware of the case at that point and had real trouble with the fact that Mr. Bowers had prosecuted it, but there were ways in which I was naive. One permitted me to say to myself that just because Mr. Bowers prosecuted that case doesn't mean that he went looking for it. If a case like that comes through his office, he handles it. Second, I didn't believe that Mr. Bowers would discriminate against me for being a lesbian. . . . I was one of the top candidates coming out of Emory Law School, and Mr. Bowers had spoken a lot during the summer that I worked there about how he doesn't discriminate and really values people for the quality of work that they do, and I believed him. When I found out that he was firing me because of our commitment ceremony, it really was a complete shock. . . . During the summer of working for his office, one thing that was important to me was to know whether or not I was going to feel comfortable working there full-time. One time there was going to be a party for the Criminal Division and I went into my supervisor's office, who I felt pretty comfortable with, and decided that I wanted to come out to her, to let her know about Fran, that we'd been together for about four years and probably were intending to spend our lives together. I told her that for me to feel comfortable working there, I would need to feel comfortable bringing Fran to parties and not being closeted about my relationship. I told her that I would like to bring Fran to this particular party and basically just wanted to get her feedback on that. She reminded me that, to begin with, this was the office that had prosecuted *Bowers v. Hardwick,* but then went on to say that some people would have problems with it and some people wouldn't, and then told me that I shouldn't bring Fran to this particular party because I was just getting to know people. So I didn't bring Fran, and maybe I should have taken that as an indicator that it wouldn't be okay to bring Fran in the future either. . . . In about November of that year Mr. Bowers sent me a form to fill out and send back to him. He'd already offered me a full-time job, which I had accepted. It was standard paperwork that would be stuffed in my personnel file asking things like your résumé, your family status, what your marital status is, and what the name of your spouse is. It also asked if you had any relatives who were employed by the State of Georgia, which is important since this could result in conflicts of interest. I really thought about those questions for a long time. What should I write on this form? And to me the honest answer was that Fran was going to be my spouse and I felt that I would be working at this job with the understanding that I was going to be honest about who I am. I didn't want to lie, so I wrote "engaged" under marital status and filled in Fran's name where you identify your spouse. I also put her name down as a relative who is working for the State of Georgia, because she was. The final part in Mr. Bowers's discovery of our ceremony was a call that I made in May or June of 1991, a few months before I was to start working in his office.

By then I had expected to hear from them about what division I was going to work in and what date they wanted me to start. As part of our making a lifetime commitment to each other, Fran and I decided that we wanted to change our last names to a common last name. The name that we chose was Shahar, which is a biblical Hebrew word which means any act of seeking God, and our primary reason for wanting the same last name was to help identify us in a more conventional way as a family unit. Now, one little problem with changing my name was that I had to contact Mr. Bowers's office and tell them. When I had worked for them during the summer, I had a contact person who I liked a lot and would have felt very comfortable calling and talking to about Fran and I having this ceremony and my changing our names. But I had a new contact person, and I didn't know him and I didn't feel comfortable coming out to him. So what I decided to do was to call over there and let him know that I was getting married, was changing my last name, and at the same time ask him in what division I'd be working and when I would start; just tie it all in together as one little neat package and get through the conversation. For most people, if you tell them you're getting married, they say congratulations, and then you go on from there. It's not a big deal. So I called. I had this conversation and I think that what happened was that my contact person got very excited. Oh, Robin's getting married! Robin's getting married! And what happened after that, I can only guess. I've been told bits and pieces of it, but of course I wasn't there to witness it. My understanding is that he very excitedly told a number of people that I was getting married, and I don't know if he had thought I was a lesbian and now thought I had reformed or what, but at some point someone in the office told him I was not marrying a man; I was marrying a women. Okay, so then the contact person brings this information to the attention of the other higher staff people and ultimately to Michael Bowers, and the decision was made to fire me. I found out that I was being fired from two senior attorneys in Mr. Bowers's office. They called me into the office and, when I got there, handed me this letter, which is written by Michael Bowers. Bowers would not meet with me personally. The date of this letter is July 9, 1991, and what it says is: "I regret to inform you that I must withdraw the State Law Department's offer of employment, which was made to you in the fall of 1990, which was to commence on September 23, 1991, to serve at my pleasure. This action has become necessary in light of information which has only recently come to my attention relating to a purported marriage between you and another woman. As the chief legal officer of this state, inaction on my part would constitute tacit approval of this purported marriage and jeopardize the proper functioning of this office. Sincerely, Michael J. Bowers, Attorney General." When I received the letter, I think I was probably in a state of shock. I had gone into these other attorneys' office, not knowing why they were calling me in, and certainly not expecting to lose my job, so it was pretty traumatic for me. I didn't think that I could be susceptible to such blatant discrimination or even to discrimination at all. I can't recall ever having experienced that in my life, and here I was graduating at the top of my class. I felt very qualified. I couldn't believe that Mr. Bowers would fire me over something as harmless as a commitment ceremony with the woman I love. I was also worried about what this would do for my career. I was just starting out as a lawyer in Atlanta, and this was really a bad way to begin. I was disap-

pointed. I had been looking forward to working for him in his office and felt I had been wronged. When I considered how to respond, as afraid as we were about the possible ramifications of filing a lawsuit, I felt I would always be very bitter if I didn't take some action to let him know that this was not okay, that we weren't just going to sit back and let it happen.

FRAN: I was working as a psychology intern at a penitentiary at the time that this letter was delivered to Robin. Just to contrast my experience to Robin's, everybody from my department was invited to our ceremony. I was completely out, and there was no problem with it. I was much freer in the prison system than Robin was in the law, which seems kind of ironic. I was standing in the psych department in the federal penitentiary when Robin called, and I was shocked. It felt like somebody kicking your teeth in. Robin and I can be pretty headstrong and we kind of decided that we were just not going to let her being fired get in our way, not in the way of the ceremony which we had worked too long and too hard on. It never occurred to us to cancel it.

ROBIN: Being in Georgia was a factor in deciding whether or not to file a lawsuit. We were pretty scared about being in a state where the Klan meets regularly and where there are a lot of white supremacist groups. I had spoken with a plaintiff who had gone through a lesbian custody case and talked to her about her experience, and she did get harassment every time she was in the media. She would get harassing phone calls and I thank God she was never hurt, but it's a risk. It felt very scary to put ourselves out there as a lesbian couple. . . .

There are three major grounds on which we're suing. The first one is freedom of religion. The second is freedom of association, and the third is equal protection. We did feel that we were facing risks in filing this lawsuit. For one thing my face was in the media and for a while I was being recognized on the street. People would come up to me and I wouldn't know ahead of time if they were friendly or not, so we were aware of the risk that someone could attack me. Fran's face was not in the media, but she was working at the prison at the time, and if the inmates or guards had found out about her involvement in this lawsuit, we were afraid that she might be harassed or even attacked at prison. A number of white supremacists are incarcerated there. We were concerned about our house and our dogs and physical violence. And as a new lawyer who was suing Michael Bowers, I wondered, Would I be blacklisted?

FRAN: One of Bowers's arguments against Robin is that our ceremony was not really a Jewish ceremony and therefore was not really religious. There is debate within the Jewish community about whether or not to recognize Jewish marriages for same-sex couples. There's debate within the Jewish community about everything. Jews disagree about many things, and unlike some other religions they don't have a final arbiter who decides that this is Jewish and everything else isn't. We both believe that Bowers has crossed the line of church and state. It is not his business to be the final say of what Jews should and should not do. We don't need Michael Bowers to be our pope.

ROBIN: What Fran and I had was clearly a religious ceremony. In fact, it was a whole weekend of Jewish religious tradition and ritual, and for Mr. Bowers to penalize me for having that infringes upon my right to practice religion. The Reform movement and Reconstructionist Jewish movements recognize these ceremonies and perform them. It is not the state's place to step in and decide for the Jewish religion which ceremonies should be recognized and which should not.

I believe that there is a similarity between the military's policy of "Don't ask, don't tell" and what Mr. Bowers wanted from me as an employee in his office. While he never stated that any gay and lesbian employees of his should not tell anyone about their sexual orientation, in retrospect it seems to me that if I had been willing to remain completely silent so that he never would have found out that I was a lesbian, then I could have worked for him in his office. . . . The Georgia sodomy law does not make me feel like a second-class citizen because it is supposed to apply to heterosexuals as well as homosexuals. What does make me feel like a second-class citizen is that sodomy is never talked about in terms of heterosexuals.

FRAN: What sometimes makes me feel disenfranchised is living in a country where there are two concurrent problems. One is the homophobic bigotry and bashing of gay people, which endangers our lives in a very direct way. But on the more subtle level there's heterosexism, which is the assumption that we all grow up the same, that we're straight, that we have one predictable pattern of life, and that if you don't happen to fit that pattern, then you are invisible and your life and your relationships and your family are not recognized. That's what makes me feel like a second-class citizen. It's not Georgia. It's homophobia and heterosexism.

A lot of men in the Navy and the Marines openly state that they don't think that women have a place on ships and in Marine squadrons, that they're disruptive. That's the context for the sexual harassment that affects lesbians and straight women alike. If you don't date, you're a lesbian. If you date a lot, then you're loose and disruptive. I've seen it happen over and over and over again to lesbians and straight women, both being characterized as who they aren't. . . . In 1987 and 1988, at that Parris Island Marine Corps Recruit Training Depot in South Carolina, Naval Investigative Services [NIS] conducted a vicious search of any woman who could be conceived of as a lesbian or might know one. The NIS put a woman they thought might be a lesbian into a room with her estranged, violent ex-husband and watched through a two-way mirror as he harangued her and said that if she didn't admit she was a lesbian, he would take their child away. The NIS investigators watched until she was ready to break. The NIS told a woman who would not say she was a lesbian that they would go to her mother's hospital bed, where she was dying with cancer, and expose her daughter as a lesbian unless she confessed. Another of their ridiculous tricks was to prepare a statement in which a servicemember allegedly confesses to being gay or lesbian. They give it to that person and say, "We want you to sign this statement," and in it there will be many really obvious typos in which their name is spelled wrong, or the *h* and the *e* are transposed in the word *the*. Every time the servicemember would come up against one of these typos the investigator would say, "Oh, I'm sorry. Will you correct that please." The person corrects it and the investigator says, "Okay, will you initial that correction." They get seven or eight of these initialed corrections, and then the person being questioned gets

to the last sentence, which says, "I am a lesbian." They object that they never made such a statement, that it isn't true, and the investigator will say, "Oh, we're sorry. We thought you did, but you don't have to sign it because obviously it isn't true." But later they'll use the document as evidence against you, saying, "Look, she initialed it seven times." . . .

It took us nine months in Congressman Studds's office to get the Defense Personnel Security Research and Educational Center [PERSEREC] report ["Nonconforming Sexual Orientations and Military Suitability"] of December 1988. This was a rather significant Pentagon report done by the Defense Research Institute out in Monterey, California. Very simply and straightforwardly, it concluded that homosexuality relates to job performance as left- or right-handedness does, period. One sentence from the report best sums up its conclusion. It says that sexual orientation has no relevance to one's ability to perform a job. The Pentagon suppressed this report. For months, I called different

Between 1987 and 1991, Kate Dyer worked on lesbian and gay issues nationally as executive assistant to Massachusetts congressman Gerry E. Studds (Democrat, 10th Congressional District). Today she is a San Francisco–based attorney in private practice who remains involved in the fight to secure the rights of lesbian and gay servicemembers.

branches of the services, trying to get them to give us a copy of the report. They denied it existed. Sometimes they said it existed but was only in draft form. People denied ever having heard of it and the next day would say they couldn't give it to us because it was "top secret." We got the runaround for nine months. We had also been pursuing unofficial leads to get it. Finally, in October of 1989, we received a copy in a manila envelope from an anonymous source. As expected, it was a very positive report for gay people, which is precisely why the Pentagon suppressed it. There were also internal memoranda from different people within the researchers' community and within the Pentagon which were really shocking—actually more interesting to us at that time than even the study's findings. . . . The memoranda exposed how the Pentagon told researchers to change the report's conclusions and showed how the researchers responded that with scientific research one doesn't know the results of an investigation before you get there, and that that's really the end. The Pentagon people then state that this report is a failure. We're not going to use it. We're not going to release it until you change it. Every single study that has been conducted by the Pentagon itself or by an investigative arm of Congress since 1957 has concluded that there is absolutely no basis for the ban on gays and lesbians, and that, in fact, it is incredibly wasteful.

I think the gay community's relative indifference to this issue is complex. Many liberal, or left of liberal, gay activists are very wary of the military, very antiinterventionist, and angry with the military industrial complex. So when someone asks them to support the idea of a military career for gays and lesbians, or asks them to march behind the American flag to extol the virtues of a gay war hero, they're

very uncomfortable. They don't necessarily consider people that fight in wars to be heroes. There's a conflict. They find it very difficult to support the military in any way, but they want gay civil rights. . . .

I think the military has been very attractive to gays and lesbians for a number of reasons. Historically, gay people isolated in small towns across America have a real need to get out of those towns—particularly if they have hostile family situations. I've talked to a lot of service members from the Midwest who knew no other gay people, and they needed a way out. Their families didn't have money, and college was not an option. The first bus up the dusty road is going to the military recruiter in the big city. This is a valid way for many people to get out of unhealthy, potentially violent situations, to get on with their lives and to meet other gay and lesbian people . . . . I've talked to people in the enlisted ranks who chose the military as a way to explore their sexual orientation. They knew there would be other gays and lesbians in the military. They would arrive at basic training, find they're not alone, talk about it, and experience a kind of coming-out process in the military. Others don't know that they're gay when they enlist at seventeen, but they know they need to leave home to broaden their horizons, learn a career, and become independent human beings. Then they figure out that it's because they're gay, and that this was part of why they needed to leave. There are many reasons people enlist—economics being an important one. . . . Many people in the officers' ranks did the same thing through ROTC. . . .

But equally important—and just as valid—there are hundreds and thousands of gays and lesbians who want to make the military their career. I think activists believe that they reflect the community in general and that everyone is as antimilitary as they are. Gay people come in every shape, size, color, and political persuasion. . . . This issue has really radicalized the gay right. There is a gay right. It's blind to say there isn't. It's just as blind to say that all of the career military gay people are right-wing. . . . There are a lot of wonderful gay people I've met who absolutely adore the military service. They want to spend their lives in it and are very, very good at it. I stand right behind them and will fight for their right to do what they want to do, because that's what freedom is. Another question to ask is, "Why do gay people do so well in the military?" It denies you a personal life. It's a pretty devastating way to live, but the people who choose to live it are so committed to their military service that they're willing to put up with that. It means they really want to be there and will therefore do a good job. The other reason they do a good job is they don't want to show any sign of weakness or draw any negative attention to themselves. They want to be the "4.0" sailor, soldier, Marine, or airman. They want to be the perfect member of that military service, and so many of them really are. The best and the brightest of both genders and races that are being kicked out from the ranks of all the services.

The relevance of the Tailhook scandal to the issue of gay men and lesbians in the military is that all we have ever said is there's no place for sexual harassment or sexual misconduct within the U.S. military. We think there should be a parity of enforcement and treatment, regardless of sexual orientation. When they say, "We can't have gays in the military because a gay soldier might look at a straight soldier and make him feel uncomfortable in the shower," we say, fine. If someone commits a violation, then get him. We don't care. We don't want special treatment for gays. But you better do the same thing to straight guys who day in and day out are doing likewise to the women in the services. I cannot walk down the hall in my office without guys commenting on my figure, did I get a new uniform, that kind of stuff, and I hate it. Now the men who run the military are scared that the same sort of roving sexual eye is going to be directed at them, and they can't stand it. They're going to keep gays out of the military rather than ever be perceived of as a sexual object. It's absolutely analogous. When it's men that might be looked at by others and don't want to be, it's a national catastrophe. Only then do we have Senate hearings. Only then do we send senators going down into the submarines to say, "Aren't you uncomfortable with a man who might be gay looking at you?" For women in the military, it seems our entire life consists of having men whom we're not attracted to looking at us. It's the heterosexual men who are doing the harassing.

28% of GAY YOUTH DROP OUT OF SCHOOL. MAKE SCHOOL SAFE FOR EVERYONE!

PASS THE GAY & LESBIAN STUDENT RIGHTS BILL NOW

Another year of sick violence unless House Bill 3353 Pa

Support House Bill "3353" It's time

GAY YOUTH

- 28% drop out of school
due to harassment

- 500,000 attempt suicide
each year. ⅓ are gay and lesbian
youth.

- 27% are forced to leave
home due to conflicts over
their sexual orientation.

MAKING HISTORY

Making History

by Dale Peck

Definitions: Ignorance, Nostalgia, and the Numbers Game

Queers are coming out younger than they ever have before. This is largely because budding queers are aware of the existence of other homosexuals and of a homosexual community even before they're aware of their own homosexuality. At some point, almost all queer youths still ask themselves the age-old question, "Am I the only one?" but for many this question is now beside the point, and for those who still ask it, the focus is often existential rather than empirical. The age-old question has an age-old answer, "You are not alone," and proof of this is now ample. Whether it be gay pride parades, Lesbian Avengers demonstrations, characters on *Real World, Melrose Place,* or *thirtysomething,* church sermons, sex education classes, or national media coverage of queer issues, homosexuality has entered the daily conversation of American life. Even when this discourse casts homosexuality in a negative light, it nevertheless underscores the fundamental message that homosexuality, homosexuals, and a homosexual community exist. With all this evidence, the more pressing concern for queer youth is how these other homosexuals can be contacted. In fact, establishing relationships—healthy, productive relationships, both sexual and nonsexual—is the key component to the mental and emotional stability of queers during their adolescence. It determines how many of them choose to come out of the closet, how many choose to stay out, how many attempt suicide, and, for those who overcome all these obstacles, how successfully homosexuality is integrated into the other aspects of their personality.

To say that making contact isn't always easy would be a criminal understatement. Widespread knowledge of the existence of a homosexual community hasn't made it easier for young queers to get to it. In fact, upon coming out, rather than finding themselves absorbed into or helped by or even welcomed by the queer community, most queer youth find themselves more isolated and more vulnerable than before they exposed themselves. In a few uplifting instances young queers are able to create communities or forums of their own. Youth discussion groups are not uncommon in major urban areas, and in some cases these groups act as more than just a forum to discuss issues such as coming out, their nascent sexuality, or the increasing level of violence against queers, especially in schools and homes. One example of further activity occurred in Boston, where a group of queer teenagers were instrumental in successfully lobbying for passage of a bill that makes discrimination on the basis of sexual orientation illegal in public schools in Massachusetts. On-line computer networks have made it possible for tens of thousands of queer youth to establish interstate electronic communities with their peers, and the circulation of thousands of 'zines serves as still another communal forum between 'zine makers and their readers. In a few cities, institutions such as the EAGLES Center in Los Angeles and the Harvey Milk School in New York serve as alternative high schools for queer youth, educational facilities free from the threat of violence or discrimination. The value of these various forms of

Overleaf: A coalition of students such as these was instrumental in lobbying for the passage of House Bill 3353. Photo by Marilyn Humphries.

community is immeasurable to the youth who have access to their services, but focusing too much attention on them distracts from the actual situation, which is this: most young queers are separated from any form of queer community. The obstacles barring their path are the generally negative forces of almost every societal institution with which they have contact, including their families, their peer groups, their schools, their churches, the medical and especially the psychological world, and the government. The organized political backlash that adult queers face in the form of antihomosexual candidates and ballot initiatives, as well as escalating antiqueer violence, is maintained by millions of conservative homophobes who have access to and control over queer youth without resorting to public forums because—literally and metaphorically—queer youth are their children, not ours.

All of this seemed to me self-evident before I began this, and as I conclude, it still seems so. What I was surprised to learn was that the most significant obstacle maintaining the separation of young queers from the homosexual community are adult queers themselves, and the political movement they have created. As a community, we are at a very specific stage in our development: we have made this country into a place that is arguably safer for adult homo-sexuals than it ever has been before,[1] but in doing so we have made it more dangerous for those persons who either are, or say they are, or are perceived to be homo-sexual and who are not adults. The one characteristic that accompanies all the freedoms we have gained is visibility, and this visibility has parents in general and the leaders of straight society in particular scared silly. As a result, the freedoms that many queer adults now take for granted are violently denied to queer youth. If it seems that I spend too much time in the remainder of this essay focusing on adult rather than young queers, it's because it's clear—not crystal clear, but shatteringly clear—that we can no longer assess the needs of queer youth without also assessing our ability to meet those needs. Some things are possible, some not, and within the framework that now confines us not much more *is* possible. It seems to me telling that the majority of queers who survive adolescent suicide attempts report that they first tried to kill themselves after they came out, and the unavoidable conclusion is not just that the adult queer community must change and provide more far-reaching services to young queers, but that change must also be effected within heterosexual society, within whose boundaries most young queers live and where they are virtually, and in some cases literally,

In 1994, the photography program at the Hetrick-Martin Institute organized an exhibition called "This Is Not the Closet," which included this photograph by Joseph Kassabian.

confined. The queer community's strategy—not fully articulated, nor even acknowledged, but implicit in virtually everything we do—has long been the futile one of trying to take queer children away from their straight parents by pretending that they can be our own, and in so doing we have created a conflict between young and adult queers of a frighteningly Oedipal nature. A large part of our effort toward this surrogate parentage is based on presenting ourselves and our sexuality as a nonthreatening alternative to heterosexuality; we do this by emphasizing the supposed similarities homosexuals share with heterosexuals, or by actually mimicking straight customs. But heterosexuality, in its own weird way, is built around the idea of difference, of exclusivity, just as much as homosexuality is. Heterosexuals do not simply consider themselves heterosexual, they consider themselves "normal," and in order for them to maintain this fiction they must have an "abnormal" to which they can point and claim, "This is not me." Queer efforts to prove that the only difference between hetero- and homosexuality is the sex of one's bedmate are, on a fundamental psychological and sociological level, completely beside the point, for this single difference is all heterosexuals need to maintain their view of themselves as superior and queers as inferior and unfit to associate with children. That such a hierarchy is morally arbitrary is, for heterosexuals, merely beside the point, and, for homosexuals, overlooked in our quest to eradicate the differences between us and them. But our strategy has failed, and we must now realize that making ourselves like them hasn't made them more accepting of us—nor, more importantly, has it made them more likely to accept their children's homosexuality.

We can no longer make ourselves like them. We must make them like us.

Now, some questions:

When are we queer? Are we born this way or do we, voluntarily or involuntarily, become this way? Is it before or after our first homosexual experience; is it before or after our first homosexual fantasy; is it before or after we are ourselves aware of our homosexuality? Is it dependent upon coming out to ourselves? To others? How do we classify persons who have homosexual experiences and later decide they're straight? What about persons who call themselves queer but never engage in homosexual acts, or even homosocial contact? What about "queer-identified" straight people? Is homosexuality a static, monolithic phenomenon, or does it change from person to person; is there, in other words, just one homosexuality with insignificantly differentiated variations, or are there in fact many homosexualities? Could it be, as some theorists still persist in arguing, that there is neither homosexuality nor homosexualities, but merely homosexual acts? And if this is even partly true, then how can we consider ourselves members of a community, and how, more importantly, can we serve that community's needs?

For a long time I've found these and questions like these to be, in general, tiresome, and, at best, beside the point. In the United States today nearly half of all

AIDS cases still affect gay men; between 20 percent and 25 percent of all PWAs are in their twenties and probably became infected in their teens, and the rate of HIV infection among adolescents is doubling every year. According to both the Department of Justice and queer antiviolence organizations, queers are the most frequent victims of bias-related violence: virtually all of us have experienced some form of harassment, nearly half of us have been threatened, and a quarter of us have actually been attacked; in half of these cases, the attackers have been men under the age of twenty-one, and, in high schools, one-fifth of all lesbians and nearly half of all gay men are physically or verbally assaulted. At a time when one in four young queers is forced to leave home because of his or her sexual orientation, suicide remains the leading cause of death among queer youth: they are two to three times more likely to attempt suicide than their straight peers, and they account for 30 percent of all completed suicides among adolescents. These statistics seem to me neither enlightening nor sobering; they are merely tabulated confirmation of what many of us already knew. They are frightening, they are enraging, and ultimately they demand only one question: what are we going to do?

Washington, D.C. July 1994

Midway through the second decade of the AIDS crisis, religious conservatives renewed their efforts to restrict accurate sex education in favor of fear-based, "abstinence-only" programs. In July 1994, the "*True Love Waits*" campaign organized thousands of teenagers to bring pledge cards bearing a vow of sexual abstinence to the nation's capital.

But who are "we"? Who are "they"? Who are these children and adolescents being beaten, infected, rejected, and killing themselves? When approaching a topic as complex as queer youth, rather than being beside the point these questions become precisely *the* point. Who are they? Perhaps it's easier to say who they're not. In postulating the existence of a group of people called "gay and lesbian youth" or "gay, lesbian, bisexual, and transgendered youth" or "LesBiGay youth" or, as I've chosen to call it, "queer youth," one also postulates the existence of its necessary correlate, "queer adults," a group about which we know, perhaps, just slightly more. This is the group of people I invoke when I write "I" or "we" or "us." More of "us" have named ourselves, more of "us" act on our particular perception of our homosexual inclinations, and, most importantly, far more of "us" have formed or joined or have access to political and social organizations in which we can collectively express our opinions about ourselves. More of "us" write books, paint pictures, produce plays, make movies, and more of "us" read those books, look at those pictures, go to those plays, and watch those movies than do queer youth. "We" possess, then, a measurable degree of economic and social mobility, a freedom to exchange ideas and to communicate with each other and with the even more nebulous group called "straight" or "mainstream" or "normal" society. But even as I list these characteristics, I'm aware of their inadequacy in describing who we, the adult queer community, really are. In the first place, the traits I've mentioned deal with our status not as queers but as adults; in order to deal with our queerness fairly, or at any rate accurately, I would need to compile

Are Your Friends Playing Safe?

Safer Sex. Talk About It.

an impossible list of each and every queer and each and every person who has ever had a homosexual thought or experience, and describe all of those thoughts and experiences. But, failing that, all I can safely write is that "we" are people who have identified ourselves; what we have identified ourselves as, in whole or in part, is homosexual, and to claim that all this means is that a homosexual is a person who is sexually attracted to people of his or her own sex is tantamount to saying that one can walk into Ben and Jerry's and order an ice cream. That the situation is infinitely more complex than mere same-sex attraction is so obvious that it is often overlooked, and because of this oversight we often use the words *homosexual* or *queer* in the blind faith that our individual meanings will have enough overlap or correspondences to make communication possible. Despite various efforts at legal, medical, political, religious, or social codification, homosexuality remains, in the end, our shared illusion. It's not my intention to be reductive. I understand that the nonqueer or not specifically queer forces that have put forth various definitions of homosexuality are formidable; contemporary queers are the inheritors and interpreters of a tempestuous discourse about themselves that is thousands of years old, and because this discourse is if anything more contested—because more important—than ever, I feel its subject must be labeled a shared illusion.

But the group we are actually trying to discuss possesses few if any of the traits we do—indeed, they're defined by this lack. Our shared illusion is barely a mist-shrouded shadow to them. Queer youth have little or no economic or social mobility; they have a difficult time exchanging ideas or communicating within or outside of their group; and most importantly they often have not or cannot or will not identify themselves. That same-sex attraction exists among children and adolescents isn't in question, nor do I mean to deny the existence of thousands of out young queers. But to suggest that the form and meaning that homosexuality has for young people is fixed, or is the same as it is for adults, would be denying the nature of growing up: children and adolescents are discovering and forming their identities and their places in the world, and for adolescents that process is acutely focused on sexuality. How many of you reading this can say that you have only ever identified with the single category homosexual—or bisexual, or heterosexual—and how many of you first began to move through these categories during your adolescence? Further, the relationship between the fluid expressions of homosexuality that occur in adolescents unconnected with the queer community, and the more fixed nature of homosexuality found in adult community members, is not just coincidental: an inevitable consequence of admission into the adult homosexual community is a reification of one's sexuality.

The importance of recognizing the amorphous nature of adolescent sexuality is revealed when one attempts a statistical analysis. The answer to the question "How many queer youth are there?" is not, as the common estimate puts it, 7.2 million,

Facing page: Contrary to popular hopes, younger lesbians and gay men have not uniformly adopted the safer sex practices that public health professionals and activists have advocated. "Are your friends playing safe?" is one example of the kind of messages that AIDS service organizations are tailoring to reach gay and lesbian youth. Poster courtesy of the Gay Asian Pacific Alliance Community HIV Project.

but rather a figure two to three times higher. To understand this figure one should examine how statistics about the gay and lesbian population are gathered. In their 1994 book *Gay and Lesbian Stats*, Bennett L. Singer and David Deschamps state that "as many as 7.2 million Americans under age twenty are lesbian or gay." They cite as their sources the 1992 edition of the *Statistical Abstract of the United States*, from which they gleaned a figure for the total number of U.S. citizens under the age of twenty (72,335,000), and "Kinsey's estimates" of the percentage of the population that is queer, or 10 percent, which I assume they multiplied into the total number of citizens under the age of twenty to arrive at the 7.2 million figure. Earlier in their book they discuss Alfred Kinsey's 1948 study of "5,300 white men," which found that "10 percent of males reported being more or less exclusively homosexual for at least three years between ages 16 and 55" and also that "37 percent of all males had some homosexual contact to orgasm"; "sampling flaws," they inform readers, "were addressed in [a] 1979 reanalysis by Gebhard et al. that yielded almost identical results of 9.9 percent and 34 percent respectively." This, presumably, is their case for men, and, by extension, for boys. For women and girls, the editors cite a 1953 Kinsey study of "5,940 white females" which found that "2 percent–6 percent of females reported being more or less exclusively homosexual between ages 20 and 35" and "13 percent of females had some homosexual contact to orgasm." But when they offer their 7.2 million estimate the editors don't state whether or not they used different percentages for the two sexes, and in fact the 1993 edition of the *Statistical Abstract of the United States* doesn't categorize its numbers by sex; it merely reports that there are 72,335,000 citizens under the age of twenty. It would seem, then, that Singer and Deschamps have, as most of us do, fallen back on the standard 10 percent figure, though they do add that "according to Kinsey, 28 percent of boys and 17 percent of girls have one or more same-sex experiences"—apparently not all of them to orgasm— "before age 20."

What can we conclude from these figures? That men are more likely to be queer than women? That it takes three years for males to be homosexual, but fifteen for women? That 7.2 million adolescents are having sex, or desire to have sex, with persons of the same sex, or that as many as three times this number desire it? If we want to speak with any certainty, we can conclude none of these things. *Gay and Lesbian Stats* is a useful tool for a society as obsessed with numbers as ours, but on the subject of queer youth it is guilty of, on the one hand, using a single statistical figure that has always struck me as having more to do with mathematical convenience than scientific accuracy, and, on the other, applying a codified definition of homosexuality that is derived from adult rather than adolescent sexual identity. The editors, like most queer adults, generalize from Kinsey's findings on homosexual behavior among adult males—white males, at that—to

The crowd cheers on a radiant contestant in a drag ball at the New York club Sally's. Photo by AP/Wide World.

the entire population and in so doing significantly and problematically undercount the number of queer youth in this country. Kinsey's numbers are categorized for a reason: that 10 percent of males and 2 percent to 6 percent of females is a specific measurement of the incidence of homosexuality as a "more or less" exclusive behavior for men and women over differing periods of time; what they specifically do not measure is the experimentation, or, to use a different term, identity formation, that is the task of adolescence. The difference between adolescence and adulthood is reflected in Kinsey's own significantly higher figures for same-sex contact among preadults—17 percent for girls, 28 percent for boys—than among adults, and the 10 percent figure should if anything be considered a prediction of adult sexual identity: perhaps 7.2 million members of the population now under twenty will, at some point, become "more or less exclusively" homosexual.

I want to argue that while a person is participating in homosexual behavior that person is homosexual; and, more to the point, I think it would seem that way to the mother who discovers her child's journal entry about his love for another boy, or to the fifteen-year-old who walks in on his friend and discovers her making out with another girl. A specific case: when I was in college a friend named Sarah told me about her four-year clandestine affair with another girl who was openly dating a male friend of mine. Now, seven years later, it's Sarah who is straight and her former girlfriend who is the out lesbian, but while I knew them, both Sarah and I believed it was the other way around. At the time of their affair both women kept it a secret for a simple reason: the stigma that heterosexual society attaches to homosexuality is focused not merely on the phenomenon, or on individuals known or thought to be queer, but on acts that are themselves considered homosexual, and the individuals who perform them.

A standard 10 percent tally denies the experiences of people like Sarah. The assumption that the additional 7 million or 10 million adolescents engaging in homosexual behavior are categorically *not* queer is a proposition as impossible to maintain as the race laws that decide how much of what kind of blood one has to possess in order to be white, black, Native American, or German—perhaps more so, for behavior is more difficult to quantify than ancestry. In their introduction to the chapter on youth and education, the editors of *Gay and Lesbian Stats* write: "Gay and lesbian youth are extremely isolated and at exceptionally high risk for suicide, drug use, homelessness, and HIV. At the same time, however, growing numbers of young people are choosing to 'come out' within the context of high schools and colleges." But the youths who "are extremely isolated and at exceptionally high risk for suicide, drug use, homelessness, and HIV" aren't merely the ones who, as they write, choose to come out; they are, rather, all youth who participate in homosexual behavior, including those who never come out, and those who later decide they're not even queer. In our binary world we don't yet have words for the experience of these people; "bisexual" doesn't even begin to do the job, and Freud's "polymorphous perversity" applies to an earlier stage of development. But when push comes to shove, we should always remember this: homophobes discriminate, but they're not very discriminating, and viruses don't discriminate at all. If, as a community, we do indeed have an obligation to those at risk of suicide, drug use, homelessness, and HIV—and I think we do—than we should accept that we have an obligation to all of them.

It is not, finally, my intention to offer a way out of this definitional conundrum, mainly because I believe its answer is practical rather than philosophical: make a world where it's no big deal for young queers to come out and we won't have to wonder who they are. Though this is an ideal to work toward, it's not particularly useful to us in our present position. We must admit the limitation of our present knowledge so that we can work honestly within its boundaries. Until we learn precisely when we're queer, and why, and what distinguishes queer people from straight people—until we learn if these things can even be known—then we're forced to accept that when we offer insights into and about "queer youth," what we're really offering are generalizations based on three things: the small brave number of out queer young people; probably faulty inferences based on psychological and statistical theorizing; and, most unreliably, our own memories of childhood and adolescence. Ignorance and nostalgia are the two beasts we are trying to tame: an undefined and for the time being undefinable group, one whose members are children we identify, rightly or wrongly, as earlier incarnations of ourselves.

The Youth Empowerment Speakout contingent at the 1993 March on Washington for Lesbian, Gay and Bi Equal Rights & Liberation. Photo by Marilyn Humphries.

Coming Out: Isolation, the Myth of Invisibility, and Denial

I worry about the arbitrary balkanization of our society. While it's undeniable that various special-interest groups have different needs based on race, class, sex, and sexual orientation, among other factors, and require different strategies to meet those needs, it's also, I think, undeniable that the Right would rather have certain of those groups divided—and, if possible, bickering among themselves—than united and challenging them. The separation of queer "youth" from queer "adults" seems to me another of those troubling divisions, and already rancor has developed between the two factions. "A Youth Movement Is Born!" is one headline in *Y.O.U.T.H., the Young Outspoken Ubiquitous Thinking Homo's Magazine*, and the article that follows the headline includes the text of a speech given by Bill Barnes, a "New York Youth," delivered at the 1993 National Gay and Lesbian Task Force's Creating Change Conference. "We were out there," *Y.O.U.T.H.* quotes Barnes as saying, "and where were you? All of the Gay and Lesbian Adults, I know were sitting in their houses making $60,000.00, $70,000.00 a year, insulated in this belief that because they were good, they we're [*sic*] there." Barnes went on:

There is no Youth member on the National Gay and Lesbian Task Force Board of Directors. There was an age and ageism workshop, that I will not go into at this moment and time, where Youth were basically told, you'll grow out of being discriminated against, but elderly people will be discriminated against for the rest of their lives. So, your issues are less important than ours. And something was said by Ms. Hollibaugh [sic] is that she has no trouble finding a large number of Lesbians in any surrounding. Well, let me tell you. As a young person from New York, I have no trouble finding Gay people, Lesbians, but I get phone calls from people around the country from people who are isolated, suicidal, depressed, who don't have the access, or the power. . . .

They don't have access to role-models from the Gay and Lesbian Community, and that's because the adults who are sitting in this room have decided it's more important to focus on domestic partnership, to focus on Gays in the Military, than to focus on the future of out [sic] movement, which is Gay and Lesbian Youth.

In adolescence, every generation creates its own language to describe its concerns; adults call this slang. A goal of slang, and indeed a primary concern of adolescence, is the exclusion of adults. Young people on the verge of adulthood need to discover and discuss their needs privately before joining with the common mass of humanity—or in this case the common mass of queers. Bill Barnes's speech struck me, not just for its power, but also for its lack of eloquence: here is a boy wrapping his mouth around words not his own. His very awkwardness emphasizes the split between queer youth and queer adults, and the fact that communication between the two groups is always fraught. One is forced either to speak one's own dialect at the risk of not being understood, or to attempt the other's dialect at the risk of not quite knowing how to say something. But Barnes's analysis comes through, and it's correct: queer youth need assistance from queer adults, not guidance. They want a space for themselves, but they can't create that space entirely on their own as they'd prefer; this, I think, accounts for the hostility that masks the inherent neediness of Barnes's address. But the split between queer youth and adults isn't permanent—young people eventually grow up—and therein lies the ameliorating aspect of this division. Though not every "queer youth" grows up to become a queer adult, those who do share one common trait: in some way, they all come out.

Coming out is one of the last rites of passage that hasn't been formally institutionalized by our society, and as such it's an invaluable experience that has as its goal the revelation of the queer in the straight and the liberation of the adult in the child. Coming out is messy, confusing, tempestuous, exhilarating, revolutionary, but the one thing it's not is a simple linear procession; it is, rather, circular. In the personal conflict between homosexuality and homophobia, the same ground is contested, often many times, as one makes insights, forgets or rejects them, and then makes them again. Like all such processes, it's inevitably dangerous. It's neither codified nor sanctioned, and, further, youth in the process of coming out are aware that those who would sanction and codify it stand on the other side of the gap they are trying to cross. The sanctioners are, as the newscasters put it, "admittedly" or even "avowedly" or simply "openly" homosexual. Youth are none of these things, and support from older queers is useful only in an anticipatory manner. In the early stages of coming out it may not even by perceived as helpful by young people, but as overwhelming and threatening, and before it can actually come to their aid, youth must first face the probable negative reaction of their families and friends, as well as any social institutions to which they might belong—their schools

Members of the Drop-In Center, a program of the Hetrick-Martin Institute in New York. Photo by Ces Nieves.

and churches especially—and the citizens of their local communities. This is because the support the queer community offers to people who are coming out, particularly to young people, is almost entirely located within the queer community itself. Within their native communities, youth who are becoming aware of their homosexuality feel confused, frightened, victimized, and, above all, alone; one study found that 80 percent of queer youth reported "severe isolation."

Looked at from a purely empirical viewpoint, this isolation seems odd: if Kinsey's figures are correct, after all, then as many as 16 million young U.S. citizens are engaging in homosexual behavior. Yet in the small body of writing devoted to queer youth, the idea of isolation, of being "the only one," comes up again and again. In *Two Teenagers in Twenty*, an anthology of essays by queer youth, contributors write: "I'm seventeen and a half years old, and I have yet to meet another lesbian" or "When I remember being a lesbian in high school, I think of feeling alone" or "I am in a town where I am the only person this way" or "It's been difficult to meet other gay teens. I sometimes feel like I'm the only one." This last comment, from a sixteen-year-old in New Jersey identified only as Chrissy, is illuminating; she knows that other queers exist, she mentions that she is aware of "support groups," and she has even managed to submit an essay to this book, but because she doesn't know any queers personally, she sometimes ceases to believe what she knows to be true. There are two reasons for her isolation. The first is simply, as Bill Barnes called it, "access": young queers are often prevented from associating with other out queers, young or old. But the main reason many young queers feel isolated is because homosexuality is considered an "invisible" characteristic, and homosexuals, as a consequence, become "invisible"; that is, they are perceived to be indistinguishable from the other members of society. But this simply isn't true; and debunking this myth is a necessary first step to ending the isolation felt by queer youth.

"Lesbian and gay male youths are an invisible population," Joyce Hunter, president of the National Lesbian and Gay Health Foundation, categorically declares. "Many do not share their sexual orientation with family, friends, or peers because they fear rejection and violence." In Hunter's account, "invisibility" is constructed as synonymous with being closeted, or "not sharing"; "visibility," then, is effected by coming out. This analysis is confirmed by many personal accounts of coming out and is echoed yet again by therapist Paul Gibson: "Lesbian and gay youth are the most invisible and outcast group of young people with whom you will come into contact. . . . If closed about who they are, they may be able to 'pass' as 'straight' in their communities while facing a tremendous internal struggle to understand and accept themselves. Many gay youth choose to maintain a facade and hide their true feelings and identity, leading a double life, rather than confront situations too painful for them." Here, as in Hunter's account, invisibility is concomitant with the closet, but Gibson's construction reveals that this "invisibility" is "maintained": it is, in his terms, a "facade," a form of "hiding," a "double life." In short, queer youth are not invisible, but disguised, and, as disguises go, this one is hardly impenetrable.

The accounts of surprised friends and family members are by no means the majority; in fact, they were difficult to find. More common were stories such as these, which I found in *Growing Up Gay/Growing Up Lesbian*, another anthology devoted to queer youth: "When he told me, I wasn't threatened or surprised. In fact, I kind of knew" or "She just laughed and said, 'What a surprise.' I guess she already knew" or "My mother had me pegged as a dyke by the age of five" or "In every case, my friends would tell me they already knew or had assumed that I was gay." Though I suspect that editorial choices have something to do with the number of nonrevelatory revelations that inhabit the pages of these anthologies, what became clear to me as I read is that queer youth are not invisible, despite their disguises—in fact, they're often visible, even when they haven't admitted to themselves that they're queer. Gary, a seventeen-year-old in Pennsylvania, remembers, "Kids would say I was gay, and I had no idea what the word really meant." Lesbian activist Barbara Gittings recalls, "One of my teachers tried to warn me that I would have a difficult time ahead in college. I can't remember the context, but she used the word homosexual as a label for me. I kind of knew what it meant in a vague intellectual sense, but it didn't seem to apply to me." Even Dear Abby has said, "A guy who's a little loose in his loafers can be spotted early, and he takes a razzing. I thought it was cruel." "Gender-role nonconformity" is the formal term for the phenomenon Dear Abby calls being a little loose in the loafers, and it's a weighty term. Though it can mean everything from being a sissy or a tomboy to full-fledged transvestism, it can also be, in our straightlaced society, as simple as making the wrong friends: one study found that children who play with opposite-sex friends are often rejected by peers of the same sex. It also found, not surprisingly, that this sort of behavior is typical of children who later grow up to identify as queer. Further, other studies have found that youth who actually identify themselves as queer are more likely to engage in gender-role nonconformity than queer adults; whether this nonconformity is willed or unconscious or some mix of the two isn't clear, though it is clear that as a phenomenon it is increasingly frowned upon by the queer community as queer youth grow up and become a more active part of it.

Queerness—and queers—are visible, even among adolescents and children. Youth who are not out are frequently identified as queer by their peers—this identification often takes the form of verbal or physical attack—and youth who are out often go to great lengths to demonstrate it. Nevertheless, despite the many and various signs that manifest homosexuality, the existence of young homosexuals is still denied by their families, friends, and communities, until it is finally denied by themselves. Until recently the existence of all homosexuals was denied by heterosexual society, even as that society used homosexuality to shape its image of itself by creating homosexual stereotypes and persecuting homosexual scapegoats. Today, queer activism has made it difficult to maintain this denial on a societal level, but as a result it's intensified in smaller population groups—particularly within nuclear families. "Parents can be blind to signs of gayness in their own children though they would immediately see such signs in others," Aaron Fricke writes in *Reflections of a Rock Lobster*. "One time my father told me Jon was so 'obviously gay' that there was no way his parents couldn't know. . . . I wanted to say, 'How can you be so blind? I'm gay too and you don't know it!'" Later, when Fricke does come out to his parents, his mother says, "'I'm so glad you were finally able to be honest with me.' She had long suspected." Fricke's mother supported him in his decision to come out, but more common is the type of story Sue Cline, a seventeen-year-old in Chicago, tells. "I haven't told my parents that I'm gay yet, and probably won't for quite a while either. I don't think they would understand. In fact, I should say that I know they wouldn't. They knew about Carla and me, and they thoroughly disapproved." Carla was Cline's former girlfriend. In other words, Cline's parents are aware their daughter is a lesbian, but since she's stopped seeing the girlfriend they were aware of and not told them of her new one, they can pretend their daughter's lesbianism has gone away. Terry, a nineteen-year-old in Salt Lake City, spells it out: "My close friends, both gay and straight, tell me that my parents already know; they just refuse to admit it." And it's not just non-queers who can refuse to admit: "I had been having sex with a man since I was fourteen," writes Mike Friedman, a seventeen-year-old in St. Paul, Minnesota, "but I thought that it was just a phase that I was going through. I thought that I would grow out of it."

The euphemism *a phase I was going through* is another way of relabeling homosexuality as heterosexuality. This ability—to deny the queer by calling it straight—is what perpetuates the myth of homosexual invisibility. I don't mean to claim that it's completely impossible to hide one's homosexuality, but I do think that once the blinders created by denial are removed, queers suddenly seem to exist in all sorts of places where formerly one would have sworn none existed at all. Clearly, maintaining these blinders is not an easy thing to do. It requires tremendous energy to compartmentalize one's consciousness so that certain things that one observes are also remembered, but other things are considered mere illusion and forgotten. What perpetuates this situation? Wouldn't it be easier either to recognize homosexuality in one's children and attempt to change them—as many parents do when they finally choose to confront their child's homosexuality—or just reject them entirely? The obvious immediate impetus of this denial is homophobia, but the mechanism that homophobia uses to maintain this denial—to keep, in other words, the door of the closet shut and locked, where its occupants exist in an out-of-sight, out-of-mind limbo—is, quite simply, terrorism, the same terrorism we associate with guerrilla warfare. It is violence with a political purpose, but it isn't systematic violence; it is, rather, random, sporadic, unpredictable violence. The terrorists can't strike at every one of their enemies, but the violence and unpredictability of their attacks are still conclusive proof that everyone is at risk. Terrorism's manifest target is the body, but its far-reaching effects are on the mind; its goal is not murder, but fear. That's why it's called terrorism.

The effectiveness of terrorism relies on the power of narrative. For terrorism to work, its targets must be aware of themselves as characters in a story that can reach a bloody crisis at any moment; the element of suspense is paramount. The victims of terrorism must continually ask themselves when the attack will come, and eventually their dread becomes self-perpetuating and paralyzing. Actual attack, in other words, isn't necessary. One need merely be acutely aware of one's vulnerability to be "demoralized, undone, humiliated by fear," as Joan Didion writes in *Salvador*. It is a sensation, as Didion notes, one does not forget, and it is a sensation that dominates the lives of many queers, and especially queer youth. We are surrounded by violence or the threat of violence. Young queers feel particularly vulnerable because two of the most common arenas in which violence occurs—school and the home—are environments they can't easily opt out of. Alternative schools such as the EAGLES Center and the Harvey Milk School are uncommon and expensive, and it's unlikely they'll ever be available to many queer youth. Further, many of the students who attend these high schools admit that although they enjoy the all-queer environment, they'd rather attend a public school free of the risk of violence. This is what antidiscrimination legislation such as that passed

Supporters of Massachusetts House Bill 3353 fill the vestibule of the State House in Boston. Photo by Marilyn Humphries.

in Boston is designed to accomplish, though it's too soon to see what effect it will have. Right now, by the time they finish high school 45 percent of gay males and 20 percent of lesbians have been physically or verbally assaulted in school, and over a quarter of these youths find it

Student supporters gather with placards inside the Massachusetts State House in Boston as they call for the passage of House Bill 3353, which extends antidiscrimination protections to include lesbian, gay, and bisexual public school students. Photo by Marilyn Humphries.

necessary to drop out because of persecution. Between 16 percent and 41 percent of all queers have been verbally harassed by their families, and 4 to 8 percent have been physically attacked. Adding to the fear this violence induces is the fact that it is perceived to lack a legal remedy: 72 percent of white victims and 82 percent of people of color didn't report being attacked to the police, mainly because of "the perception that the police are antigay" (*Gay and Lesbian Stats*, p. 71).

Terror can be created without fists or baseball bats. Take, for example, AIDS, here often construed by homophobic institutions as a punishment for being queer. "AIDS is a big threat to me," an anonymous sixteen-year-old in Maine writes in *Two Teenagers in Twenty*. Another writes, "Then the AIDS crisis began. All of the reports on TV in the mid-eighties said that many gays were being killed by this disaster. I thought that just because I was gay, my chances of getting the disease would be higher than if I was straight." Psychologically, then, the damage is being done, but let's not forget that AIDS is a physical illness, and it is a particular threat to children and adolescents in a country where, "since 1982, more than sixteen hundred school districts have adopted sex-education curricula that present sexual abstinence and monogamy within heterosexual marriage as the only sexual choices available to teenagers" (*Gay and Lesbian Stats*, p. 78). It's even more of a threat when those children and adolescents are exploring a homosexual identity. Negotiating the rules of sex is difficult enough for heterosexual adolescents, but for queer youth—and here, I think, we must use the most expansive definition of that term possible—who are questioning the morality and normality of themselves, their partners, and the act they are performing, prophylaxis is, understandably, though not acceptably, the last thing on their mind.

Finally, there is the continued threat of psychiatric treatment or institutionalization to "cure" homosexuality in young people. When the American Psychiatric Association voted to declassify homosexuality as an illness, fully 40 percent of its membership dissented from that decision; many of those psychiatrists are still practicing today. One writer, himself a therapist, states, "Perhaps no risk factor is as insidious or unique to the suicidal behavior of gay and lesbian youth [as] receiving professional help." Another writes, "Pain and suffering are inflicted on the very young, whom society is supposedly protecting, under the guise of preventing the spread of homosexuality or of treating the individual." If therapy doesn't work, institutionalization remains a popular recourse. "The legal system makes it easy," one recent article reports. "Adults threatened with psychiatric confinement, in most cases, are guaranteed an impartial hearing, but juveniles institutionalized by their parents have no such option. Institutionalizations of young people are considered voluntary, even when they are dragged kicking and screaming to their confinement." How many young queers are institutionalized? A 'zine put out by an eighteen-year-old lesbian who had herself been locked up by her parents has received letters from more than twenty-five adolescents who have been institutionalized. *10 Percent* magazine puts the number in the "hundreds." According to *The Family Next Door*, "of the approximately fifty thousand young people who are committed to psychiatric institutions each year, estimates indicate that as many as 20 to 30 percent are lesbian, gay, or bisexual," which puts the number at ten or fifteen thousand young queers who are being "treated" with, according to one lesbian's account, "visits from a local chapter of Homosexuals Anonymous, so-called visualization techniques to make her change her sexual orientation, and antipsychotic drugs. If she disobeyed the rules, [she] was punished by further isolation and threatened with electroshock."

And although it seems obvious, the point needs to be made that young people are aware of these threats to themselves because of their sexual identity. "In school, if you are a guy and you act the slightest bit homosexual—if you talk a certain way or you walk a certain way—the other kids call you a fag." This is a typical story told by Mike, a fifteen-year-old. "You get teased, you get beat on. So I am learning to act really straight. A girl walks by, I'll say, 'Hey, she's hot,' just like the other guys do. And there's a guy in class, he does act homosexual, and I tease him just like the others do. I feel like I have to do it. It keeps the teasing away from me." But in avoiding the "teasing" one avoids also the chance of contact with other queers. "I never discussed my feelings with anyone. No doubt I would have denied them vehemently if anyone had dared to ask. It turns out that my school had quite a thriving gay underground, though I was more or less oblivious to it at the time. There were a couple of fairly overt gay male teachers, and a young lesbian faculty member who was sort of 'out,' as well as a few highly closeted older teachers. I was intrigued with my lesbian teacher, but also terrified" (*Teens with AIDS Speak Out*, p. 35). We end up, then, where we began: with the queer adolescent isolated even though she knows other queers exist, not just "out there" but close by—in this case, in her own school—but choosing not to notice or associate with them because she is terrified of what will happen if she does. Terror creates an insidious circle of denial and isolation; that's why coming out is never as easy as saying, "Mom, Dad, I'm queer." It's an extraordinary and moving testament that any young person is able to break out of this circle, and it's clear that what makes coming out possible for most queer youth is the promise of a new community to replace the one that rejects most queer youth. But there is a price: coming out requires not just that one identify oneself as homosexual, but also identification with all or part of the huge body of institutions and ideologies that have grown up around homosexuals and homosexuality. A purely individual concept of self, and the freedom of behavior associated with individuality, is sacrificed for a communitarian notion of self that demands that personal behavior be modified to conform to the standards of the community. In return, the community offers protection and a forum to express certain aspects of one's personality that would otherwise be stifled.

The Forging of Community

Since World War II, queers have created an enormous edifice of institutions to facilitate first the creation and, later, the growth of a queer community. This community is explicitly considered the foundation of a political movement, and some fifty years after the period that most queer historians date as the beginning of the contemporary queer community, the *Gayellow Pages* lists two thousand five hundred organizations, ranging from the largest, the Human Rights Campaign Fund

Members of the Drop-In Center, a program of the Hetrick-Martin Institute in New York. Photo by Ces Nieves.

with its eighty thousand members, to regional lesbian softball teams and gay bowling clubs, to tiny chapters of Queer Nation or the Lesbian Avengers with just three or four members. There are clothing stores, erotic boutiques, restaurants, cafés, bars, clubs, and discos; there are travel agencies, hotels, motels, bed-and-breakfasts, and guesthouses; there are answering services, secretarial firms, accounting agencies, real estate brokerages, investment houses, insurance companies, health clinics, legal services, counseling centers, and martial arts dojos; there are chapters of AA, OA, NA, SA (Smokers Anonymous), and SA (Sexual-compulsives Anonymous); and there are art galleries, bookstores, publishing companies, magazines, cable television networks, and archival projects; there are computer supply stores and computer bulletin boards; there are switchboards and community centers; and then, finally, there are, grouped under the rubric "education and advocacy," the really big organizations—the Empire State Pride Agenda, the National Gay and Lesbian Task Force, the Human Rights Campaign Fund.

We assume this community is a good thing. Gay men, lesbians, bisexuals, and transgendered people are supposed to enjoy communicating with and communing alongside each other. Further, we expect ourselves to engage in activities that strengthen the singular tenuous bond of sexual orientation, and these activities are not merely sexual; many, in fact, are explicitly nonsexual. Still, when one sifts through the various and not insubstantial social, legal, and political products of communitarian activity, there seems to be one purpose that all the others attempt to realize: belonging to the queer community is supposed to give its members the opportunity to be—as people in general, and especially as homosexual people living in a homophobic society—happy. This seems to me the most simplistic possible definition of a community that is a civil rights movement (or several movements), a social scene (or scenes), an artistic network(s), and a web of sexual liaisons, but sometimes simplistic renderings are illuminating. The queer community can't guarantee happiness, but it should, in classic American language, allow one to pursue it. By many accounts, this is the philosophy under which the community was founded, and implicit in this philosophy is the notion that queers cannot exist happily outside of a community. According to *Growing Up Before Stonewall*, "Part of the process of creating identity was an attempt to get gays and lesbians to see themselves not in pathological individualistic terms, but as people who, when organized into some collective sense of identity, could have a happy and successful life just like heterosexuals supposedly had. What was needed was a shift from a sexual category to a human identity based on nonerotic ties, a collective culture with its own institutions and ideologies." Creating community and developing identity are mutually dependent processes, this passage makes clear; the "collective sense of identity" characteristic of members of a community replaced the identity that was seen to define precommunity queers, an identity that was not merely "individualistic" but also "pathological." The newly created community involved not just "institutions" but also "ideologies" to regulate this identity. Community, after all, is a normative concept. Certain behaviors qualify one for membership; certain behaviors disqualify prospective members or qualify current members for expulsion, and in the queer community these norms are based on political as much as moral criteria. What distinguishes the homosexual community from other minority communities is the interesting intersection between the concepts of "homosexuality" and "community." Homosexuals are the only "minority" distinguished from the "majority" by a behavior, or, at the very least, a behavioral impulse; as a result, there are individuals who are drafted for inclusion in at least a provisional sense as members of the homosexual community based on their sexual behavior, whether or not they would or even could consider themselves homosexuals. Historical figures fall into this category—Henry James, say, or Michelangelo or Sarah Orne Jewett—and Roy Cohn is a modern, uglier example. Homosexuals don't "recruit," we've long insisted, but the homosexual community does, because communities aren't static. They must change in order to remain vital. Though change might come from within, it comes more substantially from without, by the admission into the community of new members. Other minorities reproduce biologically, but for queers this isn't quite the case. We must wait for new members to join us; we must wait for them to come out. We must wait, in other words, for queer youth to take an abridged journey through queer history, which begins in the countryside of "pathological" individual identity—where the only person one answers to is oneself—and finishes in the big city of collective identity, where one is judged by, and with, millions of other people. This model is, admittedly, incomplete, but I think it illustrates how gaining access to a community organized along ideological lines by its (adult) members is going to be traumatic for adolescents who, as adolescents put these things, don't want to be "labeled," even as they search for inclusion in some new community to replace the ones they often feel have rejected them for their nascent sexuality. To youth beginning to examine their sexuality, the queer community can seem an overwhelming, all-or-nothing proposition; to youth taking their first steps toward this community, its norms can seem to represent inflexible views of sexuality. Bisexuals have long testified to this, and newly organized queer youth are adding their voices to this discussion.

Despite this trauma, the importance of the queer community to young queers can't be overstated. "Into the dark confusion of sexual self-discovery," one boy writes, "gay culture emerged to me as a guiding light. It not only assured me that there were others of my persuasion, it also gave a structure to what had been a shapeless mass of unsorted desires; it showed me how those desires could be confirmed, developed, and ultimately satisfied. The gay media gave me a sense of community that helped take the place of what were often inaccessible relationships. Almost invariably, being gay and young puts one at odds with institutions concerned with youth. The home and school may cease to be sources of emotional

217

"In
the
world
through
which
I travel
I am endlessly creating
myself."
Franz Fanon

support, or at least become diminished. . . . Such rejection, when it does not have disastrous consequences, is motivation to explore the world beyond."

This is Bill Andriette, a sixteen-year-old with apparently little access to queer people or organizations, and who is also estranged from his "home and school." Queer culture, just as the architects of the post–World War II queer community had predicted it would, is teaching Andriette how to be gay. For David, a nineteen-year-old in Baltimore, "becoming active in the gay community" is "the last stage of coming out." If coming out is, at its most basic level, an admission that one is queer, then, under David's definition, queerness has acquired an additional characteristic. Rather than merely having a desire to have sex with persons of one's own sex, queers now are also, actively, a part of the queer community. Like Andriette, David's first encounter with the queer community wasn't through queer people, but through the media, and that media served a teaching role. "I began by becoming as informed about the gay experience as possible through books, films, and other sources." Eventually, "after I felt secure enough with myself"—a security gained through knowledge of what it means to be queer— "I called the local gay community center to inquire about activities in the area."

But, despite his efforts to become a part of Baltimore's queer community, what David discovered was that most queer organizations, some of them in accordance with specific guidelines but most for reasons having to do with the place queer youth occupy in society, are more or less closed to minors, and the organizations that do accept minors aren't geared toward their needs; as a result, the community they offer is of limited use to the young people who can get to them. The exceptions to this are, of course, those institutions specifically created to serve queer youth, such as the Hetrick-Martin Institute in New York City and the EAGLES Center in Los Angeles. Hetrick-Martin publishes a directory of more than 170 organizations that provide services to queer youth; these include hot lines, support groups, and emergency services, but, it should be noted, many of these organizations are neither specifically "queer" nor specifically "young," which limits their effectiveness, or perceived effectiveness, in helping young queers. Most of these organizations are also located in major urban centers so that the majority of queer youth don't have the ability to learn about the community through them. They do so through the media or through anonymous sexual contact or, most commonly, through bars; this isn't a situation they're happy with. Joanne, an eighteen-year-old in York, Pennsylvania, expresses a common opinion when she writes, "I also hope that an alternative to the bars is developed to meet people's social needs. As a fifteen-year-old trying to sneak into bars where the drinking age is twenty-one, I was not very successful. And when I did get into a bar, I hated it, because it was superficial." But the adult queer community is also not helpful to queer youth on other fronts. Jim S., for example, is a twenty-three-year-old

Facing page: Lyle Ashton Harris, *In the world through which I travel I am endlessly creating myself* (1990).

PWA. "I went to one meeting for people with the virus, where everyone was
older than me. And not only was nobody else my age, but no one was even talking about having the virus. . . . I'm going to go back to that group, I think. But
I'd just like to talk this all over with someone who's young like me." Adults, in
the eyes of youth, seem to be concerned first and foremost with their own issues:
"There is no excuse for ignoring us," writes Matthew John Marco, the editor of
Y.O.U.T.H., "but we should understand two facets of the Adult Gay personality:
(1) For many of them, their Youth was either as painful as ours or it was passed
up. Therefore seeing us is a reminder of a negative part of their lives that they may
possibly want to forget. (2) For Adult Gays and Lesbians to advocate for us means
that they are taking a chance on being called child recruiters by the religious
reich which has made that accusation for years." In Marco's construction, this
"reminder of a negative part of their lives" is in direct opposition to community's
goals; although his reasoning here is simplistic—bad memories aren't, I think, a
significant factor in the barriers between youth and adults—there's still a ring of
truth to it. But his second point is much more compelling. Today, as vehemently
and unreasonably as ever, the myth of the homosexual as pedophiliac recruiter is
used to separate adult queers from young queers; it has become, I would argue,
the single most important barrier.

The myth of the homosexual pedophiliac recruiter deserves a close examination because, of all the barriers that separate adult queers from young queers, it's
the one impediment that isn't merely a matter of money or of location or of
parental authority; these obstacles are hardly negligible, and they need to be dis-
mantled, but adolescents in pursuit of sexual outlets have always found ways
around them. And it isn't merely a question of the laws that criminalize adult

sexual contact with minors; at one point every state had a law against sodomy, and twenty still do, five of which apply exclusively to homosexuals. Pedophilia, though, is more than this: it's not a matter of doctrine, it's a matter of hysteria. The prohibition against intergenerational sex, sparked by the incest taboo, is fanned by the twinned erotophobia and erotomania so peculiar to our culture, and then exploded by homophobia. For example: "In the summer after fourth grade," Aaron Fricke writes in *Reflections of a Rock Lobster,* "on the way to Provincetown, my mother took me aside for a talk. She warned that one day, a man in Provincetown might ask me up to his house. If I went up, terrible things would happen to me. The man might cut me up into little pieces. When I asked her why someone would do this to me she paused and said, 'Because they are what you call homosexuals.'" Fricke discusses this issue elsewhere in his book. "Another theory is that a sexual assault by an older man leads boys to become homosexual,"[2] he writes, and his phrasing reveals the homophobic basis of the myth of pedophilia: the worst thing about an older gay man sexually assaulting a boy isn't the assault itself, it's the idea that the assault will make the boy gay. And when Fricke's two accounts of contact between younger and older homosexuals are merged, what emerges is this: being queer is considered as bad as being cut into pieces. This kind of thinking reveals the fundamental irrationality of the homophobia that maintains this particular myth, but it also reveals the enormous amount of power, particularly sexual power, that straight people attribute to queers; this myth, in other words, is maintained not only by homophobia, but by erotophobia as well. It's because of this unreasonable awe that rational appeals to facts—such as, for example, a recent finding by the University of Colorado that a child is one hundred times more likely to be molested by a heterosexual than a homosexual—have had so little effect. The propagators of the myth of homosexual pedophilia aren't concerned with actual numbers because they know, as all queers know, that sexual contact does occur between younger and older queers, that at least some of that contact is coercive and damaging, and that a few sensationalized cases are all that's necessary to maintain a climate of hysteria.

As a community, we're not able to distinguish between cases of abuse and those cases where abuse isn't present; yet as a community, we must learn to do so, and we must teach heterosexual society to do so as well. Dozens of my friends and acquaintances have told me stories of sexual encounters or affairs they had with adults when they were children; the literature devoted to queer youth is full of accounts of sexual contact between adults and minors. "My first real affair was with a much older man, and he was a beautiful person"; "I fell in love with a woman! A thirty-nine-year-old woman!"; "I am grateful that I have such a caring person as my [thirty-two-year-old] lover"; "I was in love with an older female friend who was thirty-six"; "I was probably eight—making a guess—and frankly I loved that man, and when he left, it just broke me up." As with the idea of homosexual invisibility, I found a contradiction between the predominant view and the stories people choose to tell. Though there were, of course, negative accounts, most notably the case of Mike W., a fifteen-year-old who was knowingly infected with HIV by a man in his thirties, as well as David, the nineteen-year-old from Baltimore, who was molested by his uncle over a period of four years, the majority of the stories reported positive or neutral encounters between adults and minors. Nevertheless, according to many leaders in the queer community, positive encounters simply can't happen. For example, Steve Ashkinazy, founder and director of Brooklyn's Madrigal House for queer "throwaway" youth: "A relationship, however, becomes problematic. And when someone is pretending to be a mentor, but is also involved with his protégé sexually, the young person always—always—suffers." For example, Joyce Hunter, president of the National Lesbian and Gay Health Foundation: "The pedophiles say they're helping the kids deal with their problems, but in fact they're contributing to the problem. The reaction of these kids is to get very depressed, angry, and scared. In the long term they often are unable to be intimate as adults with their partners. I've never seen it where it's a good thing." The official line is that it's always bad for the children and also, and more to the point, it's bad for the community; this final example is from Kevin Cathcart, executive director of Lambda Legal Defense and Education Fund: "As a community organization, we also have an obligation not to take cases that are going to harm lesbian and gay civil rights over the long run. Our clients have to be the best of the best. . . . And NAMBLA does not fit that category."

Pedophilia, like most sexual behaviors, is neither good nor bad; branding it one or the other is reductive and useless. Its moral status isn't inherent, but is determined by the context in which it occurs. But its moral status as an expression of sexuality isn't, here, what interests me about it. What concerns me is how a phenomenon that is by anyone's estimates extremely rare has been used successfully to damn every homosexual, the homosexual community, and homosexuality itself; and, further, how this homophobic viewpoint has been adopted by the homosexual community itself. We live in constant fear of being labeled pedophiles just as we once lived in fear of being labeled queer. The defense we used against forced outing—coming out ourselves—has proven remarkably effective in shaping public discourse, but in dealing with something that doesn't exist to the extent that our adversaries claim that it does our community has become as reactionary as the homophobes who made up the story in the first place. We get defensive; we get hysterical; if we're not actually guilty, then we're sure acting that way. As a community, we shadowbox with the specter of pedophilia on a daily basis. It's behind the disclaimer "All Models Over 18" on porn videos and magazines (imagine, by comparison, if all people were required to carry a sign reading, "I don't have illegal drugs in my pocket" whenever they left their homes). It's what motivates certain parenthetical statements in personal ads: "looking for young (18+) GM or

GF for companionship, friendship, more"—and if you assumed that the person who placed that ad was an older man or older woman, then it's what motivated that thought as well. And it informs the question that we ask on first meeting someone who looks awfully young, whether or not we're interested in sex with that person: "How old are you, anyway?" When Damien Martin was trying to raise money for the Hetrick-Martin Institute, "one man," Jesse Green reports in a recent article, ". . . insisted on delivering his $50,000 cash contribution in his cowboy boots, lest anyone think he was a pedophile."

All of this defensiveness is getting us exactly nowhere. We haven't dispelled the myth of homosexual pedophilia, and our internalization of it has made it extremely difficult for adult queers to help young queers. The question remains, why do we cling to it? The answer has to do with the relationship adult queers envision themselves having with queer youth. As I wrote in the first section of this essay, adult queers have placed themselves in a surrogate parent's role for their young counterparts. This is immediately troublesome because it mimics the power inequality that exists between parents and children, but a more serious problem is the sexual conflict it creates. Even when they're not having sex with each other, adult queers exist in a sexual relationship with young queers. It's not, however, the comparatively uncomplicated relationship that exists between members of the same peer group, nor is it the abusive pedophiliac relationship that so many homophobes are afraid of. It is instead the sublimated, highly conflicted, Oedipal relationship that exists between parents and their children, in which a mutual sexual attraction exists but is consciously denied. This relationship is complex enough between children and their real parents, but it's even more complex in the surrogate-parent relationship that queer adults have created with queer youth: first of all, it's centered in the adult rather than the child half of the pair; secondly, the taboo that prevents adults and their offspring from sleeping with each other is only marginally present in the relationship between older and younger queers, and it is, as well, temporally defined. Both parties are aware of this—aware that eventually there will be no obstacles at all to a sexual relationship—but both parties are also aware that the obstacles that currently prevent a sexual relationship are artificially maintained. Queer youth know this more than adults, because they didn't create the relationship, but, as children do, follow the lead of their chosen role models and also deny the sexual nature of their relationship to queer adults. I believe that this artificially created Oedipal conflict is the subconscious fuel behind our community's internalization of the pedophilia myth.

The myth of the homosexual pedophiliac recruiter regulates the behavior of not one but two groups: queer adults and queer youth. It functions not merely to protect children from sexual assault, nor to prevent adults from having same-sex relations with minors; it aims, in its misguided way, to prevent the creation of new homosexuals. We can no longer toe the line that community leaders have laid:

viewed through this lens, pedophiles are community members who don't conform to community standards, and as such they're summarily expelled. But the eye that offends thee, when plucked out, is still thine eye; it's just not in your body anymore. Such solutions merely misplace the problem, and it seems to me we must now accept the fact that queer youth are *not* our children. They are new members of an established community, and they are our future, if not our current, sex partners. Even those of us who concern ourselves with maintaining and strengthening old-fashioned institutions like antiviolence organizations and political lobbying groups can learn a lesson from punk: "GIVE US YOUR CHILDREN: what we can't FUCK we eat" seems to me as useful, truthful, and manageable a proposition as declaring that there are not and cannot be any pedophiles in the homosexual community. If, in our fear of being labeled pedophiles, we continually glance over our shoulders as we attempt to lend a hand to queer youth, then when we're finally ready to move forward, it will only be to discover that "our children," whom we thought we were helping by staying away from them, have disappeared. The homophobes will have carried the day.

Toward a Moral Model of Homosexuality

We don't know when we're queer because we don't know why we're queer. There are theorists on this question and they have advanced theories: there are psychologists and various kinds of biologists, especially, and there are also historians, politicians, lawyers, ministers, and economists; they have all offered various and generally contradictory explanations for homosexuality, and all of the suggestions they have advanced have failed, and failed spectacularly, in pinpointing why we're queer. Nevertheless, their ideas have had an enormous effect on what it means to be queer, on how we're queer; this imprint was felt before queers politicized themselves, when the average person with same-sex attractions was searching for an ancillary meaning to attach to those particular feelings, and it has only increased since queers have organized themselves into a political unit; now, we not only want answers for ourselves, we want answers for our cause, for those who will come next, for our youth, "for the children." But because we can't say with certainty, "You are queer because . . . ," we end up saying, "Are you queer because . . . ?" and what we've given queer youth aren't answers but questions; what we've given them are contexts. For example, a biological model that claims that homosexuality in gay males is caused by a hypothalamus smaller than that found in straight males suggests that homosexuality is an innate characteristic but not necessarily inevitable or unchanging; it forces us to ask, and to debate, whether homosexuality is normal or abnormal. Is the smallness of some hypothalamuses a product of illness or injury, or is it a naturally occurring, statistically smaller, but still normal phenomenon, like blue eyes? Can it be prevented? Can it be reversed? Should it be prevented or reversed? A psychological model that claims that homosexuality is a developed

aspect of personality raises questions of mental healthiness and unhealthiness, and, again, questions of permanence. Is it a healthy response to environment or an unhealthy one? Is it irreversible or reversible? Can homosexuality be cured? Should it?

The medical model, of which the biological and psychological models are two main subsets, is the most common one in use today, but there are others, and their effects are still being felt. There is a linguistic model, in which homosexuality or homosexuals are claimed not to exist in cultures and times where no recognized words for them existed. There are various religious models. There is even an

"Born Queer" by Diane DiMassa.
From *Strange-Looking Exile*, #4.

economic model, in which homosexuality is seen as the critical factor in what kind of job one will get. And there are other models, other contexts that we have created for homosexuality, and which queer youth have learned from us. Some, such as the psychobiological medical model, are more common than others, and some, such as the economic model, are more limited in scope, but nearly all of the current models of homosexuality frame it in various binaries, the most important one being immutable vs. mutable, from which follows all of the others: normal vs. abnormal, healthy vs. unhealthy, rights gained vs. rights denied, and so on. It could be argued, and it certainly should be suggested, that all of these binaries have as their actual root

not immutable vs. mutable, but heterosexual vs. homosexual—that the construction we are relying on, in other words, is not only not helpful, it's also homophobic in origin. All of these binaries are geared toward the political, which is to say, the communitarian, cause of directing the debate over queers' status as a minority in this society. In other words, homophobic society claims we choose to be this way, it's neither normal nor healthy, and as a result we're not entitled to certain rights that everyone else is; whereas we counter with the claim that our homosexuality is an innate part of us, and because of that it's both normal and healthy and we are entitled to all the rights that everyone else in this society possesses—or possesses in

theory or ought to possess. The claim for the immutability of homosexuality, according to Richard Mohr, has a simple basis, though it's rarely articulated anymore. "If [homosexuality is immutable], gays would be, so it is claimed, relevantly like blacks—like in that one's group characteristic is not of one's own doing, with the result that in a group-based discrimination one is treated unjustly because treated without regard to what one oneself has done." But Mohr extends this argument further than most: "Even if it were conclusively proved that being gay is not a matter of choice, such a biology-based or psychology-based strategy gets morality on the cheap, indeed too cheaply." Mohr argues, correctly, I think, that "a minority

is a group treated unjustly because of some status that the group is socially perceived to possess independently of the behavior of the group's members," which is to say, in the case of queers, that "gays are viewed first and foremost simply as morally lesser beings, like animals, children, or dirt, not as failed full moral agents."

This argument interests me because, to simplify it greatly, it suggests that the medical model of homosexuality—indeed, all the models of homosexuality that attempt to locate a cause or a justification for its existence in something other than the thing itself—are merely means to an end. Queers who espouse the immutable models of homosexuality are looking for a way to raise themselves to the level of full moral agency in the eyes of a homophobic society, and they do this not by offering up their actions to moral scrutiny, but by diverting attention from their actions. Sexual orientation is fixed at conception, they argue, sexual orientation is fixed while one is still in the womb, sexual orientation is fixed in infancy, sexual orientation is fixed by the time one is an adolescent, sexual orientation can't be changed, and so on. Now, in the first place, immutable characteristics don't necessarily contain moral value—Mohr uses the example of blue eyes, which I think is a good one—but, further, "moral minority status," as Mohr calls it, doesn't need to rest on immutability—he uses the example of religious minorities, and I think that's a good one, too. We live in a society that has a tradition of at least paying lip service to the idea of protecting difference of expression, but as a community we seem unwilling to accept that, and so we seek protection for difference of circumstance. But none of these approaches is content with the one prima facie datum that we possess: homosexuality—or, at the very least, homosexual acts, like heterosexual acts—exists. Homosexuality isn't a moral condition, despite the fact that homophobic society regards us as morally inferior for being homosexual.

Seeking to create a moral status of homosexuality by locating its cause in an unchangeable psychological or biological or any other cause is a smoke-and-mirrors approach to morality; its proponents look for an excuse so that their behavior won't have to, or can't, be judged. Their position contains within it the impossible assumption that because homosexuality can in some way be considered moral, then all homosexuals must also be moral. This position forces us to claim, for example, that the sexual abusers of children somehow must not remain members of the homosexual community. Rather than merely condemning their abuses, which is all that's necessary, and attempting to prevent such abuses, we go one step further and try to define them out of existence—or at least out of our existence—and that does nothing for them or their victims. By moving away from a medical model of homosexuality to a moral one, we no longer have to judge homosexuality, but homosexuals, and more specifically homosexual acts. This is unquestionably problematic— we live in a homophobic society, after all, and the homophobes have most of the power, not us—but it has the distinct advantage of resting on a factual moral foundation, and not a supposed or fabricated or merely false one.[3]

But why am I posing a model for a moral vision of homosexuality in an essay about queer youth? Because youth, as Y.O.U.T.H. is fond of pointing out, are the leaders of tomorrow, but queer adults are the leaders of today. Though the leaders of tomorrow have their own vision, they're not going to pull it out of a hat. They're going to get it from the leaders of today, from listening to what we say and watching what we do, and what they see is this: queer youth see us as the last generation to view homosexuality in pathological terms. We're the people who wondered if we were ill or abnormal, but they see themselves as having moved beyond that: they are the people who claim to be healthy and normal. But operating within a medical model of homosexuality only allows for a minor change in the terms of the discussion; it doesn't change its nature at all. Before there were psychological theories to justify homosexuality, we wondered whether or not we were healthy; now that such theories exist, we must continually assert that we are healthy and attempt to prove it. Before there were biological theories to explain homosexuality, we wondered whether or not we were normal; now that theories exist, we must continually assert that we are normal and attempt to prove it. But normality and health, just like abnormality and illness, are generally concepts defined by the more powerful elements of a society—by straight people, not queers—and as a result the main way to assert one's normality or health is to conform to their standards: to assimilate. But assimilation functions differently for homosexuals than it does for other minorities because homosexuals are a behavioral minority. Assimilation, then, strikes me as having two possible outcomes: it's either a Sisyphean task that can never be accomplished, or, if we do accomplish it, it would only be by assimilating ourselves out of existence. The infinite manifestations of homosexuality are what make it interesting—from Boston marriages to leather bars to lesbian chic to drag balls, from Sappho to Socrates to Gertrude Stein to Marcel Proust to k.d. lang to Neil Tennant—but all these manifestations rest in some nearly intangible way on a single sexual impulse. That behavior, and everything that stems from it, is the true price of assimilation. We are being led, like donkeys, in a circle. It's time we shed our yokes and began going somewhere. In adopting a moral model, we are no longer judging homosexuality itself. Homosexuality is accepted as a given, and what we now judge are homosexual acts. What we judge now is our community. What we judge now is ourselves.

In every narrative written about queers, the community is represented by a series of static anecdotes, statistics, facts. It happens in memoir, in works of fiction, in poetry, but nowhere is it more apparent than in the literature prepared for queer youth—magazines like *Y.O.U.T.H.* and *Inside/Out*, anthologies like *Growing Up Gay/Growing Up Lesbian* and *Two Teenagers in Twenty*. A certain comfort can be taken from these unchanging stories: Rachel Corbett, for example, will always be sixteen; she will always be angry because it's hard for her to meet other queers her age; the tears will always be rolling down her mother's cheek as she tells her daughter that she's proud of her. David Johnson will always be seventeen; he will continually make his escape from Wheeling, West Virginia, to Los Angeles; he is still slipping into tight white pants and slipping out of them in empty rooms in his friend's motel. Mike W. from *Teens With AIDS Speak Out* will always be fifteen; he will always be a bit confused, always suffer from the memory of the man who infected him, but he will never get sick; he will never die. The fixed nature of these stories is patently false—perhaps *incomplete* is a better word, though I'm not sure that it is—but to a teenager whose mind and body and world is changing far too quickly for her to maintain a rational understanding of her life, these stories can serve, for a time, as rungs on a very steady ladder. The jubilant and, to my mind, false optimism that characterizes this literature is probably necessary; eventually, one hopes, youth will realize that the difficulties facing queer people are not as simple to understand or overcome as these texts suggest. But one of the great privileges of childhood—as well as one of its great myths—is the right to be sheltered from the truth.

I had wanted to add my own narratives to this community. I had wanted to tell good stories, true stories, stories of youth who came out into a world that accepted them fully, of youth who triumphed over adversity, of youth who were brutally beaten down; I had wanted, where it was appropriate, to emulate James Baldwin and offer stories from my own life in service to a larger cause. I had wanted to do this not least because it is the type of writing I do best, but also because I believe that for most readers narrative is the most effective means of conveying information. But it's not the best way: nothing beats cold hard facts, the kind that sit in your mouth like ball bearings. Narratives are subjectively rendered, and they're subjectively read as well; and as I sifted through hundreds of different narratives about queer youth, written by youth themselves, or by people like me who had once been queer youths, or by people who merely had some interest or stake in the subject, I found that this subjectivity was simply too great a hurdle to overcome. Greater writers than I have been reduced to sentimentality when writing about children—Dickens comes immediately to mind—and no one approaching Dickens's ability has yet approached the subject of queer youth. Our culture is afraid of children. Their vulnerability makes us want to protect them, but we also want to hurt them because it's so easy; the sexuality inherent in this vulnerability repels us, but it also compels us: their skin *is* soft, their bodies *are* pliable. When these children are also queer, homophobia, including the internalized homophobia present in every queer person, increases the tension a hundredfold. In the end, we adults have chosen to protect ourselves—not the children, but ourselves—by a wall whose bricks are made of sentimentality and whose mortar is hyperzealousness. In literature, where this wall isn't rendered in the text by the author, it is built into it by readers. These are children! one can hear them exclaim. These are children having sex! These are children having sex with other children of the same sex! Such exclamations aren't merely homophobic, whether uttered by straight or queer people; they're irrational as well. There are millions of children in this world, more and more of whom identify as queer, and even more of whom have sex with other children—and adults—of the same sex. But because straight people, and, to a lesser but still significant degree, queer people, regard sex as the rightful domain of adults, we regard sexual orientation as an adult possession as well. To say that both of these positions are false is begging the question: both of these positions are obviously false, and most of the people maintaining them know this.

They maintain them, as I have said, not because they believe in them, but because they think they are protecting children, when in reality all they are protecting is themselves.

In the end, I decided I didn't want to create further narratives that would merely be walled into this tiny compound of misrepresentation and misinterpretation. Instead, I chose to write what I believe to be the larger narrative describing most queer youth and their relationship with queer adults. Its parts are simple: the individual before it identifies itself; the individual as it identifies itself; the individual as it identifies with community; the individual as it problematizes the communal definition of self. Stripped to this, its most basic level, it's a narrative that isn't unique to queer people, but is shared by every person who considers himself in some way different from the defined or dominant norm of society. I phrased my meta-narrative in the form of an argument specifically to invite disagreement, dissent, other arguments, because I wanted, finally, for this to be not a finished product but the next round in an ongoing discussion. I not only hope but believe it's crucial that some of the next rounds in this discussion are new narratives, moral narratives as opposed to moralizing ones. Stories have many weaknesses, but their great strength is their ability to convey truth irrationally; as such, they may prove to be the only truly effective counter we have against the irrationality of our views about queer youth.

Language, I think, is like a sense. It's like seeing, hearing, smelling, touching, though perhaps it's most like tasting: it's a way of capturing something and bringing it inside yourself, and this capture is only a beginning. Words, like food, have to be digested. Language is both a shared and an individual experience because definitions of words are like tastes of food. What you mean by queer and what I mean by queer and what you taste when you eat asparagus and what I taste when I eat asparagus have both similarities and differences—they may even have more similarities than they do differences, but it's the differences that divide us, and it's these divisions that stories and essays like this one hope to narrow. And so, to close, a story: my first boyfriend was a beautiful young man with eyes the color of a clear, brown-bottomed pool of water and, when I knew him, a fresh pink scar that brought out the line of his left cheekbone. The time of our love affair encompassed a lazy summer in which neither of us had jobs or classes or anything to do besides participate in ACT UP and Queer Nation demonstrations and be with each other. I remember one of those summer evenings after a long hot afternoon together: we ended up somewhere and because money was short we bought only one bottle of water to share between us. The bottle was in his hand and he took the first drink. I expected him to hand it to me—I always expected him to do things like that—but instead he pulled me close to him with his free hand and kissed me and passed me the water that was in his mouth. I knew immediately that I shouldn't swallow it but pass it back to him, and I did, and he passed it back to me, and it moved back and forth between us, the water warming, its taste changing as it mixed with his saliva and my saliva, its volume shrinking with each pass as some of it dribbled down our chins and the rest of it made its way down our throats, and when the first mouthful was gone, he took another drink and the process began again. I remember it as one of the most shared experiences of my life. I think of it as the closest I have come to being inside another person. I believed that I was tasting the water exactly as he tasted it. But we couldn't drink the entire bottle that way, and eventually the summer ended and his scar faded; we got jobs and went back to different schools and these difficulties proved insurmountable. When we broke up, he moved to San Francisco. Usually I think that every cell in my body that might have been affected by that water has been sloughed off by time's erosion, but sometimes when I remember the experience, I remember also that the brain is made of cells, and that gives me hope. I'm not sure if this story is phrased as an answer or just another question; I do know that I would like to eroticize our knowledge of things and of each other, and so, rather than concluding by writing "these words have left my mouth and entered your ear" (because they haven't, after all, they've left my hand and entered your eye), I write instead: the water has left my mouth and entered yours. Now you have choices: you can spit it out, first of all, or you can swallow it; you can swallow some and pass the rest back to me; you can pass it all back to me; you can invite a third person into our chain. You can do nothing at all. There are other choices, some of which are not known to me, but, at any rate, what happens next is up to you.

Notes

1. This statement can, I think, only be made by defining the AIDS epidemic in terms that exclude the possibility of its being, among other things, a form of violence perpetuated on gay men. But I think that the epidemic is a form of violence: I think, in fact, that for many homophobes AIDS inflicts the physical damage on queers that they might otherwise inflict themselves. It is, in Catholic terms, a sin of omission rather than commission, and so, parenthetically at least, I'll revise the above sentence to read: ". . . excluding the AIDS epidemic, we have made this country . . ."

2. "I was never sexually assaulted during my childhood," Fricke continues. "There was the time when I was seven and my sixteen-year-old babysitter tried to make me touch her rear end—but I merely passed the incident off as straight whimsiness and made her give me ten dollars not to tell my parents. I don't see how this could have made me switch sexual preferences."

3. One final point: as political tools, I find these theories uninteresting and limiting; as moral yardsticks, I find them false and distracting; as I'm not a scientist, I don't know about that. Spiritually, however, I must admit they're fascinating. Human beings have always wondered where they came from, who or what made them, and what their purpose is; much of history and most of literature is about this quest for self-knowledge. But most human beings undertake this endeavor with the acceptance that on some basic level *they exist*. Queers, however, don't seem to have got this point. Every morning we wake up and pinch ourselves to make sure that we're not dreaming, or being dreamed by someone else. When we accept the fact that we do indeed exist, these myths of origin will, I think, take their proper role in our community.

The Moon Still Rises, the Seasons Change, and the Song Has Yet to Be Sung

by Malkia Amala Cyril, January 18, 1993, in tribute to Audre Lorde

Back to breaking down
I always come to why, to
the unfair, to the painful
part of life which runs through
everything like children's crayons
or mud streaked into the secret
rooms of my house.

It gets easier and easier
to sit and watch the sun set
forgetting how it rose
forgetting how the glow lifts
black children's faces toward
tomorrow and another chance
and then wanting with everything
that I am, to know the world
and fill it up with one mighty
word, one poem to rage catastrophically
on my enemies, and rain liberation on my
friends, one powerful song to fly
past silence, set complexity in its place
and bleed will into children
trapped by public schools and
private traumas
and this
is part of the prison.

Forgetting shades and shadows
and in between spaces that
deny opposition, invite chaos
and perspective, split veins that
pour nations of children nodding
melodies of action without theory,
theoretical milestones without hands.
Lives being the orchestras
that they are, the only direction
for me now is out into diversity
that is mine to decipher.

Yes, I have begun to know the
intensity of sound, all the hues of
my skin and my spirit, and Audre,
this is belief that I am learning
not to sacrifice, this is Hope
that I can't allow to be murdered
by the refusal of lives to be
changed by the word of a woman,
and still
sometimes I wake in the middle of
the night screaming
memories of dark alleys
and words hating to fit the reality
of an ex-lover's body desecrated
and buried in time for papers
to catch the story and yeah
scandals and lies and more good-byes.

That is not
I know not
the whole of life,
whole, I can't explain, is where
she took me, is where you bring me
to become the poetry of our mothers
we are the survival of our fathers
and begin to love beginnings
taking trips back to loving hands
into the vast measure of human
existence, into the sit back, yes on track
stand up way Audre had of obliterating
silence and rejuvenating quiet
so that Mid-town maniacs with billy
clubs or red ties, when grinding
us into spit, cannot deny we are still our elements
and know it,
and in pouring our dreams into the sea,
smearing our own blood on our hands
naming our futures
castrating our destinies
we are still the plenty of our love
the height of our promise and
I have known a woman who was a
movement in my life, like welcome back
to love we become the women
whose tongues have been stabbed
and sing anyway
the children who learn from
tear gas and tears how to make
a bomb cry, the soul rise
to meet the earth
who learn from broken necks
Brownstone Brooklyn babies
smashed under buses
splintered onto sidewalks
that death is not the end of life
language and change are the
beginning, I want to be a beginning
for me
for you
for every good-bye I have believed in
because every good-bye ain't gone.

Facing page: Poet, essayist, and activist Audre Lorde, seen here reading
at the Full Moon Coffeehouse in San Francisco in the mid-1970s.
Photo by Lynda Koolish.

In 1991, educator Jerry Battey founded the EAGLES Center, an alternative school for high-risk lesbian, gay, bisexual, and transgender youth in Los Angeles. After functioning for three years in a cramped five-hundred-square-foot space, the EAGLES Center moved into a space ten times that size in Santa Monica where a faculty of three currently works with forty students.

The EAGLES Center is a continuation of the Los Angeles Unified School District Options Program. EAGLES is an acronym that stands for Emphasizing Adolescent Gay and Lesbian Education Services. What we are trying to do here is to target at-risk youth whose needs have not been met by the regular, comprehensive high schools. Many of our youths are at risk of suicide, dropping out, high absenteeism, and low grade-point averages. What we are here to do is to help these youths to obtain a diploma in the most positive, safe, free haven that they can experience in Los Angeles. . . . What we're teaching them here is how to be fully functioning members of this society. They already know how to be gay. What they don't know is how to be high school students, college students, and employees. . . .

I read an article in the *Los Angeles Times* that was entitled "Latinos with AIDS." In almost every one of the cases, the women who were interviewed stated that they had become infected with HIV by their boyfriends or their husbands.

In only one case did the woman state that her husband had obtained his HIV infection by going to a female prostitute, which meant that these ladies were dealing with husbands or boyfriends who were playing both sides of the sexual spectrum. They were heterosexual, as far as their home life was concerned, but perhaps homosexual in their other activity outside the home. I was a middle-school teacher in the inner city in Los Angeles, and about 95 percent of the youths that I was teaching were Latino. As I looked at these kids, I got to thinking, we've got an insidious virus out there, and because of the culture in which these youths are brought up—because of the social pressure of machismo and because they cannot openly admit they are gay or bisexual—how many of them would actually live out that same scenario and infect a wife or a girlfriend or perhaps produce HIV-infected children? I felt that by opening this school and by being able to help these youths to be in an environment where their sexual orientation could be developed, perhaps we could save others. We could provide these youths with the correct information about protecting themselves against HIV infection. We could also protect them and their loved ones from lies and deceit in creating relationships. Indeed, if we could break this pattern that you must have a heterosexual relationship to be a man although your desires are truly for those of your own sex—and the same for women who have same-sex emotional and sexual desires—then perhaps we could save families not only from a death sentence, but from living through horrendous traumas when suddenly it comes out that you're gay. . . .

Most of the parents we deal with are extremely supportive of the school. I even have to say there's support because they allow their children to come here. I'm sorry to say there are many parents whom I haven't met, and this may primarily be due to the parents being unavailable during the daytime to meet with us due to their jobs. But we do maintain contact by phone with every one of our parents, and you can tell every time you make a call that they are so interested in having that call and being considered a vital part of what's happening. . . . I also want to stress the dire importance for parents of gay and lesbian children (particularly heterosexual parents) to be in tune to what's happening to their children, to keep communicating with them. Once they become aware that their child may indeed have homosexual tendencies, if they find that they are being harassed and ridiculed or are beginning to suffer depressions, not just to shrink back and wonder what can be done. Not only has the child maybe not come out to the parents, but when the child does, the parents have a coming out of their own to do: parents must demand that their children's needs be met.

SARAH LOMBERG-LEW

I met some students who were working on the passage of House Bill 3353. They were coming from communities that were not nearly as safe as mine and from schools where it would make a major difference if discrimination were prohibited. When I started hearing their stories, I realized that the rest of Massachusetts and the United States isn't nearly as safe as Brookline. I heard stories about people being kicked out of school, being harassed and having to leave, dropping out through no fault of their own, but just because the environment was too hostile for them. It was a reality check that told me that something really needed to be done. . . . The goal of this law is to make a public education accessible to all students. That includes straight students who are perceived to be gay. Anyone who is harassed because of their sexual orientation or because of what people think their orientation is, is being robbed of their public education. . . .

The Gay-Straight Alliance is a student group started in November 1992 with a few faculty advisers. Its purpose is to provide an open forum for discussion of any issues that are on people's minds about sexuality. For example, issues of coming out or of someone who thinks their friend is gay or even of talking to your parents about being in the Gay-Straight Alliance—all the things that worry people about sexuality and homophobia. The group's other function is to be politically active within our school. We post signs on the walls and we organize assemblies focusing on homophobia. We're dedicating the month of March to homophobia awareness as part of a year-long awareness program in our school. We're also a political action group outside of school, but our primary purpose is to provide support for students in the school. . . . The participation of straight students in the HB 3353 effort was incredibly important. It takes a lot of guts to get involved in a struggle that doesn't have impact on you directly. There wasn't any personal reason for the straight students to do it, but they did it because they cared about their gay friends and because they cared about the purpose. It means a lot to see people standing up for a cause that they believe in, especially if

In 1992, student and activist Sarah Lomberg-Lew cofounded the Brookline High School Gay-Straight Alliance, which was instrumental in organizing students throughout Massachusetts to press for the passage of House Bill 3353. In September 1994, she became an undergraduate at Smith College in Northampton, Massachusetts.

they don't have to. I appreciate their efforts. . . . The opposing arguments were classic: Gays want special rights. Why are they protecting gay kids? Why aren't they protecting kids with acne? It's not fair. We don't want gay students in our schools. One very common argument was, we don't have gay students in our schools. We don't need to protect gay students because they're simply not here—which, of course, is part of what contributes to the whole problem. . . . HB 3353 says nothing about curriculum. It doesn't say that the word *gay* even has to be mentioned in public schools. It simply says that you can't discriminate, and that only affects people who are being discriminated against on the basis of sexual orientation or perceived sexual orientation. While I would like to see multicultural curricula that include lesbian and gay issues implemented in public schools, that's much more controversial. I'm not sure I would want curriculum tied directly to the antidiscrimination law since it would give the opposition more ammunition. I think we have to hold on to the antidiscrimination protection at the very least. . . . It's possible that a lawsuit would emerge because of HB 3353, but that's not the goal. The goal is to

protect students, and hopefully even the threat of a lawsuit would deter any administration from condoning discrimination. If there is discrimination, I don't think we would hesitate to press charges, but hopefully that wouldn't have to happen more than once. . . . There hasn't been all that much response in the adult gay and lesbian community. In the past, gay and lesbian adults ignored gay youth for a lot of the same reasons everyone else does: because they don't believe that people could know that they're gay at this young age, or because they're resentful of gay young people even being out to themselves in high school. The gay newspapers in Boston both ran cover stories on HB 3353. That was fun and important, I guess. But I don't know how interested the adult gay community really is in this.

We heard about the March on Washington for Lesbian, Gay and Bi Equal Rights last year, and for months we kept saying, we should get a bus and go. We didn't do anything about it, however. Then, a month before the march we realized that we'd better get moving if we actually wanted to get down there. We managed to reserve one of the last buses in Boston, since all the other buses were already reserved. We made a big push to raise money. It was tough, and we barely made it, but everyone was so happy being there. We drove all night to get there, but everyone was on an incredible adrenaline high, surrounded by a million other people, all there for the same reason. We were in the front of the march with the youth contingent. We definitely felt like we were part of something bigger than ourselves that day. People cheered as we went by. People kept coming up to us, saying, oh, I graduated from Brookline High. We reached the Mall around three o'clock, and by the time we got there everyone just fell asleep on the grass because we were so tired. We went back the next day. We had school. It was a tiring trip.

To other lesbian or gay young people I would say, always remember you're not alone, even if you feel like you are. Part of what makes being gay different from other minorities is not being able to tell who else is gay, which leaves you without a sense of community. But there are other gay people out there. You may not be able to find them, but you're not alone. It can also be dangerous to feel prematurely empowered. You should never come out in a situation where it may not be safe. Always consider your own safety first. You have to feel out a situation before you decide how out you're going to be in it. Whether you're going to be very out or subtly hint at it or lie outright. The situation you find yourself in can justify telling a lie because it could be very dangerous. . . . The biggest difference between the gay youth community and the gay adult community is that we're not centered around bars. I know that's a stereotype, but for a long time a gay bar was the only place that adults could go to be with other gay

people. High school students don't have that option so we're forced to seek out something else. I'm not exactly sure how, but I think that makes a difference. . . .

I don't think that anyone telling me I'm too young to know my sexual orientation is worthy of a response. I know what I know, and it's awfully presumptuous of anyone to assume that they could even understand what's going on in my mind at all. However, since a lot of these people are parents, the easiest response is, "Don't you think your children know they're straight?" which of course assumes they are straight, but their parents are probably also assuming that anyway and would never question their child's heterosexuality if they were asked.

I've always believed, or at least thought I believed, that the individual could create change and that the power of the people was greater than the power of any bureaucracy. This experience clinched it. People were listening to us even though we weren't old enough to vote. It meant for me that maybe the political system wasn't just about getting reelected. Maybe people really do listen to what the issues are and care about passing laws that are good for people. I guess it reinforced my confidence in the system. . . . I guess I'm an idealist. I'd like to see the world without any prejudices or discrimination or assumptions. But since that's not likely to happen, I'd at least like to see a world where gay and lesbian young people could finish high school just being students, not having to worry about their gay or lesbian identity all the time; not having to explain themselves to their friends or teachers or be constantly faced with things they can't identify with. I'd like to see math word problems that incorporate same-sex couples. It wouldn't be much, but it's amazing what a little pronoun can do.

TROIX BETTENCOURT

Boston-based activist Troix Bettencourt was president of the Boston Alliance of Gay and Lesbian Youth from 1992 to 1994, after which he interned in the Irish Parliament with openly gay senator David Norris. In November 1994, he was an American representative to the USA-Israel International Symposium on Adolescent Health in Jerusalem.

I first thought that I might be gay when I was seventeen years old, after having a real intimate relationship with my best friend. He and I would say, "I love you," to each other. We would have sex and fool around, but he and I could say we weren't gay because we both had girlfriends at the same time. I didn't fit the stereotypes that I was taught to associate gay people with. . . . I loved my best friend very much and the time we spent together was when I felt the best. Yet I was angry at myself because I didn't know why I liked him so much. When we would fool around, even if we just kissed, there was a kind of passion that you'd think a boyfriend and girlfriend would feel. We'd start off wrestling or something, then one thing would lead to another, or we'd play stupid games like, I dare you to kiss me. But afterward I'd think about the way I felt kissing him and the way I felt kissing my girlfriend and there was such a difference. Why do I like kissing my best friend so much? . . . What made me face the reality that I was gay was when my best friend told me that he was in love with me. I was forced to question what kind of relationship he and I had, how I was feeling about him, and how it was the way I should have been feeling with my girlfriend, but wasn't. This freaked me out. The first thing I did was cut it off completely. I didn't want to have anything more to do with him. I went to my parish priest and asked him for help, saying, "I'm gay. Change me. Stop this. I don't want to be gay." I'll never forget that. I was hysterical. I was crying. I kept asking, "Why is this happening to me? I'm a freak.". . . The priest's name was Father Gomez and he was very helpful. He asked my questions back at me. "Why do you think you're gay? Why do you think you're feeling this way? If you don't want to, why do you think it's happening?" He made me

come to realize that it wasn't a choice, that this is just the way I was and didn't make me a better or worse person.

I finally had to admit that I was feeling the same way as my best friend, and I told him that I was in love with him. And at that very moment, when we said that we were in love with each other, it felt great and I felt like my life is going to be fine. There were days when I told myself, okay, I can deal with this. But then there were days when I said, I don't want to deal with this. No one knew at the time except for the parish priest. A little later on he found me a youth support group in Boston, which wasn't too far from where I lived. I decided to go there and lie to everybody, telling people that I was attending an art class in Boston so nobody knew where I was going. I lied about my name and where I was from, which made it a lot easier. Going to this youth group, I realized that I wasn't the only one. I started meeting guys and girls like me as well as guys and girls that weren't like me, but who all felt the same way about dealing with the same kind of thing. This group definitely made the biggest difference in my life. I was also seeing a guidance counselor at the time, talking to her about what was going on at home and in my relationship with my girlfriend. I also talked to her about my best friend. At the time the word *gay* hadn't crossed my mind, but I guess she concluded that I was gay by the way I talked about him. She never told me this. She never said anything to me. Instead she called my parents in for a meeting. It was two weeks before the end of my junior year. I was called down to her office without any idea what was going on. I walked into her office and there were my parents, with my Portuguese teacher, who acted as an interpreter for my father because he doesn't speak English well. My guidance

counselor was expressing her concerns about my sexuality and my confusion and was wondering if anything was going on at home that could be affecting me. It never occurred to my parents that I could be gay. They were just upset that this guidance counselor called them in and embarrassed them that way. That was my last day of school. I never went back.

Everything that I thought I had to be—the perfect little boy, the perfect jock, the perfect high school student—it all just came crashing down. I was in such denial that I didn't want to see it and I just started acting out in self-destructive ways. Right after I dropped out, I got two different jobs and I just worked all the time. I didn't want to associate with my friends or deal with my parents. I just wanted to be by myself and try to figure things out on my own. I tried everything possible to avoid everyone and it ate me up inside. I couldn't sleep. I'd watch TV all night and sleep all day. I'd start crying for no reason. I was angry at what was going on inside of me because I didn't understand it and didn't know what it was and felt like I had no one to talk to and nowhere to go. I couldn't talk to my friends because none of them seemed to

be going through this. I also felt guilty because I had this girlfriend who professed to love me so much, without my feeling it, too. I broke up with her at that point, using my parents' divorce as an excuse. . . .

The first person in my family that I came out to was my sister. She was in college at the time and she seemed pretty open-minded. It was late one night; I'd come home from the youth group in Boston. I just started talking to her about these guys that I met in the "art class." I started this whole scenario, saying, they're gay, but they're cool, testing the waters to see where she was coming from. She knew gay people in school, and she said a lot of supportive, kind of liberal things. I decided to tell her right then. She didn't believe me at first and kind of laughed about it. Then she was great. She hugged me, kissed me, told me she loved me. Then I asked her to talk to my mother about it because I didn't know how my parents would react. . . . She talked to my mother, and about a week later my mother approached me. I was in the bathroom getting ready to go to my "art class." I think my mother had started to doubt that I was going to an art class by then, and she asked me what was going on. She didn't come right out and ask if I was gay, but she was asking me if I had met anybody, what I was doing. I asked her, "What would you say if I told you I was gay?" She paused and said, "Nothing. I love you and you're my son." So I told her, just casually. I said it in such a way that if she had a bad reaction, I'd be able to say I was only joking. But she seemed all right about it. She sat down and we started talking and I was telling her about the youth group that I was going to and everything seemed pretty cool. But I knew that as soon as I left the room, she was going to burst into tears. I had such a hard time dealing with it on my own that I knew my mother wasn't going to suddenly say, "It's okay. He's my son." I knew that she was going to have to go through the same thing I went through and that it would take some time and I was thinking, "What can I do for her? What kind of support can I give her? Who can I get to talk to her?" She had a hard time trying to understand, but our relationship improved. We started talking more. I started opening up to her a lot more and she noticed. I had always been like, yeah, I'm going out, whatever. But now I was opening up and talking to her. . . . After I started getting really involved with the youth group and my whole community found out that I was gay, my close circle of friends just started drifting away. Slowly but surely, they all went away—definitely fear of guilt by association. I knew people were saying things about me. I got it directly from people in the community and from my parents and relatives who basically branded me an outcast and refused to speak to me.

After I spoke publicly at Gay Pride, people started to identify me as The Gay Teen. Once people in my hometown who might have heard my name some-where connected the face with the name, things just skyrocketed. Rumors started flying. People at my mother's work started approaching my parents, saying, "How could your son be gay? It's disgraceful. What kind of parents are you? How could you let him do this?" My friends had people saying things to them like, "Are you gay, too? How can you be friends with him? That's sick." It went on and on, and I knew it. No one said anything directly to me at first, but it was always there. Nobody wanted to talk about it, and that became a really big problem at home. . . . One morning, as I was getting ready to go out, my parents were having an argument. My name came up and the argument escalated and exploded. My mother started in about the youth group, about my going to Boston. She didn't say anything about my being gay, but she started talking about how I was never home anymore. She didn't like what I was doing. We started arguing back and forth until she finally said, "Get out of my house. Leave." I didn't know what to do. I ran downstairs and locked myself in my bedroom. She started banging on the door, saying, "This is my house, open the door." Then she called the police. When the police arrived, my mother started going off, my husband this, my daughter that, my son, etc. But as soon as she said I was gay, the police officer immediately zoned in on me and said, "Look what you're doing to your mother. If my son were gay, he'd be out of my house really fast and on his own." The whole situation started focusing entirely on me, and this police officer started feeding lines to my mother, like, you know, "Do you want him out of this house? He belongs in Boston with the fags. You don't need this shit. If my son were gay, he'd be out on the street." My mother started crying, "Get him out! Just get him out of my house. I can't deal with this anymore." The officer took my keys to my house and made me leave. I was crying and I asked him where I was supposed to go. He said, "That's not my problem. You want to live this way, you figure it out." I started walking down the street. I had no idea where I was going. He climbed into his cop car and started following me slowly as I walked down the street. I started running. He drove faster. He kept following me until I ran into the woods. I went to the house of a friend of my sister's and called all my friends to find someplace to stay. My friends all said, you can't stay here, my parents wouldn't let you. But I knew it was because they were afraid of what people would think of them.

I called the Department of Social Services, where kids are supposed to go when they're kicked out or thrown out. When I explained to them what had happened to me, I figured this was my last resort. They wanted to know exactly why this happened, why I was being kicked out. When I said it was because I was gay, the woman on the phone said that they didn't have any services that could help me and hung up the phone on me. I kept calling back until finally a man got on the phone; he must have been a supervisor. He said to me, "Look, we don't have any services for gays, we can't help you." I was crying and I asked him, "Where the hell am I supposed to go?" He said, "Well, isn't there some kind of community center you can go to?" I had no idea what that was going to do for me. He hung up the phone and I had nowhere to go and nowhere to stay. I was homeless. That night and the next night I slept behind my mother's house, down by the river. I hardly slept, but when I finally got up and started walking around, there was all my stuff in front of

the house. My mother had thrown it out for me to pick up sometime. I didn't know what to do. The only place I could go now was Boston. I got on a train, not knowing what the hell I was going to do. I went to the youth group, but I didn't tell anybody what had happened at home. Finally I told a friend of mine, who let me stay at an apartment he had just moved out of but still had for two more weeks. . . .

I threw myself into social service trainings that were just beginning to happen around gay and lesbian youth. That's when I heard about House Bill 3353. I could testify, I could go to the House and the Senate, I could go on *Beacon Hill*. I could say something because I had nothing to lose. I didn't have to worry about my parents or my friends finding out because I had already lost them all. . . . I first got involved with HB 3353 two years ago as the president of the Boston Gay and Lesbian Youth. I was asked to represent the bill in the hearing before the Massachusetts State Legislature. I testified, telling them my story and what happened to me in school, how I felt there, and how this bill might have kept me from dropping out of high school in the first place. From that moment on, I realized that I was in a perfect position to be outspoken. As president of the youth group I wasn't just representing myself but a whole group of people. We weren't asking them to tell their parents about it. They didn't have to sacrifice anything. So I gave testimony after testimony. Soon people began testifying, as students, without having to be out about their sexuality but talking about situations and friends and circumstances. As time went on, people who felt they could be out began testifying as well, and the next thing we knew, two years elapsed and we had a whole youth contingent—gay and straight, but mostly gay—lobbying at the statehouse, saying, "You've let this die two years in a row. We're not going to let it happen a third time. You can see us now. We're your children. What are you going to do?"

HB 3353 is an amendment that adds sexual orientation to an existing student rights bill alongside such criteria as sex, ethnicity, religion, etc. It protects students in public schools who may identify as gay or lesbian. It can be used to protect gay and lesbian students who want to start a support group or a rap group after school; or if a student wants to bring a same-sex partner to a prom, and their school says, "That's going to disrupt the prom." Students now have the right to say, "It's your job to protect us because this is our prom." It protects students who are in any way being harassed because of sexual orientation, even if they're not gay. That student can say something to a principal, and instead of the principal writing it off as two kids fighting, now they're forced to do something. They have to protect that student regardless of their own bias. . . . A similar bill passed in Wisconsin some time ago, but we didn't know that until after we passed ours. . . . It's not promoting homosexuality in any kind of way. It's protecting the kids who do identify as gay or lesbian. Let's say that there's three hundred students in a school and one of them is in a wheelchair. Just because there's only one student in a wheelchair, does that mean you're not going to build a ramp at that school? That student has as much a right to equal access in education as everyone else. It's the same with gay and lesbian students. . . .

There aren't many support networks available for gay and lesbian teens. Around the country there are small support groups and a very few larger organizations, like the EAGLES Center in Los Angeles, Los Angeles GLASS, and the Hetrick-Martin Institute in New York, and I think this is the responsibility of the adult gay and lesbian community. But there's the fear of being cast as pedophiles, especially when you have organizations like NAMBLA around. . . . I wanted to show the adult gay community who we were, that we are powerful in numbers, and that we can make change happen. I wanted to elicit their support. When I first got kicked out of my house, I turned to organizations like GLAAD and Gay and Lesbian Defenders because I was looking for an attorney. They said, "Sorry, we don't provide adolescent services." I fought for the longest time to make the adult gay community realize that although they're afraid of being labeled pedophiles, if they don't help gay youth now, then this cycle will just continue. People will continue to come out seeking support without finding it. I've noticed that many adult gay men and lesbians try to forget what it was like to grow up gay. They want to forget the pain and the isolation. But you can't change anything by forgetting. It just keeps on happening. By doing that they only neglect us, the next generation and the ones who are going to come after.

Series Titles and Credits

The Question of Equality was produced by Testing the Limits for the Independent Television Service with funds provided by the Corporation for Public Broadcasting and Channel Four, UK. Additional support was provided by foundations and individuals.

Program One: **Out Rage '69**
Producer/Director/Writer: Arthur Dong
Associate Producer: Susan Levine
Story Consultant: Allan Berube
Editor: Roger Schulte
Assistant Editor: Tia Lessin

Program Two: **Culture Wars**
Producers/Directors/Editors:
    Tina DiFeliciantonio, Jane C. Wagner
Co-producer: Suzanne Wright
Additional Editing: Sylvia Waliga
Assistant Editors:
    Joyce Haverkamp, Keith Croket,
    Robert Perkins

Program Three: **Hollow Liberty**
Producer/Director: Robyn Hutt
Producer: Bennett Singer
Editor: Richard Gordon
Additional Editing: Jonathan Oppenheim
Assistant Editors: Julie Berg, Ben Jorgenson

Program Four: **Generation Q**
Producer/Director: Robert Byrd
Associate Producer: Kurt Wolfe
Editor: Richard Gordon
Assistant Editor: Cyrille Phipps

Executive Producer: David Meieran
Series Senior Producer: Issac Julien
Senior Production Consultant: Richard Kwietniowski
Co-executive Producers: Sandra Elgear, Robyn Hutt
Supervising Producer: Craig Paull
ITVS Executive-in-Charge: Mark Lipson
Series Associate Producer: Esther Cassidy
Production Manager: Tina Berger
Production Office Coordinator: Maria Elena Grant
Production Coordinator: Ryan Kull
Postproduction Coordinator: Sarah Sheffield
Music: Anton Sanko, Bill Laswell
Principal Photography:
    Richard Numeroff, Wolfgang Held, Bobby Shepard
Series Development: Susan Levene, Bennet Singer
Consulting Producers:
    Sam Pollard, Lillian Jimenez, Tina DiFeliciantonio
Contributing Producers:
    Louis Erskine, Heather MacDonald, Frances Negron
Creative Consultant: David Deitcher
Research Director: Tanya Steele
Researchers: John Flinn, Richard Meyer, Holly Price, Valerie Lombard, Jennifer Romine, Deborah Wasser, Rebecca Llorens
Interns: DM Reznik, Betsy Radmore, Mathew Curlewis, Victoria Lind, Jennifer Fixman, Kathy Allen, Jenine Lurie, Kristen Cassidy, Mike Israel, Jennifer Thompson, Rudi Furst, Susan Strine, Abbey Williams, Helen Hong, Gina Dicaprio
Assistant to the Executive Producer: Cleve Keller
Administration: Darrylyn Bonaparte, Jack Waters
Promotion: Niq Shelbi
Legal: Peggy Brady, Roz Lichter
Communication Director: Rob Davis
Outreach Coordinator: Nadine Smith
The 'In Their Own Words' interviews were conducted by the producers/directors of the indivual shows.

Photo and Illustration Credits

Pages 4, 5, 40–41 (bottom), 68–69, 71, 73, 78, 123, 129, 130, 132, 133, 144, 150, 169, 175, 176–77 (insets), 182, 184, 186, 191, 238, 240, 243, courtesy Testing the Limits; 12, 16–17, 20, 24–25, 30–31, 67, Diana Davies, courtesy Rare Books and Manuscripts Division, New York Public Library, Astor, Lenox, and Tilden Foundations; 18, 42, 43, 46, 60, 101, 138, 139 (top), 152–53, 168, 181, courtesy JEB (Joan E. Biren); 22, photos by Nancy Tucker, courtesy Lesbian Herstory Archives/Lesbian Herstory Educational Foundation, Inc.; 28, 39, 40 (top), 51 (bottom), 59, 74, courtesy Bettye Lane; 32, photo by George Desantis, © 1970 *QQ Magazine*; 34, 36–37, courtesy Ellen Shumsky; 35, 38, courtesy Lesbian Herstory Archives/Lesbian Herstory Educational Foundation, Inc.; 42 (top), courtesy Tia Cross; 44, 45, 80, 126, 236, courtesy Lynda Koolish; 48 (inset), 50, 51 (top), 115, courtesy Rink Foto; 48–49, courtesy Mel Cheren; 52, 53, 106, 166, 179, 204, AP/Wide World Photos; 54–55, © 1993 Robert Kirby and Orland Outland, courtesy Giant Ass Publishing; 58, courtesy Ira Tattelman; 62–63, 64, 139 (bottom), 143, 145, 154, 155, 194–95, 206, 212, 213, courtesy Marilyn Humphries; 65, courtesy Michael James O'Brien; 82–83, 84, © 1994 Carolina Kroon/Impact Visuals; 85, courtesy fierce pussy; 86, courtesy Cheap Art; 90, © 1991 Jim West/Impact Visuals; 91, © 1991 T. L. Litt/Impact Visuals; 92, © 1990 T. L. Litt/Impact Visuals; 93, © 1989 Eli Reed/ Magnum Photos; 94, © 1991 Donna Binder/Impact Visuals; 97, courtesy Frank Herrera; 100, © 1989 Signifyin' Works; 102, © 1992 *The New York Times*; 103, © 1987 Steve McCurry/Magnum Photos; 104, © 1992 Marv Bondarowicz/ *The Oregonian*; 105, © 1992 Donna Binder/Impact Visuals; 107, © 1993 Philip Jones Griffiths/Magnum Photos; 109, courtesy Dyke Action Machine; 111,

© 1992 Dana E. Olsen/*The Oregonian*; 112, courtesy Shan Gordon; 113, courtesy Tom Boyd; 119, courtesy the Bayard Rustin Fund; 120, © 1993 Jetta Fraser/Impact Visuals; 134–35, © 1987 Rick Reinhard/Impact Visuals; 136, © 1993 Costa Manos/ Magnum Photos; 137, courtesy QUASH; 140, 151, courtesy Jane Rossett; 142, © 1989 Ellen Neipris/Impact Visuals; 146, courtesy U.S. Supreme Court Historical Society; 157, courtesy Tee A. Corinne; 159, courtesy Estate of Peter Hujar; 162, © 1993 Linda Eber/Impact Visuals, 164, © 1992 Tom Mckitterick/Impact Visuals; 167, © 1993 Stacy Rosenstock/Impact Visuals; 171, © 1993 Loren Santow/Impact Visuals; 172–73, courtesy Bureau; 174, © 1993 Donna Binder/Impact Visuals; 176–77, © 1993 Rick Reinhard/Impact Visuals; 178 (top), © 1993 Ellen Shub/ Impact Visuals; 178 (bottom), courtesy Cathy Cade; 197, Joseph Kassabian, courtesy the Hetrick-Martin Institute Photography Program; 199, courtesy AIDS Community Television; 200, courtesy the Gay Asian Pacific Alliance Community HIV Project; 203, courtesy Rosamund Felsen Gallery; 208, 215, Ces Nieves, courtesy the Hetrick-Martin Institute Photography Program; 218, © 1990 Lyle Ashton Harris, courtesy Simon Watson; 220, © 1993 Donna Binder/Impact Visuals; 225–29, © 1994 Diane DiMassa, courtesy Giant Ass Publishing.

Index